O9-AID-810

THE CONGRESS DANCES

Earlier books by Susan Mary Alsop

Yankees at the Court
Lady Sackville
To Marietta from Paris: 1945–1960

LE CONGRÈS.

The congress dances, a contemporary cartoon. (*Bibliothèque Nationale, Paris.*)

THE
CONGRESS
DANCES

Susan Mary Alsop

HARPER & ROW, PUBLISHERS, New York
Cambridge, Philadelphia, San Francisco, London
Mexico City, São Paulo, Sydney

1817

For my two dear traveling companions,
Marietta Tree and Charles S. Whitehouse

THE CONGRESS DANCES. Copyright © 1984 by Susan Mary Alsop. All rights reserved. Printed in the United States of America. No part of this book may be
used or reproduced in any manner whatsoever without written permission except in the case of brief quotations embodied in critical articles and reviews.
For information address Harper & Row, Publishers, Inc., 10 East 53rd Street,
New York, N.Y. 10022. Published simultaneously in Canada by Fitzhenry &
Whiteside Limited, Toronto.

F I R S T E D I T I O N

Designer: Sidney Feinberg

Library of Congress Cataloging in Publication Data
Alsop, Susan Mary.
  The Congress dances.
  Bibliography: p.
  Includes index.
  1. Congress of Vienna (1814–1815) 2. Napoleonic
Wars, 1800–1814—Influence. 3. Napoleonic Wars,
1800–1814—Treaties. I. Title.
DC249.A47 1984   940.2′7   83–48781
ISBN 0-06-015280-X

---

84 85 86 87 88 10 9 8 7 6 5 4 3 2 1

Contents

Illustrations

Acknowledgments

I owe my first thanks to Frances Lindley, my brilliant editor, and to Cass Canfield, who not only paid me the honor of asking me to write *The Congress Dances* but whose wise suggestions much strengthened the book.

The following works have, as the reader will realize, been of immeasurable value to me in this undertaking: *The Letters of Lady Burghersh; A World Restored,* by Henry A. Kissinger; *The Congress of Vienna,* by Harold Nicolson; *Les Dessous du Congrès de Vienne,* by M. H. Weil; *Clemens Metternich-Wilhelmine von Sagan, Ein Briefwechsel 1813–1815,* edited by Maria Ullrichová; and *Metternich and the Duchess,* by Dorothy Gies McGuigan. My other sources are listed in the bibliography to be found at the end of the book. I owe a special debt to Mrs. McGuigan, who helped me so generously despite her grave illness.

My British publisher, George Weidenfeld, has been a tower of strength throughout the years of writing, as has my literary agent and friend James O. Brown. My invaluable editorial assistant, Mary Buell, has given me badly needed advice and unlimited support. Other friends to whom I am very grateful are Teymuraz K. Bagration, Olivier Bernier, Evangeline Bruce, George Carver, Anne Crile, Millicent Fenwick, Frank and Katherine Giles, Marilyn Gillet, Edward Glover, Stella K. Hersham,

Alastair Horne, Hugh Newell Jacobsen, Dorothy R. Kidder, Henry A. Kissinger, Bettina Looram, Lynn Pedigo, Louise de Rougemont, Liliane de Rothschild, Paul Ruddick, Evelyn M. Tehaan, Hans von Urbanski. The book is dedicated to Marietta Tree and Charles S. Whitehouse, who lovingly accompanied me on my first research trip. Thanks to their enthusiasm we found the background to my story not only in Vienna but also in Czechoslovakia, Poland, and Hungary.

THE CONGRESS DANCES

Lady Burghersh's Adventure

Priscilla Anne Burghersh was off. She had declared her intention of accompanying her soldier husband abroad. For an inexperienced young woman of barely twenty to fling herself into a winter campaign in the heart of Europe in the year 1813 seemed not merely hazardous, but mad.

During the twenty years that Great Britain had been at war with the French, the island had been completely isolated from the continent of Europe, with the exception of the brief Peace of Amiens in 1802. Then had come the years of Napoleon's tremendous Continental victories. Britain's mastery of the seas was never seriously doubted after Nelson's triumph at Trafalgar in 1805, but in that year began a succession of disasters in central Europe. First came Napoleon's defeat of Austria at Ülm, swiftly followed by the great battle of Austerlitz in December 1805, in which the armies of both Russia and Austria were crushed. The French juggernaut rolled on irresistibly. The battles of Jena and Auerstedt in 1806 all but brought Prussia to her knees. The next year she fought beside the Russians at Friedland, where both powers again met defeat. When Austria was once more vanquished at Wagram in 1809 and obliged to accept a humiliating peace, it appeared to all the world that Napoleon was unbeatable.

What was his greatest moment of supremacy? The historians

argue, but surely it was after Friedland at the triumphant meeting at Tilsit with his former enemy, Alexander I, tsar of Russia. In the middle of the river Nieman, the conqueror and the conquered met on a canopied raft while all the world watched and the observers wrote amazedly of the camaraderie, the affectionate rapport that sprang up between the two emperors. At the end of two weeks of fêtes and mutual exchanges of compliments, the pair parted, each well satisfied with the result of the "summit conference." Europe had been divided into spheres of influence, and Napoleon had been the one who drew the map. The young and impressionable tsar was grateful for the French promises of future cooperation, and the terms of the Treaty of Tilsit were infinitely more generous toward Russia than were those meted out to Prussia despite the efforts of Louise, the lovely Prussian queen, who attended the conference to fight for her country. Napoleon wrote to Josephine from Tilsit: "She was full of coquetterie toward me . . . do not be jealous. I am an oilcloth off which all that sort of thing runs. It would cost me too dear to play the *galant*."[1]*

In the next year Napoleon overextended himself. A defeat in Spain following a popular rising demonstrated for the first time that the French armies were not invincible. However, the damage appeared to be contained when the French emperor himself arrived in Spain to take command.

In 1812 he went further, and this time the overextension was fatal. That great tool, that superb machine, the Grande Armée, of which the heart was the Imperial Guard, which Napoleon called "ma Vieille Garde," followed him indomitably into Russia, 400,000 of them. Only 60,000 returned, stumbling, falling in their tracks, and, when they did so, dying almost instantly of the cold. Those who survived staggered with the exhaustion of failure and despair. They were abandoned by the emperor, who left them and raced across Europe in order to prepare Paris for

*Source notes will be found beginning on page 211.

the effects of the terrible Twenty-ninth Bulletin, which announced the disaster.

Emboldened by the failure of the Russian campaign in the previous year, heartened by the knowledge that a British army under Lord Wellington was driving the French out of Spain, a coalition was then formed of Russia, Austria, and Prussia, who bound themselves to end Napoleon's domination. Thus, by the autumn of 1813, all Europe north of the Alps was in arms against Napoleon, and the leaders of the three allied Continental powers had gathered with their armies in Germany to plan their next move.

Fully engaged on the Spanish front, British troops could not be spared for the central battlefield, but the prime minister, Lord Liverpool, and his cabinet in London could and did increase their already generous subsidies of money to the Allied cause, and a handful of diplomats and military officers were dispatched to advise the Allied sovereigns and their ministers for the purpose of negotiating some sort of peace settlement with Napoleon when the time was ripe. One of the officers was Priscilla's husband, Lord Burghersh, who was assigned to the emperor of Austria with the nominal title of British liaison to the Austrian army.

Lady Burghersh came from a powerful military and political family, the Wellesleys, who were accustomed to serving the British empire in the remotest corners of the globe. One of her uncles, Richard Wellesley, had been a celebrated governor-general of India; another was Arthur Wellington, the hero of England, who was at this moment forcing his tired army across the Pyrenees to outflank Napoleon's forces in France. Yet even this adventurous tribe blanched at Priscilla's decision. Possessed of a fiery and determined nature, passionately in love with her husband and adamantly refusing to be left behind, she succeeded in getting her way. She embarked in September with her husband and an entourage that sounds extraordinarily luxurious by today's standards, but was then considered perfectly normal. There was a private secretary, a stout English coachman for the traveling carriage—a large berlin made in Norwich—two footmen and six horses. An elderly Frenchwoman, Madame Legoux, who had been befriended by Priscilla's mother, volunteered to serve as maid, nurse, and companion. Her courage and resourcefulness were often gratefully mentioned in Priscilla Burghersh's letters to her family.

Owing to Napoleon's Continental Blockade, it was very difficult to get from England to Germany. The Burghersh party took ship to Sweden, crossed Sweden overland, re-embarked to traverse the Baltic, and landed at the Prussian port of Stalsund. Lady Burghersh's first letter was written from Gothenburg in Sweden on October 11, and her second from Berlin on October 27. They had traveled fast over bad roads through bare country in weather which already hinted the approach of the bleak northern winter, but from Berlin she assured her mother that she was "not in the least tired although I have just spent thirty hours in a carriage." She was immediately stimulated by the atmosphere of the Prussian capital.

> It is a most interesting moment to be here. Everybody is so enthusiastic and there is a patriotism and eagerness of which we have no idea in England, nor have we a conception of what these poor people have sacrificed in the good cause, the poverty and wretchedness to which they have reduced themselves is quite shocking. There are thirty-eight thousand wounded in this town, and many of the Princesses and ladies have sold their jewels to assist them. I hear that at Princess Radziwill's there is an assembly every night where they all scrape lint to send to the hospitals.*

What Priscilla Burghersh was seeing was Prussia's reaction to something that had happened when she was a girl of thirteen: in 1806 Prussia had been all but annihilated by the great

---

*This and subsequent extracts of her letters are from *The Letters of Lady Burghersh*, edited by Lady Rose Weigall. London: John Murray, 1895.

French victory at Jena. The king, Frederick William III, a weak and rather stupid man, of whom it has been written, "He was always able to display a doglike if somewhat bewildered devotion to the winning side," [2] could only just stay afloat as he was swept along by the ruthless Napoleonic torrent. The Treaty of Tilsit had compounded the pitiful state of the nation that had been a mighty military power under Frederick the Great, reducing its territory and its population by half. The people became as despairing and frightened as the king. Yet, inspired by the heroic Queen Louise and supported by the youth of the country, a popular movement of nationalism and rebellion came to revive this seemingly flaccid and exhausted people. The surge of patriotic enthusiasm forced the reluctant king to join the Russian and Austrian alliance, and on October 17 and 18, 1813, just ten days before Lady Burghersh arrived in Berlin, the combined armies, aided by Bernadotte and his Swedes, defeated the French at the fearful battle of Leipzig.

At the news of this tremendous event, Lord Burghersh hurried on ahead to Allied Headquarters at Frankfurt, and his wife set out to join him, alone but for Madame Legoux. For the first time in her young life she saw the cruel face of war at very close quarters, and noted her experiences in a sort of journal to her mother, jotted down at her stopping places. It is a remarkable document:

> We did not go through Leipzig, it was in such a state from the unburied bodies remaining from the battle that we were advised not to approach it, but God knows, we saw horrors enough without seeking more. All along the line of the French retreat the roads are covered with dead horses and the remains of dead men. The latter, I am told, we shall see many of between here and Frankfurt, particularly at Hanau, where Wrede fought a sanguinary battle a fortnight ago. No language can describe the horrible devastation these French have left behind them, without seeing it no one could form an idea of the country through which such a retreat as theirs has been

made. Every bridge blown up, every village burnt, the fields completely devastated, the orchards all turned up—we traced their bivouacs all along and saw every horror you can imagine.

None of the country people will bury them or their horses, so there they remain lying all over the fields with millions of crows feasting. We passed quantities, bones of all kinds, hats, shoes, epaulettes, a surprising quantity of rags and linen. Every kind of horror. They told us that the French soldiers had been in such a state of starvation that they took the earrings from their ears and implored for bits of bread, which none of the inhabitants would give them. The consequence is that the rivers are full of bodies.

We found Halle full of wounded, 14,000 in that town. There was only one room to be had at the inn there, which was also full of wounded Russians and smelling—Oh! I got that room for myself and Madame Legoux. I took precautions before leaving Berlin and got some sulphurous powder which is burnt in the hospitals to purify the air, I also wear quantities of camphor and my dear little aromatic vinegar box, and make Madame L. do the same.

They pressed on for Frankfurt and the next night she reported:

In this room, on one of the coldest November nights, I lay down on the carriage cushions on the floor and covered myself with a greatcoat. . . . I slept well, caught no cold, and set off merrily the next morning. The horrors of the road increased every step as we approached Hanau. We made the post-boys holloa out when we were coming to any dead bodies [so that she wouldn't have to look at them] but I saw four or five stripped of all clothing. In some places the stench was horrid. Anyhow at Hanau it all ended in my joy at finding B. again. The town is as full as it can hold [Frankfurt]. Kings and Princes without end. We have very bad quarters, and with great difficulty got any at all. Tomorrow we are to change. Is it not extraordinary that after such a journey of nine days, getting up every morning two hours before daylight, and travelling until eight, nine, or ten at night, I am not only not in the least tired, but have grown fat. Pozzo* was quite struck with my looking so much better than in London.

In that vivid piece of war reporting there was no pity for the French soldiers whose corpses littered the countryside through which Priscilla Burghersh traveled, but it must be remembered that she had been born and brought up in an England that for a whole generation had been engaged in war to the death with France. Every English nanny of the time would threaten her charges with: "Eat up your porridge, or Boney will get you." Fear and awe of "the Corsican ogre" had kept many a small English boy and girl awake at night. It would have been too much to expect that Lady Burghersh should have felt mercy toward the implacable enemy.

Those gray, gaunt dead faces upturned to the sky on the fields of Germany were the remains of Napoleon's second Grande Armée led by the Imperial Guard. This superb elite corps was the most admired force in Europe. The guardsmen had to be tall, to be able to read and write, and to have fought in three campaigns. Young men under thirty, they carried themselves with pride and were politely addressed as "Monsieur" by their officers.[3]

Their unshakable morale set an example for the whole army. Napoleon himself looked back on Austerlitz as his proudest victory, and it was in that 1805 campaign that the quality of the Grande Armée had first been fully tested. It had been drawn up at Boulogne, preparing for a possible invasion of the British Isles, when in a sudden change of plan the emperor threw it across Europe by forced marches, a blitzkrieg that brought it to the Rhine in twenty days, to Ülm in Bavaria a few weeks later, and on to Austerlitz in what is now Czechoslovakia. There, near the town of Brünn, the French met and conquered the strongest Allied force that had ever been put into the field.

*Count Pozzo di Borgo was a Corsican who had joined the Russian service. He had been much in England and was a friend of all Lady Burghersh's family.

Napoleon believed that fortitude was the most important quality a soldier could possess, and for greater mobility the army carried no baggage trains, lived off the land, and slept out of doors without tents in the iciest weather. Every military historian has criticized Napoleon's supply system. The men were ill-shod, ill-clothed, ill-fed, and frequently short of ammunition. There was no medical corps, and standing orders dictated that the wounded were not to be removed from the field during a battle. Eventually an apothecary, frequently drunk, might perform amputations on the more serious cases after giving the patient a swig of brandy. Disease carried off ten soldiers for every death in combat, with typhus so widespread that the hospitals in the towns in the rear frequently could not contain a tenth of those who crawled to them only to be turned away.

The Grande Armée had arrived at Austerlitz sleepless and half-starving, to be flung into action immediately. What was the explanation of the extraordinary spirit that was the envy of the world? The British historian, Alastair Horne, has written: "Like so much else, the explanation had its roots in revolutionary times . . . the French soldier alone felt that he had a personal cause worth fighting for. . . . But Napoleon, of course, grafted his own special—indeed unique—morale-boosting magic onto the Revolutionary stock."

His magic touch had deserted him in Russia, but he was reluctant to admit that his genius could fail him again. Somehow, he raised a second Grande Armée within five months and lunged eastward once more. Showing much of his old temerity and resolve, he was victorious against the Allied Coalition at Lützen and Bautzen in the month of May 1813, and again at Dresden in August. But he could no longer follow up his successes. Lacking cavalry, weakened by deserters and stragglers in the ranks of the new army, his marshals increasingly sullen and war-weary, he faltered. The cost of this campaign, which culminated in the terrible defeat at Leipzig, was 300,000 men out of an army of 700,000.

Caulaincourt, duc de Vicence, Napoleon's most loyal supporter, expressed the prayers of his countrymen during an abortive peace conference at Prague that summer when he whispered to the Austrian foreign minister, Count Metternich: "Get us back to France, whether it be by war or armistice, and you will earn the gratitude of thirty million Frenchmen."[4]

Such then, in barest outline, was the situation when Priscilla Burghersh arrived in Frankfurt on December 3 after her ghastly drive from Berlin. Nearly half a million Allied troops under the command of the Austrian general, Prince Karl Philipp von Schwarzenberg, waited for orders east of the Rhine while the sovereigns and their ministers, glowing from the success at Leipzig and for once united in amiable concord, discussed what their proposals should be. The French emperor had withdrawn like a wounded lion west of the Rhine on November 2.

The three British ambassadors attached to the sovereigns at Allied Headquarters were generous hosts. One night there might be a dinner at Lord Cathcart's, the next evening Lord Aberdeen would entertain, and on the third night the party would be at Sir Charles Stewart's. The last named plenipotentiary was half-brother to the foreign secretary of England, Lord Castlereagh, and an old friend of Priscilla and her husband.

"Consider how odd for me to be the only woman among fifteen to thirty men . . ." she wrote home, clearly savoring every moment of her unique position. Not only was she reunited with her beloved "B.," but the news from her uncle, Arthur Wellington, was excellent. Having crossed the Pyrenees, he was now pressing the French army under Marshal Nicolas Soult hard in the faraway Basque country, driving for the town of Bayonne and the road beyond it to Bordeaux. She loved "Arthur," as she called him, and he in turn considered her his favorite niece.

Soon she met all the celebrities gathered in Frankfurt. She wrote home that she liked the emperor of Austria, whom she found a "kind, although wizened old man." He was forty-five years old, but it must be remembered that she was only twenty. She even warmed to the king of Prussia; that dim and eternally bewildered figure had now been adopted by the tsar of Russia, whom he revered, calling him "my divine friend." Politically, it was extremely convenient for the tsar to have Frederick William of Prussia attached to him as a sort of tame bear on a chain, and he could easily rationalize the master-servant relationship between them by saying that Queen Louise, who had died in 1810, had loved them both and would have wanted him to look after her husband. Alexander I was a duplicitous man, but he usually succeeded in clothing his falsity in a coat of sentiment.

Lady Burghersh did not like Alexander, which is surprising, as he was highly admired in England. She wrote to her mother of a fete given by the tsar at which the soldiers of his own regiment paraded before him, superb, gigantic men who afterward sang in deep bass voices which profoundly stirred her. She found the whole Russian show astoundingly romantic— the bands, the stout little horses from the steppes, the long, slanting lances of the Cossacks. But the tsar—"I never was so disappointed as in the Emperor Alexander. He is the image of —————— only fair instead of red, and also very like W. the dentist. He certainly has fine shoulders, but beyond that he is horribly ill-made. He holds himself bent quite forward for which reason his Court imitate him and bend too, and gird in their waists like women. His countenance is not bad, that is all I can say."

This description of the savior of Europe, as the English had thought of Alexander since Napoleon's disastrous Russian campaign, must have astonished Lady Burghersh's family. In defense of the tsar, it must be pointed out that he leaned forward in conversation because he had been deafened in the left ear in early youth by being forced to listen to the cannonades as his insane father's troops marched back and forth day after day before the despot in never-ending review to the sound of heavy artillery.

It was fortunate for Priscilla Burghersh that she had been brought up by a French governess, of whom she had been very fond, and as a result had learned to speak French fluently. It is impossible to exaggerate the importance of that language in the society into which she was now thrown. The tsar himself always spoke and wrote in French to his German wife, and she replied in kind. This was also the case with his favorite sister, the Grand Duchess Catherine, and his mother, the dowager empress. His Russian aides all spoke and corresponded with him and each other in French, and so did the generals. Even old Marshal Michael Kutuzov, that great stout oak, the most Russian of Russians, had invariably written his reports to the emperor in French.

What a cosmopolitan group assembled at Frankfurt in November 1813! Baron Heinrich Friedrich Karl vom und zum Stein, the patriot who had done so much to lead Prussia into her victorious War of Liberation, and was currently serving the tsar as adviser, was a Rhinelander, not a Prussian at all. Whereas Friedrich von Gentz, an Austrian adviser, was by birth a Prussian. Prince Karl August von Hardenberg, chancellor of Prussia, was a Hanoverian. Emperor Francis I of Austria had been born in Italy, where his father reigned as grand duke of Tuscany. Having spent his boyhood in Florence, he was always more at ease speaking Italian or French than German. Prince Clemens Metternich,* the greatest foreign minister in Austrian history, was the son of an ancient Rhineland family and never saw Austria until he was thirteen, nor did he live there until he was seventeen. Educated in Strasbourg and Mainz, brought up in Brussels where his father held high office under the Austrian government, he was equally at home in German, French, English, Italian, and Russian, although he preferred French to the other languages.

Metternich in 1813 was, in effect, the prime minister of the Allied Coalition, and he deserved to be considered so. But his

---

* Earlier referred to as Count Metternich, the foreign minister was given the hereditary title of prince by the emperor after Leipzig.

contemporaries and many later historians have been hard on him, especially the English.

"Most intolerably loose and giddy with women," wrote Sir Edward Cooke, a senior British civil servant who knew him well at Vienna.[5] Dr. C. K. Webster, the eminent historian, described him: "A timid statesman, though fertile in diplomatic expedients, he was an opportunist, pure and simple."[6]

A very handsome man in his portrait by Sir Thomas Lawrence, he appears the eighteenth-century grand seigneur that he was. In the portrait he is gazing serenely at the world, the jewel of the Golden Fleece hanging from his cravated neck; his fine torso encased in the resplendent uniform of a Knight of Malta. He was as smooth and shiny and ornamental as the richly decorated enamel eggs that the jeweler Fabergé contrived for the last Imperial Court of Russia, toys that contained many a hidden coil and spring. There were indeed complex coils and springs beneath Metternich's gleaming surface, but it was to remain unmarred throughout his long life by the cracks and chips of self-doubt. "Error," he remarked in his old age to François Guizot,* "has never approached my mind."[7]

He was highly attractive to women, and his mistresses were invariably important and influential. Yet his love letters could be unbearably pretentious and self-centered. To Princess Dorothea Lieven, whose political letters to him from London make excellent reading today, he replied with diffuse, ponderous protestations of everlasting love, full of rhetorical passages. To many observers, he appeared vain, pretentious, humorless, and devious. Politically, he saw things rather mechanistically: the concert of Europe was like a game of chess in which the pieces could be neatly assigned to their places on the board. He had been brought up on the eighteenth-century belief in a rational system. If only man would conduct himself according to the rules of this perfect system then harmony in human affairs would be as possible to attain as it would be for a practiced

---

*François Pierre Guillaume Guizot, 1787–1874. French historian and statesman, premier of France, 1840–1848.

clockmaker to build a faultless clock. The secret of the political mechanism, the heart of his policy, was the equilibrium of Europe.

In pursuit of this goal, he was capable of infinite tenacity and resolution. The diplomacy he employed to gain his ends during the years 1805–1814 was as courageous as it was brilliant. Without this seemingly cold, unoriginal man, there would have been no gathering of Allies at Frankfurt to discuss the terms to offer Napoleon.

His early career in the Austrian service had taken him to Dresden in Saxony as the envoy of the emperor, and in his first diplomatic report from there, written when he was only twenty-eight, he described his concept of the balance of power: "The power of France must be reduced; Austria and Prussia must forget their recent past . . . not competition but cooperation is their natural policy. An equilibrium is possible only through a strong Central Europe backed by England. . . ."[8]

Metternich held steadily to his course during the difficult years that followed. His career was a splendid one—Berlin and Paris were his embassies after the Dresden post, and in 1809, when he was thirty-six, the emperor named him minister of foreign affairs. The French triumphs had been followed by such harsh peace treaties that it appeared impossible that the bankrupt power of Austria could ever again present a military threat. Emperor Francis, a man of pedantic and indolent nature, accepted his humiliation passively. He was content to lead a placid life far removed from events taking place on the great stage of Europe; his one desire was for peace at any price.

Metternich, on the other hand, had long decided that war was inevitable. Much as he disliked the thought of it, he saw no other way to achieve the balance of European power that had been his lifelong aim. However, to lead his master into war and to form the forces with which to fight it without arousing the suspicions of Napoleon was to require diplomatic maneuvering of the utmost delicacy.

As the ally of France, Austria was required to send an auxiliary corps to assist in the Russian campaign of 1812. Metternich saw to it that the corps was raised and made combat-ready, but at the same time he made a secret proposal to Russia that, while the Austrian troops would be sent, they would be kept on the sidelines instead of participating in action to back up the French. The astonished Russians naturally asked that this offer should be confirmed in writing, which Metternich coldly refused to do. At the same time he shrewdly proposed that Russia send forces into the Austrian border province of Galicia. This seeming threat would not only justify Austrian inaction on the Russian front but would also provide an excuse to create yet another army corps "for the defense of Austria." [9]

Thus the Austrian army grew into a powerful force during 1812 with the complete approval of the unsuspecting Napoleon. In a letter oozing with deference, Metternich wrote to him that a hundred thousand men would be mobilized: "Ranged on the flanks of the enemy, they are designed to intimidate Russia and to inspire even England with caution." [10]

Napoleon agreed with every word, and when Metternich offered Austria's services as neutral mediator for a general peace settlement he agreed with that also, but not without demanding the doubling of the Austrian auxiliary corps so that, should the peace efforts fail, France could count upon an even stronger ally in Vienna.

By March 1813, Metternich had advanced another step on the road to his ultimate objective: the formation of a new Allied Coalition against the French, led by Austria. He succeeded in maneuvering Prussia into formal alliance with Russia. This meant that when the two great armies, French and Allied, moved into central Europe in May their forces were nearly equal. Austria was in a pivotal position: her weight on either side would be decisive.

Metternich had played a weak hand superbly, but the game had been full of risks. At any moment Napoleon might have seen through his laborious planning and turned to crush him.

That he did not was partly because Napoleon was never quite the same man after the Russian ordeal. His clarity of vision was clouded, his capacity for self-delusion stronger. And Metternich, who had studied the French emperor closely during his years at the Paris embassy, counted on another factor. Napoleon not only considered that Francis of Austria was a coward, but his Corsican sense of family loyalty blinded him to the possibility that his father-in-law would ever declare war on him.*

To have gone from French ally to armed mediator in the short space of seven months was an achievement that amazed his future allies, but that Metternich did not now take the last step and join the coalition exasperated them. Charles Stewart, writing to Castlereagh from Prussian headquarters on May 31, expressed his worries: "Our operations have been conducted with implicit faith in Austria. We have . . . committed ourselves to a narrow strip of country where existence for an army becomes very doubtful. We have abandoned Breslau, the direct communication with Kalish, and have thus given over Poland to Bonaparte's influence; and still Austria does not declare. . . . I am by no means pleased with the manner things are going, both in the councils and on the battlefield." [11]

Sir Charles could not know of the anguished appeals that Metternich was addressing to the Emperor Francis—pointing out in forceful, heartfelt letters that now at last Austria had her great chance. She would become the strongest power in the center of Europe, in a position to establish an equilibrium which would prevent the dominance of either France or Russia. The emperor resisted his arguments with mulish obstinacy. He would not go to war again, abandoning the security of isolation for the dangers of combat. Surely there must be some way to compromise with Napoleon?

Therefore Metternich was obliged to make Napoleon appear so irrevocably adamant that even Francis I would see that there

---

*Napoleon had married the Archduchess Marie Louise of Austria in 1810.

was no alternative to fighting. He accomplished his purpose in the third week of June by the application of a fresh and dangerous tactic.

This maneuver was to offer Napoleon a document known as the Treaty of Reichenbach, the terms of which stated that Austria would be obliged to join Prussia and Russia in war unless France accepted certain conditions. They were moderate conditions, concerning the redrawing of various boundaries that were not of cardinal importance, and Bonaparte should have accepted the terms at once. He did not, and historians still point to his refusal of the treaty as an example of his blind intransigence.[12] It would have been awkward in the extreme for Metternich had Napoleon agreed to the Reichenbach treaty. Emperor Francis would have been able to say, "I told you so," and the already worried Allies might well have lost their nerve.

On June 26, 1813, Napoleon summoned Metternich to his headquarters in a villa just outside Dresden. It was a terrible confrontation.

The emperor was in a towering rage. "So you want war? All right, you shall have it. I crushed the Prussians at Lützen, I destroyed the Russians at Bautzen; now you want your turn. Very well—we shall meet at Vienna."

Metternich suggested that the decision between peace and war lay in the hands of France. "You want me to dishonor myself?" Napoleon replied. "Never! I know how to die, but never shall I relinquish territory. Your sovereigns, who were born to a throne, can afford to be beaten twenty times, and will always return to their capitals. I cannot do that—I am a self-made soldier."

During the conversation, which lasted for nine hours, Metternich told the emperor that, if he rejected the Treaty of Reichenbach, an Austrian army of 250,000 men was ready and waiting. This boast was a wild exaggeration and Napoleon knew it. When he doubted the figures, Metternich offered the ultimate insult; he dared to question the strength of the Grande Armée.

"I have seen your soldiers—they are children. And when these infants are killed what will Your Imperial Majesty have left?"

The remark stung Napoleon as no other criticism could have. Flinging his hat into a corner, he all but screamed at the Austrian foreign minister: "You are not a soldier. You can know nothing of what goes on in a soldier's mind. I grew up upon the field of battle, and a man like me cares little for the lives of a million men."

Metternich did not pick up the emperor's hat, which was lying on the floor. Instead he leaned calmly against a little table by the window and said in measured tones: "If only the words that His Imperial Majesty has just uttered could be heard from one end of France to the other!"

This insolent sentence had the effect of an icy douche upon the emperor. Growing quieter, he began to pace the room. Noticing his hat in the corner, he picked it up and said, as if speaking to himself, "I may lose my throne, but I shall bury the whole world in its ruins."

At the end of the interview, the emperor led Metternich to the door almost affectionately. Tapping him on the shoulder, he said, "No, you will never make war on me." Metternich replied, "Sire, you are a finished man."

Outside, the French marshals and ministers, who had been waiting all day in breathless anticipation, rushed to Metternich as he left the chamber. Louis Alexandre Berthier, prince de Neuchâtel, murmured: "Remember that Europe needs peace—France most of all."

This account, taken from Metternich's memoirs written years later, has been doubted by serious historians. Henry Kissinger gives it only a few lines, although he grants that it is psychologically correct. To this writer it seems most unlikely that Metternich, or anyone else, ever dared to say to Napoleon, "You are finished."

On the other hand, Metternich was playing for very high

stakes and just might have deliberately decided to abandon his habitual tact in order to outrage Napoleon and determine him to reject the Treaty of Reichenbach. The dates are interesting; Metternich knew that the full text of the treaty was to be presented to the emperor the next day, June 27. It is an intriguing question, to which the answer will never be known as there were no witnesses to the conversation in the villa outside Dresden.

What does carry the ring of truth is Napoleon's lament about being a self-made soldier in contrast to the Habsburgs, established for five hundred years upon the Austrian throne. He was never to lose his dread of being called "a Corsican upstart." An example of his deep sense of insecurity can be found in his first meeting with Talleyrand in 1797, following his return to France as a young general who was covered with glory from the campaign of Italy. All Paris longed to greet the hero of the battle of Rivoli, above all Talleyrand, a somewhat tarnished relic of the *ancien régime,* who wanted to attach himself to the rising star. And yet Bonaparte opened the conversation with Talleyrand rather shyly, saying: "I believe that your uncle was the Archbishop of Rheims? I also am the nephew of a bishop, who much influenced me during my bringing up in Corsica." This was as if to say: "I know that your name is Talleyrand-Périgord and that your family tree goes back a thousand years, but we are both gentlemen, aren't we?"

On returning to his lodgings in Dresden, Metternich sent an express to Prince Karl Philipp von Schwarzenberg, Austrian commander in chief, asking how long it would take to put the army on a war footing. Schwarzenberg answered that if he could have twenty days, the troops already mobilized could be increased by 75,000. After some anxious weeks and some futile conferences, bonfires were lit around the town of Prague on the night of August 12, 1813, to inform all Bohemia that the Austrian empire had gone to war against France.

If this story were being written as a play, it would fall neatly into acts. Having formed the Allied Coalition in Act I, Metternich was to remain very much on center stage. But now he was to share the footlights with a new actor in the drama, Robert Stewart, Viscount Castlereagh, the foreign secretary of England; and it was the Englishman who was to be the more formidable of the two protagonists in the second act.*

* Castlereagh's titles can be confusing. Born Robert Stewart in 1769, he was given the courtesy title of Viscount Castlereagh in 1795. In 1816 he became the Marquess of Londonderry, but some contemporary records continued to refer to him as Lord Castlereagh.

Into France

LORD CASTLEREAGH had no intention of leaving England to assist his ambassadors in Frankfurt in concluding the negotiations with Napoleon. Lord Aberdeen,* although only twenty-nine, had had considerable diplomatic experience and seemed competent enough, besides which he was seconded by Lord Cathcart† and Sir Charles Stewart. Both were soldiers by training, but Castlereagh knew his half-brother Stewart to be highly intelligent, if a touch hot-tempered and erratic. He loved this younger man as he did no one else in the world with the exception of his fat, dowdy wife, Emily.

The first sign of trouble was implied in a patronizing letter from Aberdeen to the foreign secretary, dated September 12, 1813: "Do not think Metternich such a formidable personage. Depend upon it, I have the most substantial reasons for knowing that he is heart and soul with us; but, my dear Castlereagh, with all your wisdom, judgement and experience . . . I think you have so much of the Englishman as not quite to be aware of the real value of foreign modes of acting." [1]

A less modest man than Castlereagh would have been highly irritated by the tone of this letter. As it was, perceiving that the young ambassador had clearly fallen victim to the charms of the

*George Hamilton Gordon, 4th Earl of Aberdeen, 1784–1860.
†William Schaw Cathcart, 1st Earl of Cathcart, 1755–1843.

Austrian foreign minister, he studied the dispatches from Frankfurt with increased attention. Once more his careful instructions went out to Aberdeen, repeating the litany which every British diplomat was supposed to carry engraved on his heart: the primary national interests of England were (1) that she be assured of maritime rights throughout the world, (2) that the Lowlands (today Holland and Belgium) remain in hands friendly to Great Britain in order to secure the English Channel.

At that time Castlereagh had never met Metternich and had had no opportunity to judge at first hand the divergence in their views on the peacemaking. He, as foreign secretary of England, represented the one country that had been at war with France continuously since 1793 except for the brief truce previously mentioned. It was thanks to the Royal Navy that Napoleon had been prevented from expanding his empire beyond the European continent. His defeat was the goal of British policy and it was toward that end *alone* that years of bloody effort and 700 million pounds had been poured out. Metternich, on the other hand, dreaded the Russians as much as he did the French. Thus, in order to retain a strong France as a counterweight to Russia, he was prepared to offer Napoleon lenient terms and to permit him to retain his throne.

It was soon all too apparent that Lord Aberdeen agreed with this policy. A sensitive, cultivated man, he had been taken by Metternich to visit the devastated German countryside over which Lady Burghersh had driven, and together the two men had toured the battlefield of Leipzig, a sight which appalled Aberdeen. The memory of the horrors that he had seen may well have nurtured the profound desire for peace which now led him to disregard his instructions. Without informing his colleagues, Cathcart and Stewart, he agreed to proposals which included offering Napoleon what were known as the "natural limits" of France: the Rhine, the Alps, and the Pyrenees, as well as certain other concessions.[2] These terms would have meant the surrender to France of the port of Antwerp on the Scheldt, and whoever controlled the mouth of the Scheldt controlled the Narrows. Such a basic British strategic interest was simply not negotiable.

Once more, Napoleon's obstinacy saved the day. The proposals were turned down. On December 2 the emperor changed his mind and sent Caulaincourt to accept them, but it was too late. The cumbersome machinery for the invasion of France had been set in motion, and the Allied armies were moving toward the Rhine under their commander in chief, Prince Schwarzenberg. Priscilla Burghersh, moving with them, had by now established a traveling salon and received every evening after dinner in the exiguous quarters assigned to her and her husband at each stop. Somehow she always managed to maintain a large supply of tea from England, a welcome drink on cold winter nights.

Besides the English attached to headquarters, including Charles Stewart, who was to remain her close friend, there were the Prussians, the Austrians, and the Russians, all eager to shake the snow from their field boots, toss their greatcoats into a corner of the little apartment, and settle down to discuss the news of the day. Of the Prussians the most impressive was Prince Hardenberg, the august chancellor, but Hardenberg was already in his sixties and much handicapped by deafness. Baron Wilhelm von Humboldt and Baron Stein were easier company; the latter sparkled with fierce energy. Obliged to flee Prussia under threat of arrest by Napoleon, he had joined the Russian service and it was largely due to the force of his energetic persuasion that Alexander had moved westward in 1813. Ugly little Friedrich von Gentz, with his sharp-featured face and malicious tongue, was the most diverting of the Austrian team under Metternich. Gentz was not popular, but he was admired for his acute political acumen. His conversation, however controversial, was the kind that keeps a party on its toes. And if the talk ever flagged, it was a comfort to have the jolly Russian staff in the room—kind Count Pozzo di Borgo, who had been the first old friend to greet Lady Burghersh on her arrival from England, and Prince Nikita Volkonsky, the dashing aide-de-camp to the tsar who was, if possible, even more agreeable than he had been during his years at the Russian embassy in London. There he had been inhibited by the presence of his wife, Princess Zénaïde. That temperamental Slavic beauty, her high cheekbones scarlet and her slanting black eyes glowering, used to slash her lips with a sharp knife each time she discovered that her husband had been unfaithful to her. As Volkonsky was incapable of constancy, Zénaïde generally appeared in public with fresh scars. The Russian foreign minister, Count Karl Nesselrode, was another charming young man. Just married, he was desolate to leave his wife in Basel as headquarters moved forward, but, as fashionable society considered Countess Nesselrode a blue-stockinged prig, he probably was more popular without her.

Surrounded by the best masculine company in all Europe, Lady Burghersh bubbled with enthusiasm:

Freiburg,
December 19, 1813

My dearest Mama,

I have just learnt that Lord Aberdeen sends a courier off tonight. It is now late, but I will write a line. . . . Such plans, orders, and counter orders, indecisions etc; but at last the Austrians have prevailed. I believe the troops have already marched. . . . The next headquarters are not quite fixed yet, but will probably be at a short distance from here. Lörrach or between Lörrach and Basle. Schwarzenberg has just been dining here; there never was anything like his attention and care of me. He has given me the best of his own chasseurs, mounted, to be always with my carriage and in my anteroom, and he will be of great service to me in moving and taking up quarters. . . .

Lörrach,
December 22, 1813

My dearest Papa,

    We have halted here at a small town, one mile from Basle, to give time for the troops to come up and pass the Rhine before we proceed towards Berne. . . . This town is little more than a village, therefore you may imagine the state of it, with all Schwarzenberg's headquarters in it. Our quarters consist of one room, where we eat, drink, and sleep. Yesterday 30,000 Austrian troops passed through the town and crossed the Rhine at or about Rheinfeld, and today the whole Bavarian army, about 40,000 infantry and cavalry, with artillery, have gone through. They are remarkably fine troops, all young and in the best condition . . .

    God knows what Buonaparte will do to oppose this force!

She was totally without apprehension. Another writer, René de Chateaubriand, described the troops moving warily, following their officers steadily but somberly. One would not have guessed that this was a conquering army. "The name of Napoleon was still so dreaded that the enemy armies crossed the Rhine with terror; constantly looking behind them as they did so as if to make sure that retreat was still possible."[3]

Meanwhile, in London, Lord Castlereagh continued to be disturbed by the reports he was receiving from his ambassadors. The Frankfurt proposals were blessedly behind them, but he did not like the sound of the state of the coalition. The prime minister, Lord Liverpool, agreed that the time had come when the foreign secretary must himself take charge. To this end, Castlereagh left England on December 26. He stopped for a few days in Holland on official business, where he left his beloved Emily. They were a childless, deeply devoted couple and she longed to accompany him, but he refused to permit her to risk the dangers and discomforts of the journey. With a ministerial colleague, Frederick Robinson, as his assistant, his private secretary, Joseph Planta, and two Foreign Office clerks, he plowed on for Switzerland, a cold and tiring drive. With the exception of one night, they slept in their carriages and stopped only to change horses. Six days later found them in Basel, where Metternich was eagerly awaiting his English opposite number.

Aberdeen's last dispatch, written on January 6, 1814, had removed any lingering illusions that Castlereagh might have held as to the atmosphere he would find on arriving. Having lost his former cocky assurance, the ambassador now longed for his master's help:

"With relation to the enemy, our situation is as good as possible, among ourselves it is quite the reverse. Everything which has been so long smothered is now bursting forth. Your presence is absolutely providential. . . ."[4]

Castlereagh was in the fortunate position of having a very free hand. Lord Liverpool was interested in foreign policy only so far as it affected votes, and his colleagues, with the exception of the secretary for war and colonies, Lord Bathurst, cared little about the reconstruction of Europe. While giving lip service to the principle of Allied unity, what they really wanted was a speedy victory with British rights protected. The prince regent, with whom Castlereagh was on excellent terms, backed him completely and the Whig Opposition was, for once, quiescent. Thus the foreign secretary was able to draw up his own instructions, which were based on the policy of William Pitt, the great prime minister who had been the mentor of the young Robert Castlereagh.

While the ship carrying the foreign secretary and his party had been lying fogbound at Harwich before leaving England, a letter from Lord Wellington to the Cabinet had been brought to him. Wellington wrote that his army was being warmly received by the French in its path as it turned northward for Bordeaux. He therefore suggested that perhaps it was time for a prince of the House of Bourbon to show himself in France. The Cabinet approved of this policy.

Castlereagh was the last person to dismiss Wellington's advice, for they were close personal friends as well as colleagues who much admired each other's abilities. But, in the six-day journey over the icy roads to Switzerland, he had a great deal of time to think. It would be impossible to postpone a decision on what sort of French government would follow the defeat of Napoleon. There appeared to be only two choices: restoring the Bourbons or retaining Bonaparte under some form of safeguards. The former was the solution desired by popular opinion in England as well as by the prince regent and the Cabinet. Now Wellington suggested that he also supported it. Yet Pitt, Castlereagh's revered master, had always declared that it would be a grave mistake for the British or any other power to impose the Bourbons on France unless and until the French people themselves "manifested a strong and prevailing disposition" for their former dynasty.[5]

These words, weightier because they came from the other side of the grave, were much in Castlereagh's mind. Did the French really want the return of their former dynasty? Perhaps Metternich, the best-informed diplomat in Europe, would enlighten him. Castlereagh had been disturbed the year before when Austria's long delay in joining the coalition had seemed to show dangerous irresolution, and Metternich's role in the recent Frankfurt negotiations had further shaken his confidence in the Austrian minister, but he awaited meeting him with an open mind. Aberdeen's dispatches suggested that Metternich was so much at loggerheads with the tsar that the alliance was on the point of dissolving. What was the justification for Metternich's suspicions of the Russian Emperor?

When Castlereagh reached Basel, the situation was clarified by a series of conferences between the two men. Tsar Alexander had been foolish enough to dash on ahead to Langres, over the French frontier, leaving a polite note for Castlereagh and the field clear for his opponent.

Metternich made the most of his opportunity. He told Castlereagh that in his view the Bourbons had been so long out of power that a monarch named Louis XVIII would mean nothing to the present generation, besides which the king and his brothers were a feeble lot. If restored, they could not possibly last and might well be overthrown by another Jacobin revolution. A France weakened by social turmoil would leave the Continent open to the power of Russia. He sketched an ugly picture: France in chaos, Poland annexed by Alexander, central Europe at his mercy. To Castlereagh this scenario at first seemed exaggerated. He had not thought of Russia as acquisitive, and in his dispatches, he had spoken of her as being, like England, "a satisfied power." This again was the legacy of Pitt. It had been Castlereagh's cruel duty to journey down to see the ailing prime minister at Bath to inform him of Napoleon's victory at Austerlitz in December 1805. It was the death blow, and Pitt's famous order to his niece the next month, "Roll up the map of Europe, it will not be wanted these ten years," had proved remarkably prophetic. But now the ten years had nearly passed. If Metternich was to be believed, the map of Europe risked being altered in the most dangerous manner. Pitt would have been appalled at the contemplation of Russia as the dominant power in central Europe, and so was Castlereagh.

The more the two foreign ministers talked, the more worried the Englishman became. Metternich's picture of an unstable emperor of Russia, bent on aggrandizement at the expense of European equilibrium, was a most unpleasant one. And it was disturbing to hear that Alexander was waffling on the question of a future French government, now advocating a republic, now a regency under the soft and ineffective Marie Louise, now a monarchy under the unreliable ex-French Marshal Bernadotte, king of Sweden. As for Russian designs on Poland, the future of that unhappy, partitioned country had not seemed of immediate concern when viewed from London, but Metternich opened wider horizons as he expounded his views.

Castlereagh was already far less insular than the government he represented. Furthermore, in human terms, the rapport between him and Metternich was immediate. "I cannot praise Castlereagh enough," reported Metternich, "his attitude is excellent and his work as direct as it is correct. I cannot find a single point of difference with him, and assure you that his mood is peaceful, peaceful in *our* sense."[6]

This was the beginning of a cooperation that would last until Castlereagh's death. That an Anglo-Irish peer should be as keen a European as the foreign minister of Austria was extraordinary, but Castlereagh *was* an extraordinary man. If Metternich flattered himself that the foreign secretary of England had fallen under his spell he was wrong; a letter from him to Liverpool written a month later showed that while he wished to collaborate closely with Metternich, whom he regarded as highly intelligent, he was not blind to his faults.[7]

Castlereagh then threw his whole immense energy into the crucial task of holding the alliance together. Risking the displeasure of his government at home, he told Metternich that, while England preferred a Bourbon restoration, he was prepared to back the Austrian policy of retaining Napoleon on the throne of France with limited powers. It was therefore in perfect agreement that the two ministers proceeded to Langres to meet the tsar.

They left Basel in the early afternoon of January 23, after a quick meal at Metternich's house in the company of Priscilla Burghersh, who was invited to follow them on the long drive across the frontier to headquarters at Langres, a town between the Seine and the Marne in the heart of eastern France. The two statesmen raced ahead through the night in Metternich's fast campaign carriage. Lady Burghersh and her companion, Madame Legoux, were soon left behind to sleep as best they could in the swaying berlin that had come so far. "Oh, my dear English carriage," wrote Lady Burghersh, "all these miles and miles and not even one single nail loose."

The cold was intense. Priscilla Burghersh thought it the most bitter she had ever known. However, her physical discomfort was forgotten in the excitement of waking at daylight to find herself bowling along the frozen roads of the France she had never seen. She realized that she was not far from the home of dear Mademoiselle, the governess who had brought her up with tales of how lovely this part of the country used to be: cows grazing in the rich meadowlands beside the poplar-lined banks of the Seine, prosperous farms, pink-cheeked children dressed in blue pinafores playing in their yards. There could be no question of pausing to look for Mademoiselle's house—the coachman was straining to catch up with the galloping cabriolet ahead. Priscilla Burghersh wrapped her fur-lined traveling cloak more tightly about her and glued her pretty head to the window, horrified at what she saw. In the bleak villages she noted "multitudes of miserable-looking women; one never sees a young man, and I am particularly struck with not seeing any babies whatever . . . all women and children, for of spare men there are none." When they stopped to change horses, crowds of begging women followed them. "If you give money to one, the rest falls on her and then begins a regular fight." She thought that she had seen dreadful poverty in Ireland, but France was far worse. "The number of beggars surpasses Dublin." The hollow-eyed peasants stared after the carriage numbly, without curiosity except at one place where the women and the old men came running out to look at "la petite princess anglaise," as she heard them calling her.[8]

They reached Langres after nearly forty-eight hours of hard driving through increasingly piercing cold. It was not much of a place, and Metternich was to write home that he was obliged to work in a room in which the temperature was only 6 degrees above zero. What was more, he told his wife, wolves had appeared in packs near the town, coming so close that an Austrian courier arriving by carriage had to chase them away with pistol shots and blows of the coachman's whip.[9]

Resilient as always, Lady Burghersh wrote to her parents on January 26, the day after her arrival: "We are twenty-four hours journey from Paris, and as yet we hear of no preparations to check us. . . . Peace will probably be signed within a very short time. The treating begins immediately, and no one has yet expressed a doubt of the issue."

While she was penning these cheerful lines, Metternich and Castlereagh were calling on the tsar of Russia. The last meeting between Alexander and Metternich had been highly unpleasant. The occasion for the row had been Austrian insistence on forcing neutral Switzerland to agree that the Allied invasion of France should be launched from Swiss soil. The tsar, shocked at this arbitrary decision, had objected strenuously. Metternich, unmoved by the morality of the issue, supported the strategic opinion of the commander in chief of the armies, the Austrian Schwarzenberg. He had won the argument and the operation had been a success, but the final conversation between the two men had been a bitter one. Metternich recounts in his memoirs that the tsar had been "extremely agitated" by the news that the Austrian and Prussian forces had safely crossed the Rhine between Schauffhausen and Basel. This is an understatement. Alexander had been in a violent rage. When he had calmed down he took Metternich's hand and said: "Success crowns the undertaking; it remains for success to justify what you have done. As one of the Allied monarchs I have nothing more to say to you, but as a man I declare to you that you have grieved me in a way you can never repair." [10]

This was highly characteristic of the tsar's style. He would never forgive Metternich, and the episode wrote "finis" to their already tenuous relationship, but it was very like him to take Metternich's hand and to sound, in his sanctimonious way, more hurt than angry. One can almost see the benign smile on his face as he dismissed the minister, while inwardly burning with resentment. Naturally secretive, his early life had made him more so. Under the rule of his insane father, he had had no authority although he was given a mass of honorary titles and positions. Emperor Paul was capable of sending for him at any hour of the day or night to castigate him for the sloppiness of a sentry's stance on duty, or the angle at which a guard wore his hat—any meaningless trifle which had caught the attention of the demented monarch. As a man of twenty, Alexander still lived in dread of his father, and in a childish attempt to make amends would write him abject letters of apology, submission and respect: "The reproach that you have made me pierces my soul. . . ."[11]

Small wonder that in all his relationships he always seemed to be acting a part. He would never recover from the night of his father's murder at the hands of a conspiracy of officers. Appalled, he had cowered on the ground floor of the Michael Palace listening to the screams over his head. When they brought him the news of Paul's death he collapsed completely. Others had accomplished what he had hoped would be done, and he felt that by his tacit consent he was guilty of the most craven kind of parricide. As he sat sobbing, Count Peter Alexeyevich Pahlen, governor of St. Petersburg, intervened brusquely: "C'est assez de faire l'enfant. Allez régner. Venez vous montrer aux Gardes!"[12] After further exhortations from his young wife, Elisabeth, he managed to stumble to the balcony of the palace to show himself to the excited soldiers below.

As an intelligent, eager boy he had been the favorite of his grandmother, Empress Catherine the Great, who had encouraged the Swiss tutor, Frédéric Césai de La Harpe to instill in the idealistic pupil the most liberal of views. La Harpe, seeing himself as the guardian of a philosopher king in the Platonic mold, filled Alexander's head with the principles of the French eighteenth-century philosophers who had formed his own thinking. Together they planned a constitution for a free and democratic Poland, they discussed emancipation of the serfs and the formation of a free press in Russia, they foresaw the day when the equality of man could become a living reality within the bounds of the empire. It was heady stuff, a secret inner existence and escape from the brutality of his father. While there seldom seemed anything true and lasting about Alexander's emotions, his affection for La Harpe was to remain as genuine later on as it had been when he was an impressionable boy, and the greatest struggle of his life was to equate the liberal ideals of which he saw himself the champion with the ugly reality of his inherited and inevitable role as autocrat. The resulting mixture fascinated and confused the cleverest men—Napoleon, having given the matter thought, could only say: "There is a piece missing somewhere in Emperor Alexander, and I don't know what it is."[13]

A more subtle observer, the French ambassador to Russia, Count Pierre Louis de La Ferronays, wrote:

> Understanding Alexander's character is a task that I find more difficult the more I know him. A conversation with him leaves you with a most favorable impression. You go away convinced that here is a prince who unites the qualities of a true knight with that of a great sovereign; a highly able man possessed of vital energies. He reasons brilliantly, he explains himself eloquently and with passionate conviction. And yet, all experience of him, the whole story of his life shows that you cannot count on him. His multiple acts of weakness prove that the energy he puts into his words hardly exists in his character, but on the other hand this weak character can all of a sudden know bursts of violence and irritation . . . he can then adopt very dangerous measures, the results of which are incalculable.[14]

Caulaincourt, who knew him well, warned Napoleon: "They believe him to be weak, but they are wrong . . . underneath his appearance of good-will, frankness and natural loyalty, there is a core of dissimulation which is the mark of an obstinacy which nothing can move."[15]

The meeting at Langres on that cold January day of 1814 between this complex ruler and the foreign ministers of England and Austria was not immortalized by the brush of a portraitist, which is a pity. Alexander, despite Lady Burghersh's earlier quoted unflattering description, was a handsome, fair-haired man of thirty-seven, whose manners were deceptively simple and elegant. Metternich at forty and Castlereagh at forty-five were two of the best-looking men in Europe. Today a hundred cameras would have caught their expressions as they greeted each other, but we have only a written record.[16]

Alexander was in a martial mood, very much the soldier-emperor. While professing himself delighted to receive his guests, he said that he could not imagine what business they had to discuss. Everything had come clear to him during the days and nights that he had stood on the bridge, hatless and coatless, watching his stalwart army cross the Rhine. God was with them. Alexander always interjected God into his conversations with a monotonous regularity that set the teeth of Metternich and Castlereagh on edge. These two fastidious and urbane products of the Age of Reason found emotional invocations of the deity embarrassing. Sometimes the tsar called him "le Très-Haut," sometimes "le Tout-Puissant," occasionally "la Providence."

"Le Tout-Puissant" had led Alexander into France. France—the country to which he, as the pupil of La Harpe, owed so much. Liberty, equality, fraternity—there in three words was the true political faith. If they cared to meet the great La Harpe, he was right there at Russian headquarters. Alexander had brought him out of his retirement in Switzerland in order to thank him for having instilled in him the knowledge that he was born to be not only a conqueror but also a liberator.

During the last two weeks, Alexander had been extremely active, as an energetic leader should be. (Possibly a hint here that while Castlereagh and Metternich had been lounging around Basel having tea with the likes of Lady Burghersh, he, the emperor, had been on the job?) No matter what the weather —his grandmother had taught him that to forswear creature comforts while on campaign was the mark of the great sovereign—he had engaged himself in the task of aiding his generals by riding from regiment to regiment encouraging the troops. Morale was excellent. He deeply regretted the uncouth behavior of certain units of the Cossacks, the Kirghizes and the Kalmucks as they passed through France (they had pillaged and raped in every town and hamlet they had come to), but those fierce warriors from the steppes were being sternly disciplined and order would be restored by the time they were in Paris. And what was to stop the advance? The towns of Strasbourg, Saverne, Epinal, Lunéville, and Nancy were already occupied. The time had come to march on Paris. "I will make no peace while Napoleon is still on his throne." [17]

It was clear to everyone in the conference room exactly *who* was going to lead the march on Paris. Castlereagh wrote to Liverpool later: "He [the tsar] has a personal feeling about Paris distinct from all military and political considerations. He seems to seek the occasion for entering with his magnificent Guards the enemy's capital, probably to display, in his clemency and forbearance, a contrast to that desolation to which his own [capital] was reduced." [18]

This was a shrewd comment. It was natural for Alexander to have in his mind a vision of the smoldering ruins of Moscow as he planned his benevolent conquest of Paris. However, there were certain practical points to be faced, and as it was impossible for Metternich to hope to succeed in persuading the tsar, Castlereagh then took the lead in conversation.

Quietly, he reminded Alexander that Napoleon and two army corps, however much diminished, lay at this moment between the Allies and Paris. Even in the event of a speedy victory, there would inevitably be a certain confusion as the coalition was not yet prepared to decide on Napoleon's successor. Could His Imperial Majesty give the foreign minister of Austria and himself the benefit of his thoughts on this matter?

Impatiently, the tsar shrugged off the interruption. Forget Napoleon, press on, leaving the future to the merciful will of the All-Highest. What was the matter with Bernadotte? And, still faithful to La Harpe, he brought up the possibility of a republic.

Castlereagh listened respectfully to the unrealistic tirade. Then he gently pointed out the obvious objections and suggested that it should not be impossible to find a solution satisfactory to everyone. Surely it would be wise to open peace negotiations with Napoleon, at the same time continuing the splendid march forward? If Bonaparte refused terms, and this time they would be far more stringent than the Frankfurt proposals, they could then replace him with a government acceptable to the French people.

After three days of hard negotiating, during which Castlereagh was obliged to strain his diplomatic skills to their utmost limits, the level of tension among the allies dropped back to manageable proportions. On January 29 an agreement known as the Langres Protocol was signed by all of them. In it the coalition agreed to treat with Napoleon as *de facto* ruler of France for as long as his people accepted him as such and to remove themselves to the nearby town of Châtillon-sur-Seine to commence negotiations with the sore-pressed foreign minister of France, Caulaincourt, Duc de Vicence. The Langres Protocol is a forgotten document, but as an illustration of Castlereagh's perseverance and tact, it deserves mention. It had been only eleven days since he had arrived from England, but somehow his presence had transformed the charged atmosphere of which Aberdeen had written so despairingly.

Castlereagh was naturally a shy man, so poor a public speaker that despite his immense prestige his own party in the House of Commons winced when he stood up to address that body; he was perfectly unacquainted with the European personages with whom he had to deal and handicapped by his awkward schoolboy French. There was nevertheless something tremendously confidence-inspiring about his tall figure, his quiet voice and his cool manner. During the next unexpectedly dramatic weeks, his imperturbability was to be an invaluable asset to his allies.

On January 26, the day that Priscilla Burghersh had written

her triumphant letter from Langres ("We are twenty-four hours journey from Paris"), Napoleon, his back to the wall, had turned over the government to a Council of Regency headed by Marie Louise and was already on his way to assume command himself of his army in the field.

The Campaign of France, as it is known in the history books, has often been compared for dash and brilliance to his early campaigns as a young general in Italy. "Excellent, quite excellent," the Duke of Wellington later murmured approvingly, as he studied the disposition of Bonaparte's limited forces.[19]

After a preliminary Allied victory at La Rothière on February 1, the Prussian commander, General Gebhard Von Blücher, and the Austrian, Prince Schwarzenberg, foolishly allowed themselves to become separated, with the result that the Prussians were defeated at Champaubert, at Montmirail, at Château-Thierry, and again at Vauchamps. Napoleon then turned on the Austrians, who were threatening Fontainebleau, and threw them back across the Seine at Montereau. His army consisted partly of hardened veterans, but mainly of untrained conscripts. These wretched boys reached the army only to perish, having no powers of self-defense. Marshal Auguste Marmont related afterward to a friend that at Montmirail, in the heat of the battle, he saw a conscript standing calmly at ease.

"What are you doing there? Why are you not firing?"

"I would fire as well as anybody," replied the fifteen-year-old boy, "if I knew how to load my gun."[20]

In those days there were no war correspondents on the scene, and therefore Priscilla Burghersh's letters are particularly valuable.

> *Châtillon-sur-Seine*
> *February 19, 1814*
> The headquarters have returned to Troyes, which is only three or four hours from here, and B. has promised to come tomorrow. I don't know what they mean to do, but I know that

Buonaparte is employing all his energy, all his activity, and all his power, and that we are dilatory, uncertain, and (entre nous) frightened—Alexander as much as any, for all his bravado.

By early March Napoleon had lost his momentum, and an Allied victory at Laon on March 10 under Blücher turned the tide decisively, but in two further letters Lady Burghersh reflected the shaken atmosphere at headquarters. On March 13 she wrote to her father complaining of "the heavy machine . . . we stand so differently now, (God knows why) from what we did two months ago."

A week later she wrote:

The negotiations ended yesterday, and the Congress [Châtillon] is broken up, so there is an end to all my fondest hopes of a quick return home, for I cannot look forward to a swift termination by the sword, seeing the same weakness, inconsistency, and timidity prevail among us. However, the final breaking up of the negotiations may inspire us with a little more energy, and make Buonaparte more moderate, seeing the Allies will not make peace upon his terms.

In this report she was furious with Schwarzenberg for ordering a retreat "just upon hearing that the enemy is within striking range." As the Duke of Wellington's niece, Priscilla Burghersh was unlikely to be kind about generals who retreated when attack was indicated.

Writing from Châtillon during the most critical moments of the Campaign of France, she described Lord Castlereagh: "I am quite delighted with Cas. I never knew he had such fun in him." Fun in him, and at such a time? Largely because he was so shy, his contemporaries usually called him reserved, cold, aloof. Evidently the twenty-year-old English girl could bring out another side of him. She loved his appearance: "You never saw such a *beauty* as Lord Castlereagh has become. He is as brown as a berry, with a fine bronzed colour, and wears a fur cap with gold, and is really quite *charming*. There never was anybody so looked up to as he is here."

Priscilla Burghersh would have been extremely annoyed could she have known that in return for these compliments, Castlereagh was making fun of her in a letter to his bored wife who had been left behind at The Hague. He reported that Lady Burghersh was "obliged to fly from Chaumont and live in a bivouac with all the heavy baggage of the army, without the possibility of changing her chemise unperceived, except the ceremony was performed in the dark of the night."[21]

A Frenchman, the Baron de Vitrolles, gave us a glimpse of Castlereagh during the campaign. He was wearing red breeches, jockey boots, a blue tunic with a white cape thrown over his shoulders, the gold-trimmed fur hat upon his head, eating a hurried lunch in the courtyard of the Château de Vandoeuvre when the baron came upon him. Tall as he was, he was standing on tiptoe to eat the meal (salmi of partridge and champagne) which had been placed on the rumble of his traveling carriage.[22]

Castlereagh knew little public popularity throughout his career. Yet the men who worked for him were devoted to him, as were his family. Ever loyal to his friends, as secretary for war in 1808 he defended Sir Arthur Wellesley when all England was calling for the head of the general who was considered responsible for the debacle in Portugal that year. "That Arthur Wellesley's career was not broken then and there on the rock of Cintra was largely due to Castlereagh and Spencer Perceval."*[23] Wellesley, later Duke of Wellington, wrote to Castlereagh: "If I had been your brother, you could not have been more careful of my interests than you have been in the late instances. . . ."[24]

Born in Ireland in 1769 of an ancient family, Castlereagh lost his English mother when he was a year old, but his childhood was not unhappy. His father remarried and the young Robert Stewart was brought up by a kind and beautiful stepmother who treated him as one of her own large brood. Early letters

---

* Spencer Perceval, 1762–1812: chancellor of the exchequer, 1807–1809.

show him as lighthearted and merry, full of jokes, writing to his young step-aunt, Lady Elizabeth Pratt, with whom he was a little in love. At the age of twenty-five he fell properly head over heels in love with a girl of twenty-two, Lady Emily Hobart, and their marriage was a wonderfully happy one. His public life was at first absorbed by the affairs of his beloved Ireland, which he handled with what William Pitt called "true impartiality and devotion." Moving into the larger stage of Westminster, he brought to the high offices with which he was entrusted "immense industry, an ability to absorb detail without getting lost in it, and a drive and enthusiasm. . . ." [25]

He was no dull bureaucrat. Political passion led him to challenge his rival, George Canning, to a duel in 1809, in which Canning was slightly wounded. As his biographer, Wendy Hinde, has pointed out, like most very reserved men, when Castlereagh did lose his temper he did it thoroughly. [26] Leaving the government, he then enjoyed two and a half years of comparative freedom, during which he relished the lack of responsibility of a parliamentary backbencher.

Public opinion was on the whole on his side over the Canning affair, and when he again took office as leader of the House of Commons and foreign secretary in 1812, the response was reasonably warm at home. Abroad, he was perfectly unknown.

However, the astonishing fact remains that during the worst weeks of the Campaign of France, while the sovereigns and their ministers were obliged to scramble from place to place with undignified haste to avoid Bonaparte's lightning strikes, while the tsar went to pieces and the king of Prussia moaned away like Cassandra, it was Castlereagh, the Englishman, who took command with quiet competence. Gathering Metternich, Hardenberg, and Nesselrode beside him, he pursued the task of negotiating with Napoleon through the French foreign minister, Caulaincourt.

This decent, honorable man, desperately trying to save the

emperor from his own folly, failed completely in his effort to persuade him to seize his last chance to keep his throne. The conference at Châtillon wound on its weary way through the month of February and into March. Napoleon, intoxicated by his victories, talked of "having annihilated his enemies and being at the gates of Munich within a few weeks." In vain Caulaincourt protested: "We must make sacrifices, and we must make them in time." [27] It was useless to attempt to restrain Bonaparte's optimism. He was soon saying to an aide: "I do not read Caulaincourt's letters, tell him that they tire and bore me beyond limit." [28]

The shrewd Friedrich von Gentz, Metternich's assistant, wrote of the peacemaking at Châtillon: "In spite of all obstacles Metternich would have succeeded had it not been for Napoleon himself. The behavior of the man was the height of madness. Like an actor in a tragedy, Napoleon, given the slightest and most transitory success, thought he had won the game and sank into a world of delusion." [29]

Nevertheless, while the Châtillon conference was a failure, the Treaty of Chaumont, signed by the foreign ministers on March 1, was an important accomplishment. It was Castlereagh's first great diplomatic success, the reward for his fortitude. By its terms a Quadruple Alliance was pledged, its members promising to continue to contribute men and money until their objectives were achieved, and to work together for twenty years after the end of hostilities. Thus Britain was brought into Europe, and a firm foundation laid for the reconstruction of the battered continent. Castlereagh, permitting himself a flourish of pride, always referred to it afterward as "my treaty." Despite the shock of Napoleon's lunge forward and the ensuing panic, he had managed to extract a firm declaration of unity.

One important result of the negotiations at Châtillon was that Metternich at last perceived the futility of seeking a settlement with Napoleon. Now convinced that the risk of establishing a weak French government was a lesser danger than the continued rule of the irremediably obstinate emperor, he reluctantly decided by the middle of March that the restoration of the Bourbons was inevitable. Politically, this came as a great relief to Castlereagh. While still personally cold to the imposition of the dynasty, in the tradition of Pitt, he was now under extreme pressure from Lord Liverpool to accept the solution. The House of Commons, reflecting a surge of anti-Bonaparte sentiment in the country, would hear of nothing else, and the prince regent was strongly in accord.

The time had come when a decision had to be taken, for after Laon on March 10 there was nothing between Schwarzenberg's armies and Paris but the weakened forces of Marshals Marmont and Edouard Mortier. Ordered to cover the capital, they were still fighting hard, giving ground inch by inch, but the end was in sight. In mid-March, the Baron de Vitrolles, a loyal adherent of the Bourbons, met with the Allied leaders. He was received by the tsar, Nesselrode, Metternich, Hardenberg, and Castlereagh, and was to write in his memoirs that he found the last-named handsome, but noncommittal and cold. Metternich was hardly warmer, but the message Vitrolles carried with him had an electric effect on the gathered Allies.

This was a minuscule scrap of paper, folded and refolded, which Vitrolles handed to Count Nesselrode. It contained one short paragraph, written in invisible ink. Holding it up to the flame of a candle, Nesselrode recognized the writing as that of his cousin, Emmerich Joseph de Dalberg, who was known to be working closely with Talleyrand.*

The message read: "The person I am sending you is entirely in my confidence, listen to him and be grateful to me. It is time to be clear. You are walking as if with crutches, use your own legs and you can have what you want." [30]

Only one man in all Europe would have dared to dictate such

---

* Nesselrode and Dalberg are typical of the cosmopolitan aristocrats who come into this story so frequently. Both Rhineland Germans, one had entered Russian service and the other French.

an invitation, informing the Allies that Napoleon was finished and that they could walk into Paris when they chose. Charles Maurice de Talleyrand-Périgord, Prince de Bénévent, Grand-Dignitaire de France, and member of the Council of Regency that had been entrusted by Napoleon with total authority for the government of the country when he left Paris to take command in the field, had now committed his supreme betrayal.

Metternich, who knew him better than the other stupefied men who heard the words that Nesselrode read aloud to them, must have been amused that Talleyrand should have employed Dalberg to write the message. It would have been suicidally dangerous for him to have written it himself, for if Vitrolles had been captured and searched, the famous handwriting that Talleyrand called "ma mauvaise petite écriture" might well have been recognized and the writer shot at dawn. To force Dalberg, who was not known for his courage, into the role of secretary had taken considerable pressure, but the need was urgent.

Talleyrand had been born in 1754 to one of the greatest families in France. As the eldest son, he was destined for a splendid military career in the army of King Louis XVI. However, a typical product of an age in which aristocratic parents were as heartless toward their young children as they were ambitious for them, he had been left as a baby in the charge of a wet-nurse. This simple peasant woman let him drop from the top of a chest of drawers when he was only a few months old, breaking his foot. Too ignorant or too frightened to inform his family of the accident, she paid no attention to the fact that the little boy could hardly learn to walk. When, four years later, his parents remembered his existence and sent for him again, the child was hopelessly crippled and would drag his poor deformed foot for the rest of his life. Goodbye to the brilliant prospects before the heir to the Talleyrand-Périgords. As a "safe" solution, the cripple was forced into the arms of the church, for which he had no vocation. Nevertheless, his family's position assisted his rapid rise in the ecclesiastical hierarchy, and he was named bishop of Autun by the time he was thirty-four.

In those days of clerical laxity, the duties of a bishop of a faraway see were hardly taxing. While he made official visits to Autun from time to time, Talleyrand's life in the golden years just before the Revolution was centered on Paris. Of his physical appearance as a young man, we have few descriptions. We know that he was of middle height, that his nose was "retroussé," that his expression was haughty, and that he limped. His face must have been attractive, for Arnault,* who disliked him, said that he concealed the heart of a devil under an angel's face.[31] Loved by many women in the brilliant world in which he lived, he had the reputation of being a libertine; yet he also enjoyed the friendship of great ladies who were models of virtue. One of them, the Marquise de la Tour du Pin, wrote that, while she disapproved of his morals, she found his charm and wit irresistible.

Still, the carefree life of an aristocrat under the *ancien régime,* delightful though it was, was not enough to satisfy Talleyrand. Clever and ambitious, somewhat embittered and already restless, he flung himself into the cause of reforming the abuses of the outmoded system of the day. At the beginning of the Revolution he broke with the church and took his place in the National Assembly, of which he became president in 1790. As a moderate, his fight against the growing dominance of the more radical leaders was to be a futile one. Abandoning the struggle for control of the extremist tide, he found his way to exile in America and did not return to France until 1796. Wittier, more bitter, more ambitious than ever, he then met Bonaparte and, immediately seeing his potential, threw his weight behind the young general.

The combination of the two men was highly felicitous for both. Napoleon needed the wisdom and experience that the

* Antoine Vincent Arnault, 1766–1834. French author of dramas and memoirs.

older man could give him and found Talleyrand invaluable as minister of foreign affairs. Indefensibly venal, the minister made a fortune out of the bribes that his position easily brought him. But there was more to his attachment to Napoleon than the satisfaction of achieving immense wealth and power. He was genuine in his admiration for the bright comet blazing across the European sky. As a proud French patriot he rejoiced in the conquests of the early years.

It was not until 1805, the year of Ülm and Austerlitz, that as foreign minister he began to feel grave concern over the consequences of Napoleon's ever-growing megalomania. His punitive measures against defeated enemies appalled Talleyrand, and with great courage he addressed a succinct, farsighted memorandum to the emperor pointing out the dangers inherent in creating a revanchist Austria. Napoleon was momentarily impressed, but it was too late for counsels of moderation to stem the inexorable current of heady success. Few men would have had the audacity to tell Bonaparte that he was wrong once, let alone twice, but six weeks after the first memorandum Talleyrand followed up with another, even stronger paper along the same lines. Once more he failed, and from then on his opposition to what he saw as the fatal policy of unlimited expansion was implacable. Resigning as foreign minister in 1807, he nevertheless continued for a time to hold high office as vice-grand-elector and when, in 1808, Napoleon went to Erfurt to meet the tsar, Talleyrand accompanied him.

At Erfurt he first betrayed his master. Throughout his career he always found it easy to attract influential women to his side when he needed their help. In this case the Princess of Thürn und Taxis was delighted to arrange nightly meetings in her drawing room at which Talleyrand could converse discreetly with the tsar over a cup of tea. Here he employed all his remarkable powers of persuasion in order to undermine Alexander's faith in his ally, Napoleon.

"Sire," he said at one of the earliest meetings, "It is in your power to save Europe, and you will only do so by refusing to give way to Napoleon. The French people are civilized, their sovereign is not. The sovereign of Russia is civilized, and his people are not: the sovereign of Russia should therefore be the ally of the French people." [32]

Amplifying this statement, he told the tsar that the French people wanted only one thing—peace. "Unless the Tsar, for there was nobody else in a position to do so, constituted himself the mediator between Napoleon and his people, they would continue to be dragged as victims in the wake of his chariot to their ultimate destruction." [33]

Alexander, flattered and impressed, felt that he had heard the true voice of the French people. Four years later, in 1812, a sleigh carried Napoleon and his aide, General Caulaincourt, on their grim journey back to Paris after the disasters of the Russian campaign. Ruminating on the past, the emperor remarked to his companion that he still wondered what had caused the tsar's abrupt change of tune at Erfurt. According to Jean Orieux, the French historian, Caulaincourt froze with horror. He had known of Talleyrand's deception, and, as a man of peace, he had heartily approved of it. During the ensuing conversation, it emerged that Napoleon suspected Marshal Lannes of being the villain. Orieux writes that it is highly unlikely that Caulaincourt would have argued the point.

It had been treachery all right, but what courageous, magnificent treachery! Had he thought only of himself, Talleyrand would never have taken a risk that might have cost him his place, his wealth, probably his neck. Talleyrand was a patriot, and the cause for which he was fighting was France.

Now, six years after Erfurt, by the message sent through Vitrolles, he hoped to spare the lives of the last battalions of soldiers who would have been inevitably thrown into a prolonged, last-ditch struggle. Once more Talleyrand was betraying Napoleon for the sake of France. Nesselrode wrote later that the Allies would never have marched on Paris as soon as they did without Talleyrand's interference. He was probably right. The aura of Napoleon, even a Napoleon at bay, still enveloped his opponents in a nimbus that froze their wills. Much of the confusion that characterized the Campaign of France on the Allied side arose from the fact that, while everyone from Schwarzenberg to the greenest trooper knew that logically Napoleon was beaten, their minds still could not take in the incredible fact.

Having thrown his bombshell, the Baron de Vitrolles, a thin-lipped earnest sort of man, then engaged the attention of the company with a description of the flaming enthusiasm for the royal dynasty that filled the hearts of the Paris populace. At the merest glimpse of the Allied flags on the horizon, millions of people would be on the streets to welcome the liberators.

Alexander, who had been rendered rather quiet by recent events, returned with an instant *volte-face* to his role as soldier-philosopher-emperor. "Monsieur de Vitrolles," he said, "the day that I enter Paris I shall recognize no other ally than the French nation. I assure you that this meeting will have great results." [34]

He was already convinced that the "Très-Haut" himself had decided what his conduct must be. Rising, he adjusted his uniform and announced his intention of immediately marching on Paris. [35] He had even decided on the horse that the Divine Will desired him to ride in the victory parade: it was to be a fine gray thoroughbred called Eclipse, a gift, in happier days, from his friend and ally, Napoleon. Alexander had not been endowed with good taste.

In hindsight, it seems odd that those two shrewd statesmen, Metternich and Castlereagh, should have remained behind in Dijon, thus allowing the tsar to precede them into the capital. Emperor Francis of Austria, who did have good taste, refused to participate in a public triumph at the expense of his defeated son-in-law, but Metternich could have replaced him. The historians have said that neither he nor Castlereagh wished to associate themselves too closely with the restoration of the Bourbons, but surely they must have been severely torn between this feeling and their natural apprehension over what the volatile Alexander might do when he arrived in Paris. The British staff, Lord Cathcart and Sir Charles Stewart, expressed open concern over the decision.

Nonetheless, they stuck to it, and Lord Castlereagh even put about the story that the road to Paris was too unsafe for him to risk traveling on it, which was a flimsy excuse indeed as all the world knew his courage. He was annoyed to learn that his young friend, Lady Burghersh, eager to be at the center of action, had set off in her carriage without guards and accompanied only by Madame Legoux. She made a safe journey, after three days and nights was reunited with her husband, and remained a sharp spectator of the interesting scene during the Paris spring of 1814.

Paris in the Spring

For the inhabitants of Paris, the worst part of the Campaign of France was the complete lack of news from the battlefront during the final weeks. Napoleon's earlier victories had been reported by the government-controlled press with wild enthusiasm and an infinite number of euphoric details. However, after March 10, when the French were known to be about to face Prussia's Marshal Blücher at Laon, the war totally disappeared from the pages of the newspapers. On March 30, 1814, the day Paris fell, the most important paper in France, the *Moniteur,* printed nothing but a literary article on the works of a minor writer. On that same day nervous crowds gathered around the house of the man who was supposed to know everything: Charles Maurice de Talleyrand-Périgord, Prince de Bénévent. They could not guess that the master of the house was as ill-informed as anyone else, nor that, as the Parisians shuddered at the sound of artillery in the outskirts of the city, the statesman was engaged in writing to his mistress in a fury of frustration:

> *March 30, 1814*
>
> Dearest one, they say that this morning's attack was only a reconnaissance and that the enemy are moving off. It is shameful that under such circumstances we should be so un-

informed. The question of the defence itself, this crucial question, is still undecided. Some want to defend—others oppose this course. There is great agitation, but all anyone does is to argue; I do not think that a body of men has ever found itself in such a humiliating position before. I will be sure to come to see you early—for the moment I am staying here waiting for news; I love you with all my soul, and to know that you are anxious and troubled desolates me. My angel, I love you, I love you.[1]

The student of the period owes a considerable debt to Anne Charlotte Dorothea, Duchess of Courland, the lady to whom the above was addressed. The notes that Talleyrand sent her, often twice a day, are the most fervent love letters he ever wrote; torn off in a great hurry in his own hand. They convey the urgency of the times far more immediately than do his own magisterial memoirs, written later. His position was precarious, and these bulletins, following events almost hour by hour, demonstrate both his fear and his patriotism. Although he was sixty years old and she fifty-three, his passion was true and genuine, and his feeling comes through more clearly than if he had been writing in a quieter time, when he would have conformed to the literary convention of the eighteenth century, filling his letters with well-turned phrases of tender gallantry, felicitously and elegantly expressed. Instead, his first letter written during the campaign, dated January 25, consisted of less than a page, tersely announcing the departure of the emperor to join his armies. The last hurried lines read: "I find everything bearable when I am near you. YOU! YOU! YOU!"

Again and again he implored the duchess to burn his "billets" immediately after reading them. She never did so. During the winter he sent her to the château of Rosny, sixty kilometers to the west of Paris, and most of the letters were addressed there. The other two people he loved most in the world, the Duchess of Courland's youngest daughter, Dorothea, who was married to Talleyrand's nephew, Edmond de Talleyrand-Périgord, and a young girl, Charlotte, his adopted child, were also living in the comparative security of Rosny.

Napoleon had long suspected his former minister of foreign affairs of treachery, but in his dire need he swallowed his pride and resentment and offered him the position once more before leaving for the front. Talleyrand turned down the Foreign Ministry, but remained a member of the trusted Council of Regency during the absence of the emperor. In that position he was often at the Tuileries Palace, helping Empress Marie Louise and Queen Hortense* pass the time by playing whist, with the Comte Louis-Mathieu de Molé making a fourth. The royal ladies laughed over the droll stories of Allied successes in the field, which the English newspapers were said to be inventing, and the Prince de Bénévent smiled benignly as he listened to the gossip. Like other wise and brilliant men (Benjamin Franklin is an example), Talleyrand talked very little in company.

No one was more annoyed by his reserve at this particular time than an old friend, Aimée de Coigny, a staunch supporter of the Bourbons, who had been enlisted by the royalists to persuade Talleyrand to make a statement in favor of their cause, and this charming woman begged and begged for just one word. He teased her and turned away. It was a time for prudence—Napoleon had left orders for him to be closely watched by the police, and the slightest indiscretion might have been fatal.

Through the memoirs, his own and others, he appears as a smooth, imperturbable figure throughout the weeks of strain—limping up the steps of the Tuileries for his whist party; receiving guests in his fine house on the rue St. Florentin; showing the more favored among them the treasures of his library. His letters to the Duchess of Courland reveal a different side of him:

---

*Born Hortense de Beauharnais, Napoleon's stepdaughter, she became the wife of his brother Louis, king of Holland.

February 9, 1814

They have removed the stocks of gunpowder that were at Essonnes and have taken them to Vincennes. Four hundred cannons that were at Vincennes have also been moved, half of them to the Invalides and the rest to Montmartre, which sounds as though the Emperor wants to defend Paris. This terrifies everyone; I am more than ever grateful that you have left. At least the person I love the most in the world is safe. . . .

February 10, 1814

Things are in the same state of horrible uncertainty. I beg you to take care of Charlotte. See that her excellent education is finished: try to mold her character on your own. . . .

February 15, 1814

How can anyone with a drop of French blood watch the pain and humiliation which our poor country is undergoing without suffering tortures. . . .

Talleyrand was very much a Frenchman. Considered by the world to be lazy, selfish, dishonest, and thoroughly cynical, it seemed to amuse him to cultivate this image of himself. He let it be known that he considered hard work deadly boring and rather middle-class, and his famous maxim during his years at the Foreign Office had been "Surtout, Messieurs, pas trop de zèle." ("Gentlemen, above all, beware of zeal.") Yet, as we have seen above, there was another Talleyrand, the patriot who had been so appalled by Napoleon's insatiable appetite for conquest that as early as 1806 he had dared to address to him two long, powerful letters critical of the emperor's policy. Those letters had been dictated, corrected, redictated, and recorrected many times before they were sent.

Talleyrand could work very hard indeed when he wished to, and by the end of March he was grimly preparing to do so once more. He regarded the Bourbon restoration as a *pis-aller* (last resort), but what alternative was there? Best to get it over with, he felt. By March 24 he had brought his mistress and Dorothea back to Paris and was dashing off impatient notes to the duchess about Schwarzenberg's incredible slowness: "It is quite inconceivable—Marmont and Mortier are incapable of sustained resistance and still the Austrians linger. . . ."

Even as he wrote the hurried lines the sound of guns could be heard approaching the city and the last of the last reserves were being ordered out: the students from the École Polytechnique—that great institution formed to train the best engineering and scientific minds in France. The boys, pink-cheeked and eager, threw away their school books and rushed to the support of the beaten remnants of the Grande Armée. Few of them survived the fighting in the suburbs of the capital.

On March 29 the empress and her three-year-old son, the king of Rome, left Paris for Blois on the Loire. This was not an act of cowardice on the part of Marie Louise. She was following her husband's orders, for Napoleon had written to his brother Joseph that, should Paris be in danger, his wife and son were to be removed before the city was encircled by the enemy. Naturally, the members of the Council of Regency would accompany them.

Talleyrand made every preparation to follow the regent and the heir to the throne into exile on the following day, March 30. As the letter with which this chapter opens shows, he was still totally uninformed of the situation on that crucial morning. The roar of artillery from Montmartre and Pantin and La Villette sounded alarmingly close. By midday it seemed to diminish. Could the French have surrendered? No, there was still fighting here and there and word came in that Marshal Marmont had refused to give in. However, by early afternoon there was a fresh and more certain report: capitulation would be declared before morning.

The Prince de Bénévent decided that this was the moment to go—and to return. Having arranged the ruse carefully, he drove out of Paris, just as he should have done, on his way to Blois and his duty at Marie Louise's side. A crowd had gathered outside the Hôtel de Talleyrand. The people watched, silent and awestruck, as the carriage containing the great man and his secretary, Perrey, swung out of the high portal on the rue St. Florentin and proceeded across the Place de la Concorde and turned right at the Seine. Passy, four kilometers to the west, was the gate chosen by the Prince de Bénévent. There was a barrier erected there, under the command of an officer of the National Guard, François Marie Charles de Rémusat. The Rémusats were close friends of Talleyrand, and he had found the time for a quick and very private conversation with Madame de Rémusat earlier that day. To the surprise of the onlookers, the carriage was stopped at the barrier and the coachman told to turn on his tracks. Everyone overheard the ensuing argument between the apparently furious statesman and the obstinate commander of the guard. Having made quite sure that his protestations had been so loud and clear that no witness could have missed them, Talleyrand gave in with an air of haughty resignation.

It did not take long to drive back from the "barriére de Passy" to the rue St. Florentin and it was still afternoon when, the little plan successfully effected, Talleyrand's carriage re-entered the courtyard it had left only a few hours before. News travels with miraculous speed in Paris and the great house was already bursting with people: well-wishers, place seekers, news-hungry citizens, friends of both sexes, some of whom had kept themselves at a distance while the barometer of Talleyrand's power had shown a reading of "stormy and uncertain." Now the staircase and the antechambers were jammed with an antlike crowd, pushing and shoving to reach out and shake his hand. One of the first to come forward was Bourrienne,* one of Napoleon's oldest intimates.

---

*Louis-Antoine de Bourrienne had been a schoolmate of Bonaparte's at Brienne.

That evening Talleyrand slipped out quietly to see Marshal Marmont, who was due to sign the order of capitulation during the night. He found him unhappily conferring with the tsar's representative, Colonel Michael Orlov. Asking for a few moments private conversation with Marmont, he succeeded in convincing the uneasy marshal that there was no other solution for France—no alternative to anarchy but immediate acceptance of the surrender terms. On his way out he bowed to the Russian aide: "Sir, would you be good enough to lay before His Imperial Majesty, the Emperor of Russia, the profound respects of the Prince of Bénévent." Colonel Orlov replied that he would not fail to carry the message.[2]

The next morning at six o'clock the household at the rue St. Florentin suffered the shock of their lives. Talleyrand, who never arose before eleven, was up, ringing peremptorily for his valet, Courtiade, and demanding that he should be made ready for action. His stunned servants did their best, but when Nesselrode, foreign minister of Russia, walked into the house he found the host still smothered in dressing gown and shawl and Courtiade in the middle of doing his hair.

> For once, Talleyrand lost his sangfroid. He jumped up, dragging his towels and his deformed foot and threw himself into the arms of the tsar's emissary, smothering him in a cloud of powder. Thus the great day of the capitulation opened to the perfume of orange blossoms.[3]

At eight o'clock that same morning, March 31, Alexander I of Russia, who had been staying at the outlying château of Bondy, mounted his beautiful thoroughbred Eclipse to take the road for Paris. His staff, surrounding him, felt that they were entering the promised land, for most of the officers had been brought up by French tutors. Their orderlies had been up since before dawn, shining the buttons of the well-brushed uniforms, giving a last polish to the gleaming boots of finest Russian leather. Leading the parade into the vanquished capital was the regiment known as the tsar's Red Cossacks, followed by the royal Prussian hussars and the Russian Imperial Guards—those giants who had so impressed Priscilla Burghersh when she first saw them in Frankfurt. Then came the tsar, the king of Prussia and Prince Schwarzenberg, representing the emperor of Austria. A suite of generals accompanied them, Blücher in the lead. Behind the Austrian and Russian grenadiers came regiment after regiment of Russian infantry.[4]

The tsar wore the uniform of an officer of the Guards, with the blue order of St. Andrew across his chest, and a tight black belt about his waist. Heavy gold epaulets widened his already fine shoulders—he always made a point of instructing his tailor to exaggerate the epaulets—and his high, stiff collar was embroidered in gold. Under his beplumed two-cornered hat, his face was pale, solemn, and benevolent. Observing the crowds closely he noticed that in the workers' quarters through which they first passed the atmosphere was cold, even hostile, but became visibly warmer after the Porte St. Denis. According to the armistice agreement made the night before, the regular French army had been evacuated from the city, leaving only the National Guard. In their red and blue uniforms these troops cleared a passage through the streets for the enemy of the preceding day. Behind them thronged the Paris crowds, pressing for a look, peering from every window, the younger among them climbing the trees on the route. Occasionally, bedsheets hung from the balconies in honor of the Bourbons, for white was their emblem. As the parade approached the Champs-Elysées, a chorus of acclamation began: "Vive Alexandre!" "Vivent les Alliés!"[5]

At the entrance to the Champs-Elysées the royal party paused to review the whole army. For five long hours the troops of different nationalities paraded before the sovereigns and the crowds went wild as twenty thousand Cossacks and Kalmucks passed, lances in hand. It was Asia in the heart of Paris!

Happier and prouder than he had ever been in his life, the

tsar waited until the last soldier had gone by and then crossed on foot to his new residence. This was not to be the Elysée as had been planned. A rumor had got about that the palace was probably mined. The Tuileries Palace was also considered to be insecure. What could have been easier and safer than that beautiful house on the corner of the rue St. Florentin and the rue de Rivoli, known as the Hôtel de Talleyrand?

It is an attractive contemplation, that walk of Alexander's across the axis of what is surely the most triumphant example of urban design in Europe. It was a clear day, astonishingly warm for the season, and windless. There is no sky so high as that over the Place de la Concorde, and on windy days the clouds careen across it in dizzy, proud exuberance. But this was a quiet afternoon. The chestnuts and plane trees along the Champs-Elysées were not yet in full leaf, but veiled in a nimbus of fragile green, anticipating the glory of the full spring yet to come. It is perhaps the most beautiful moment in all the year to see Paris for the first time, as the architectural bones emerge as pure and uncluttered as they lay on the drawing boards of the geniuses who planned the concept.

The emperor and his party emerged into the great square between the Chevaux de Marly, those dashing, prancing horses which stood and stand high on their pedestals, straining to be off. Behind was the long, straight perspective leading uphill to the then unfinished Arc de Triomphe. Before them, straight as a die, the unbroken line continued forever and ever, so it seemed, through the Tuileries Gardens with its geometrically placed ornamental pool and allées. To their left, the pale end-of-March sun illuminated the vast buildings which are the masterpieces of the great architect, Jacques Ange Gabriel: the Hôtel de Crillon and the Ministry of the Navy. Built of the warm off-white stone of Caen, perfect in their proportions and seamless in their unity, their majestic colonnades dominate the vast space without overwhelming it.

There were many people in the square; a crowd of curious

onlookers had remained when the parade was over in order to stare at the victors. Alexander, still exhilarated by his tremendous day, was at his most charming and informal as he accepted their salutations. Then he led the way into the courtyard of the house at the corner of the Place de la Concorde and the rue de Rivoli. Its master was waiting on the steps, a slight but elegant figure, leaning lightly on his gold-headed cane.*

Out of sight, in the subterranean gloom of the vast kitchens, Monsieur Antonin Carême and his underlings were toiling. The famous chef had been informed by Talleyrand only a few hours before that he was to prepare dinner for the emperor of Russia, the king of Prussia, their suites, and other guests—thirty or forty people, all told. It was the sort of challenge Carême enjoyed, and such was the smooth organization on which he prided himself that it is unlikely that there was any more pandemonium below stairs than there was in the quiet vestibule.

The tsar and his suite crossed the black and white marble floor to the wide straight staircase, which led first to the entresol containing Talleyrand's own apartments, surprisingly sober in decoration and low of ceiling for such a *grand seigneur,* and up one more flight to the twenty-foot-high glory of the apartments arranged for the tsar's reception. Of these, the Salon de l'Aigle was chosen for an immediate conference.

Facing the Russian emperor and his advisers alone, Talleyrand listened quietly, as was his way, to Alexander's exposition of his views. To Metternich and Castlereagh they would have been wearily familiar. The tsar had not come to Paris to impose an outworn monarchy on the French people. How was he to know they wanted a restoration of the Bourbons? There were other solutions: a regency, Bernadotte, a republic. Talleyrand, speaking gravely and respectfully, told the emperor that only

---

*In his memoirs, Talleyrand wrote that he could not have been more surprised to learn about the rumored mining of the Elysée Palace. This is hard to believe. He almost certainly had had the rumors put about in order to get the tsar into his own house and so be perfectly situated to influence him during the next crucial days.

the Bourbons could re-establish what he called "a France that would be wise and strong at the same time." He emphasized the importance of the principle of legitimacy, "Louis XVIII is the incarnation of the principle, as the legitimate King of France,"[6] What was more, he could prove what were the true desires of the French people by convoking the Senate, which he would do immediately. The vote of the representatives of the people would be the determining factor, and the tsar's very natural respect for democratic procedures could be satisfied.

It was soon time to end the talk. Ever sensitive to atmosphere, Talleyrand knew that this was not the moment to press the Russians. Instead he suggested that they rise from the conference table and stretch their weary legs before dining. Perhaps it would amuse them to look at the view? Gratefully, the participants filed over to the tall windows. The Salon de l'Aigle was an immense drawing room at the western corner of the house. It overlooked the Place de la Concorde and, in the distance, for the days were lengthening now, the setting sun fell on the radiant golden dome of the Invalides far across the river. As in the rest of the house, the gold and white of the paneling was restrained in its elegance, but the architect had let himself go in the modeling of the eagle over the fireplace which had given the room its name. This eagle was not martial nor was it severe like its Napoleonic or indeed its Russian relatives. It was a typical rococo bird of the time when the house was built, in the reign of Louis XV. Decorative, languorous, seductive, from its graceful wings fell golden garlands of flowers, delicately carved. To the young Russian aides-de-camp, brought up to revere French taste, the Salon de l'Aigle and its breathtaking view epitomized all that they had come so far to see.

The room into which Talleyrand now led the party was as harmonious as the one they had just left. Named the Salon des Quatres Saisons after the ravishing nymphs who reclined above the doors representing the seasons of the year, it was a happy room, made for convivial dining, very grand yet totally unpretentious. The dinner guests were the conquerors who had entered Paris that morning—sovereigns, generals, aides—plus a handful of intimates of the house. The Duchess of Courland was there, as was her daughter Dorothea de Talleyrand-Périgord. Princess de Talleyrand must have been there, for she could hardly have been kept out of her own house on such an occasion. Blowzy, vulgar, and tactless, she was the only one of her husband's many mistresses whom he should not have married, and for years they had lived apart.

Bored as he was by his embarrassing wife, Talleyrand was never cruel to her, and it would have been inconceivably cruel not to have permitted her to have joined his glittering dinner table on the night of the capitulation of Paris, or to have forbidden her to accompany the party to the remarkable occasion that followed immediately afterward: an opera gala.

The opera house was filled when Talleyrand showed his royal guests into their boxes, their suites behind them. Outside, the crowd had already given the foreign sovereigns the warmest of welcomes as the train of carriages approached—"Vive Alexandre! Vivent les Alliés!" It was again one of those rare, warm moonlit nights with which the extraordinary week had been blessed. Inside the house the audience consisted of the grandest of the grand of Paris society, the men wearing full dress and the women their jewels. They rose as one to cheer. Among the audience obliged to listen to the ovation for the emperor of Russia—the applause for Frederick William was polite but perfunctory—were Lord and Lady Burghersh and Sir Charles Stewart. The two men had been sent on by Castlereagh as observers while he remained with Metternich at the Hôtel Dampierre in Dijon. (Priscilla Burghersh, having pushed on to Paris, was already established in a well-furnished house with a competent staff of servants.) To the English, it was intolerable to witness the Russians monopolizing the triumph, and triumph it was.

French historians have described this occasion with shame and embarrassment. "Indecent" is the adjective that recurs in their writings. Duff Cooper, the distinguished twentieth-century diplomat and historian, wrote more compassionately:

> On their appearance [Talleyrand and the royalties] the whole house burst into frantic cheers. The French are certainly not less proud or patriotic than other nations, and that they should have spontaneously applauded the masters of foreign troops upon their native soil, standing in the place so often occupied by their own Emperor, proves how profound their discontent had been. Not without reason could Talleyrand maintain that he never conspired, except when he had the French nation as fellow-conspirators."[7]

Yet there were many men and women inside Paris and out who suffered intensely when Paris fell. Far away in Switzerland, the exuberant Madame de Staël, a passionate Francophile who usually employed fifty words when three would do, could only gasp out one short sentence when she heard the news: "Oh, God, not Cossacks in the rue Racine."*

Chateaubriand, historian and patriot, wandered the streets reflecting that what he called "this inviolable city, this capital of glory," had not fallen since the Franks had entered it in the year 496. "Now I had to watch Caucasian hordes setting up their camp in the court of the Louvre. . . . I felt stupefied and strangely without identity, as if they had already torn away the name Frenchman and replaced it with the number with which I would be known as a prisoner in the Siberian mines. At the same time I felt my exasperation mounting towards the man whose desire for glory had reduced us to this state of shame."[8]

An eyewitness, who had never known a sense of patriotism before, had tossed in her bed while she, too, thought of the Cossacks, and her account is all the more interesting because she was not a great writer like René de Chateaubriand or a tremendous personality like Germaine de Staël. Her name was

---

*The rue Racine is a small street on the Left Bank of the Seine. Just the sort of street for which a true lover of Paris would have mourned.

Adèle de Boigne, and she was a fashionable grass widow living with her parents in a house just under the heights of Montmartre. The daughter of a diplomat, the Marquis d'Osmond, she had been born in 1781 and brought up almost literally on the knees of the royal family at the court of Versailles, where her mother was a lady-in-waiting. The revolution brought emigration to England and near-destitution. To save the family fortunes, Adèle married the very rich and very unpleasant General Comte de Boigne. In 1804 young Madame de Boigne and her family returned to Paris. Her husband, who disliked Paris, his wife and her parents, set them up comfortably before retiring to sulk in his château in the South of France.

Attractive and perfectly uninterested in politics, immensely sociable and gossipy, the Comtesse de Boigne opened a successful salon and had a very good time during the height of the empire. Professing to loathe Napoleon, she nonetheless much enjoyed going to the Tuileries and admitted that she was charmed by the emperor, who put himself out to be delightful to the daughter of the Marquis d'Osmond. She saw representatives of every party and her circle included the most attractive members of the diplomatic corps: Count Metternich, Count Nesselrode, Count Nicholas Tolstoy, and Count Pozzo di Borgo. Perhaps just because she cared little for issues in an age when many women were relentlessly political, she was a popular figure in Paris during the years that preceded Napoleon's fatal invasion of Russia.

During the last weeks of the Campaign of France, the seriousness of the situation began to penetrate the brain of this charming and frivolous woman of thirty-two. Discussions were held as to whether the family should leave Paris; but the Marquis d'Osmond stoutly refused to budge. He ordered that the house should be stocked with provisions and, in order to glean some news of what was really happening, encouraged his daughter to visit her cousin, Fanny Bertrand, the wife of Napoleon's devoted grand marshal, General Henri-Gratien Bertrand.

Madame de Boigne wrote down a description of visiting the Tuileries Palace:

> The government officials were completely disorganized. . . . One morning I saw an officer arrive, coming from the Emperor's army, then another sent by Marshal Soult, then an envoy from Marshal Suchet, all bringing news of disastrous events. Poor Fanny was on thorns. At length, by way of culmination, an Illyrian official appeared.* He proceeded to tell us how he had been tracked through Italy, and with what difficulty he had reached the French frontier. Fanny could no longer hold out, and said to them with extreme vivacity: "Gentlemen, you are all wrong. Last night excellent news came from every quarter, and the Emperor is entirely pleased with all that is going on." Each man looked at his fellow in astonishment, and it was clear to me that this remark was intended for myself.[9]

Madame de Boigne returned thoughtfully to her home after the last of her visits to her unhappy cousin and spent the next few days working with her mother to give aid and shelter to the wretched young conscripts, wounded in the retreat, who were wandering homeless and despairing through the streets.

She wrote a vivid description of the night that Paris fell: March 30–31. It must be remembered that she lived in a quarter of the city that then, as now, was normally almost as noisy by night as by day:

> The weather was magnificent, the town entirely calm, and my mother and I stood at the window. Our attention was attracted by the noise made by a very small dog gnawing a bone at some distance. From time to time the silence was broken by the challenges of the sentries of the Allied army, who answered one another as they made their rounds upon the heights which overlooked us. *It was these foreign accents which first made me feel that my heart was French.** [10]

---

*Illyria, now Yugoslavia, was a province of the Austrian empire that had been conquered by Napoleon.

* Emphasis added.

After a few hours of uneasy sleep, she and her mother were once more at the window. To their horror they saw a Russian officer accompanied by two soldiers coming down their street, and what was more they heard the officer asking a terrified neighbor for the house of the Comtesse de Boigne. Then there was a knock on the door. In a state of frozen dread they braced themselves to face the barbarians with what dignity they could muster, and went downstairs to endure God alone knew what nameless horrors.

To their amazement they found a handsome young man chatting amiably in perfect French with the Marquis d'Osmond. He introduced himself as Prince Nikita Volkonsky, aide-de-camp to the tsar, who had been sent by their old friend, Count Nesselrode, to see if they were all right and to find out if they needed anything. For their protection he would leave two sentinels outside the front door, and Count Nesselrode himself hoped to be along later in the day. In fact, if it was convenient, he would like to come to dinner.

Immensely relieved, Adèle hurried off to watch the victory parade from the balcony of a friend's house which overlooked the Avenue des Champs-Elysées. She wrote in her memoirs:

> Must I admit that the anti-national faction had concentrated in this spot to welcome the foreigner, and that this faction was chiefly composed of the nobility? Was it right or wrong? I cannot now decide, but at that moment our conduct seemed to me sublime. . . . None the less, in the midst of our hatred [for Napoleon] and our momentary infatuation I considered as entirely foolish and unnecessary the conduct of Sosthène de la Rochefoucauld, who went to put a rope around the neck of the statue of the Emperor Napoleon in the Place Vendôme in order to drag it down from the column.[11]

Rochefoucauld, the scion of an august house, was restrained from his absurd gesture by officers of a crack Russian regiment, the Semionovski, who were horrified by his lack of decorum. Another enthusiastic aristocrat, the Comte de Montreuil, drove around Paris with the Legion of Honor, Napoleon's revered Order of Merit, attached to his horse's tail. Every Napoleonic eagle which could be reached on the public buildings was hastily festooned with a white silk cravat, and tricolored flags, proud emblems of revolutionary France, were bundled away into garrets and cellars.

Madame de Boigne of course attended the opera gala, and had the grace to admit in her memoirs that she was ashamed of having done so and was also embarrassed to have been present at the many similar festivities that followed. Yet how hard it was to resist the conquerors:

> We were at dinner, when the door of the dining room opened noisily and a Russian general suddenly burst in. He waltzed around the table, singing, "Oh, my friends, my dear, dear friends!" Our first idea was that he was mad, and then my brother exclaimed: "Why, it's Pozzo!" [12] [This was the charming Count Pozzo di Borgo so often mentioned by Priscilla Burghersh in her letters.]

While most of Paris slept better than they had for weeks at the close of that endless day, March 31, there were some who did not sleep at all. Before leaving for the opera with the sovereigns, Talleyrand had given swift instructions to his most trusted lieutenants. Throughout the night they galloped about the city, rousing aging senators from their beds in order to convince them that they must meet the following day to establish a provisional government which would be followed by the return of the monarchy. It was not an easy task; many of the senators were old republicans, nostalgic for the heady days of their Jacobin youth. Out of 140, only 63 went to the Senate; the others remained in bed, declaring that they were ill. However, the 63 voted unanimously as Talleyrand had asked them to do, and by the evening of that day, April 1, 1814, France had a provisional government bound to establish a constitution, a chamber of representatives to vote the laws, and a temporary head of government: Talleyrand. The tsar was impressed; at last, he said, he had heard the true voice of the French, and he bowed before their decision.

Napoleon, abandoned at Fontainebleau, his brothers bolting for Switzerland and his wife and son about to leave for Vienna, made one more try. He sent Caulaincourt to see the tsar, offering abdication in return for the acceptance of a regency in favor of the little king of Rome. Twice Talleyrand managed to prevent the meeting, but at last Caulaincourt caught the tsar as he was leaving the Salon de l'Aigle after a conference. It was a poignant moment, for Alexander genuinely liked and respected Caulaincourt. Regretfully he told him that he had come too late. The French people themselves had elected to return to a monarchy, under Louis XVIII. The Duc de Vicence turned on his heel and left the Hôtel de Talleyrand for the last time. From then on events moved rapidly.

Napoleon signed a formal act of abdication on April 6, and remained in Fontainebleau, where he bungled a suicide attempt a few days later. By the time Metternich and Castlereagh arrived from Dijon on April 10, a new constitution, or charter, had been rushed through the Senate, and dispositions for the future of Napoleon and his family had almost been decided. Financially, the arrangements were generous. The former emperor was to receive an annual revenue of two million francs a year from French funds. Marie Louise was to receive the duchy of Parma with reversion to the king of Rome. Provision was made for annuities to be made to members of the Bonaparte family, including an annual pension of one million francs to the former Empress Josephine. Thus, the Treaty of Fontainebleau, as the arrangement was called, seemed eminently dignified and suitable to the British and Austrian foreign ministers with one crucial exception. The French emperor's destination, as agreed by the Russians and Prussians, was to be Elba. Castlereagh refused to sign this part of the Treaty of Fontainebleau.

He had no very good alternative to suggest. During the days

of his self-inflicted isolation with Metternich in Dijon, various proposals had reached their ears. The tsar, in his new, benign mood, had offered to take Napoleon to Russia, "where we should treat him as a sovereign." No one warmed to this suggestion. England was out of the question—Napoleon himself had suggested that, but Parliament indignantly rejected the very thought of housing the monster. America? Nice and far away, but the unlucky War of 1812 between the English and the Americans was only now winding to a close—one could hardly ask the Americans for a favor. And Elba sounded so convenient. Admittedly, the island lay only just west of Leghorn in Italy, far too close to the coast of southern France. Metternich, for his part, contended that to send Napoleon to Elba would be to invite another war within two years.[13]

But with the British navy encircling it? Surely it was the best solution. Napoleon would settle down quietly and write his memoirs, establish a miniature court, be watched over by the Allied commissioners in whose charge he was. General Schoulov of Russia, General Köller of Prussia, and Lord Burghersh of England would escort him into exile. Lady Burghersh did not take the news calmly.

Paris, April 13

I am in the greatest rage that ever was tonight! Only conceive, just as I was beginning to enjoy myself, and be quite happy here, thinking all my lonely hours at an end for ever, Burghersh is named to attend Napoleon to the Isle of Elba. He is to be escorted by a Russian (General Schoulov), an Austrian (General Köller) and an Englishman (B.) I would go with him with all my heart, but that they will not allow, and I suppose, indeed, I could not do so, as they will travel with him, dine with him, etc. It will be just like guarding a wild beast. They set off tomorrow and are to embark on the sixth day, so B. will probably be back here in nine days. There never was anything so hard on me; we were so happy here. . . . I do think

it is a cruel thing on me, but it is a curious mission to be sent
on.

Today Prince Esterhazy and Prince Wenzel Liechtenstein
returned from Fontainebleau, where they had been sent by
the Emperor of Austria to Marie Louise. They dined with us
today and gave me an account of her. She cried very much, but
consented to leave Buonaparte, for which I think she is a
monster, for she certainly pretended love for him, and he always behaved very well to her. She said she would not see
him before he goes, for that if she saw him and that he asked
her to come with him, she knew she could not refuse him; but
that to obey her father, and for the good of her child, she
agreed to go to Vienna. She showed them the King of Rome,
and they say he is the most beautiful child they ever saw. She
is to have the duchy of Parma and Guastalla. I think it is quite
disgusting in her to abandon him in his misfortunes, after
pretending, at least, to idolise him in his prosperity, and I feel
exactly the same about all his marshals, etc. who have left
him.

Priscilla Burghersh subsequently changed her mind about
Marie Louise and became her friend during later years in Italy,
where she found the former empress a good and warmhearted
person. Warmhearted she certainly was. Emperor Francis had
sent one of the greatest noblemen in the Austro-Hungarian empire to bring his daughter home—Prince Paul Esterházy—accompanied by a handsome young general, Count Adam Neipperg. The party had hardly been on the road two days before
Marie Louise and Neipperg became lovers. Napoleon himself
had been astounded by his bride's sexual appetite on their
wedding night in 1810. He had naturally expected to find the
little Austrian archduchess a trembling, frightened figure when
he took her to bed for the first time at Compiègne.

Handsome Neipperg was to remain a great solace to Marie
Louise. Meanwhile, the famous scene in the Cour du Cheval
Blanc took place. On April 16 the Allied commissioners who

were to conduct the Emperor of the French to the coast arrived at Fontainebleau. Lord Burghersh, to the infinite relief of his wife, had been replaced by another British officer, Colonel Neil Campbell. At midday on April 20 Napoleon descended the curving, horseshoe-shaped palace stairs to the courtyard where the Imperial Guard was drawn up. The emperor made them a short, dignified address, embraced their commander, General Jean-Martin Petit, and for a moment buried his face in the standard of the guard. He then signaled for his carriage to advance and was driven off for the south at a gallop.

In Paris the weather continued to be beautiful. The Comtesse de Boigne wrote:

> No events in this town, no battle, foreign occupation, revolt or disturbance of any kind, could influence or restrain the toilettes of the women. . . . They wore their elegant costumes to visit the bivouacs of the Cossacks in the Champs-Elysées.
>
> Strange to both sight and thought was the spectacle of these inhabitants of the Don peacefully pursuing their habits and customs in the midst of Paris. Most of them were sewing, darning their clothes, cutting out and preparing new uniforms, repairing their shoes or the harnesses of their horses. . . . They readily allowed people to approach them, especially women and children, and the latter were frequently on their shoulders. . . . They had every reason for remaining near their horses, for never under any pretext would they take a step. When they were not sitting on the ground they were on horseback. To go round the bivouac from one group to another they would mount their horses. . . . these nomadic customs seemed to us so strange that they keenly excited our curiosity, which we satisfied all the more readily as we were persuaded that our affairs were proceeding excellently. Partisan success hid from us the bitterness of a foreign bivouac in the Champs-Elysées. I will do my father the justice to say that he did not share this impression, and that I never could induce him to go and see this spectacle, which he always insisted was sad rather than curious.[14]

All Paris was deeply impressed by the dignity and modesty of Emperor Alexander. He continued to go about without any escort and almost alone, winning all hearts. He visited the wounded French soldiers at the hospital, he drove out to Malmaison frequently to call on the failing former Empress Josephine, and stayed to comfort her the night before she died.

Madame de Boigne wrote:

> He was simply adored by his own subjects. I remember arriving one night at the theater just as he was entering his box. The door of it was guarded by two great giants of his army, who observed so strictly military an attitude that they did not dare move to wipe their faces, which were bathed in tears. I asked a Russian officer what had happened for them to be in such a state. "Oh," he answered carelessly, "The Emperor has just passed by, and probably they managed to touch him."[15]

The spring of 1814 belonged to Alexander, whose popularity contrasted sharply with that of the king of France. Louis XVIII's return to his country was a grisly anticlimax. He took his time about leaving England, arriving in Paris only on May 3.

Chateaubriand wrote:

> I can see the scene as if it was yesterday. As the government wished to spare the King the sight of foreign troops, a regiment of the Vieille Garde formed a line from the Pont-Neuf all the way to Notre Dame, along the Quai des Orfèvres. I do not think that human faces have ever expressed such menacing hatred. These grenadiers covered with wounds, the conquerors of Europe, were forced to salute an old king, invalided by time and not by war, protected by an army of Russians, Prussians and Austrians, in Napoleon's capital. . . . When they presented arms it was a movement of fury, and the sound of those arms made one tremble.[16]

On the way to Paris Louis XVIII had stopped at Compiègne, to which palace he summoned Talleyrand. The meeting was an icy one between the obese monarch and the statesman who had done so much to facilitate the restoration. The shadow of too many old scores lay between them. Alexander, the next visitor to be received, was treated so brusquely that he refused to spend the night at the château, as had been planned, and returned to Paris as soon as dinner was over. It is curious that Louis XVIII should have been so clumsy. Despite his gout and his appallingly overweight body, he was an intelligent, shrewd man. Perhaps the loyal entourage that had surrounded him for so long in England had concealed from him the fact that the younger generation could hardly remember the name Bourbon, and that many of the older survivors of the Revolution were ambivalent in their feelings toward him, his brother, the Comte d'Artois, and his niece, the Duchesse d'Angoulême, the last living child of Louis XVI. Nothing could have been stiffer than the manners of the latter, and she annoyed Madame de Boigne and her friends by arriving dressed in English clothes, which she continued to wear although French and English fashions were worlds apart.

A happier occasion surprised the Parisians the day after the return of the royal family. Without fanfare or fuss, the Duke of Wellington rode into the city wearing a plain frockcoat, white neckcloth, and top hat. He had been appointed British ambassador to France and did not wish to enter Paris as a red-coated conqueror.[17] The news was around in a flash, and the crowds shoved and fought their way to catch a glimpse of the famous man riding quietly between his half-brother, Charles Stewart, and Castlereagh.

Stewart gave a ball to celebrate the occasion. All Paris society was there and Adèle de Boigne described the glorious moment when the duke entered the room with his niece, Priscilla Burghersh, on his arm. Unluckily the historic evening was spoiled, according to Madame de Boigne, by an unfortunate contretemps:

It was at this same ball that the Grand Duke Constantine,*

---

*Constantine was Emperor Alexander's brother and heir to the Russian throne.

after the departure of the Emperor Alexander, asked for a waltz. He was just beginning to dance it when Sir Charles Stewart stopped the orchestra and asked for a quadrille, which Lady Burghersh wanted. He was devoted to her.

The conductor hesitated, looked at the Grand Duke, and continued the waltz.

"Who has dared to insist on having this waltz played?" asked Sir Charles.

"I," answered the Grand Duke.

"I alone give orders in my house, Monseigneur," said Sir Charles. "Play the quadrille," he continued, turning to the conductor.

The Grand Duke went away very angry, and was accompanied by all the Russians. This made a great stir. . . .[18]

There were so many balls and receptions during that month of May that the statesmen assembled for the purpose of drafting a peace treaty with France found it difficult to get their work done. "Paris is a poor place for business," wrote Castlereagh to Lord Bathurst, apologizing for being such a bad correspondent.[19] In fact, he and his colleagues succeeded in producing a remarkably wise and generous document which was known as the First Peace of Paris, signed on May 31. The Allies believed that it was much in their interests to support the frail new Bourbon regime, and, while France had to give up Napoleon's conquests, she received some not inconsequential additions to the frontiers of 1792. There was to be no army of occupation, she was to retain much of her colonial empire, there were no reparations demanded. The looted art treasures from all over Europe were to remain in the Louvre.[20] It was anything but a punitive peace settlement and a far wiser one than that made just over a hundred years later by the peacemakers of 1919 after the next gigantic conflict, World War I.

However, the great task of European reconstruction, the complex problem of establishing what Castlereagh called "a real and permanent balance of power," was postponed. It was decided that a congress to settle all possible disputes would be held in Vienna in a few months time.

In retrospect, it seems incredible that two such experienced men as Metternich and Castlereagh could have worried as little as they seem to have done about the general invitation extended in Article XXXII of the peace treaty, by which "all the powers engaged on either side" in the recent wars were asked to send plenipotentiaries to Vienna. This meant that all Europe, from the Baltic to the Illyrian provinces, from the pope in Rome to rulers of the tiniest German principalities, was invited.

Metternich did write urgently to his wife, giving her detailed instructions about redecorating the Chancellery reception rooms and hurrying on the architects who were working on his private villa in the Rennweg in preparation for the parties which the Metternichs would be obliged to give, but he and Castlereagh both thought that the congress would last a matter of weeks—two months at the most. The four powers, Russia, England, Austria, and Prussia, had made a secret agreement which was not published openly in the text of the Treaty of Paris, but was confided to Talleyrand. This agreement made it clear that all major decisions were to be made by them, and the smaller powers were to have little share in the more important conclusions reached by the congress. Talleyrand accepted this news with his usual impassivity, and it was possibly then that he started to prepare the thirty pages of instructions of his own which Duff Cooper has rightly said should be essential reading for all young diplomats.

It was hoped that much would be settled in London, whither the emperor of Russia, the king of Prussia, their ministers and Metternich were now proceeding. But it cannot be too often reiterated that the future congress was intended to be *only a ratifying instrument of the decisions of the four great powers.*

Metternich and Castlereagh were to prove to have been overly sanguine. The Congress of Vienna lasted for nearly nine months instead of a few weeks, and so bitter were the disputes that once more Europe was brought to the threshold of general war.

Visit to England

THE ROYAL VISIT to England commenced on June 6, 1814. Originally it had been planned to invite the tsar alone, but Lord Castlereagh disagreed:

"The Tsar," he wrote to the prince regent, "has the greatest merit and must be held high, but he ought to be grouped and not made the sole feature for admiration."

The emperor of Austria refused to be "grouped" and sent Metternich to represent him. It was a great relief to him to have the excuse of being needed in Vienna to make arrangements for the coming congress. Although he hated public occasions, he was prepared, as the head of the ancient house of Habsburg, to do his duty this time. Metternich had assured him that the congress would last only four to six weeks. That would be endurable, although it made Emperor Francis distinctly nervous to overhear his foreign minister discussing which of the greatest dancers and singers in Paris should be engaged to provide entertainment for the delegates and taking advice from Talleyrand about whether or not the painter, Jean Baptiste Isabey, was the very man to undertake the official portraits and also lend his talents as decorator in charge of the celebrations.

Nevertheless, the emperor was not without a certain pride. Four times during his lifetime the Austro-Hungarian empire had been at the mercy of the French. Now, at last, the French would come crawling to his capital hoping for a seat at the conference table. Bankrupt as the exchequer was, it was perhaps time to repaint his immense but shabby palace, the Hofburg, and put on a show. There were plenty of officials to see to the details; he must remember to have a word with Prince Trauttmansdorff, master of the horse, about supplying smart carriages for the visitors. Shiny dark green would be nice, with the Habsburg arms in yellow on the doors. He himself could look forward to a peaceful summer, pursuing his favorite hobby of making toffee in his private kitchen.

The king of Prussia was delighted at the prospect of padding along in the wake of his "divine friend" Alexander, and with him came Hardenberg and Blücher. This arrangement suited Castlereagh very well. Surely in peaceful England, he thought, there would be time to gather his foreign colleagues together and to "methodize" (one of his favorite words) the problems that would confront them at Vienna. In Paris it had proved impossible to pin Alexander down on the most thorny issue: the future of Poland. London should provide the opportunity.

It was, therefore, with the highest hopes that the visit of the sovereigns and their suites opened in Dover where they landed on a sunny evening. Eager crowds thronged the beaches, and the Scots Greys and three other famous regiments were drawn up on the quayside, every button shining and each soldier standing smartly at attention. The next morning a train of carriages carrying the visitors set off for London, where a vast multitude had gathered to welcome them.

For twenty years the people had been waiting to celebrate the coming of peace. "The Emperor of Russia," wrote an English lady, "is my hero, and everybody's hero!"[1] Since Napoleon's retreat from Moscow, she and most of her compatriots had burned with an almost hysterical enthusiasm for all that was Russian. Their fervor had been increased by the descriptions from Paris of the modest and democratic manners of the godlike emperor during his stay there. The English newspapers had reported his visits to the wounded French soldiers, his tenderness toward the dying Empress Josephine, his charming way of walking unescorted through the streets. To liberal thinkers he incarnated their hopes for a new and better world. It was known that he had resisted the restoration of the Bourbon monarchy; that he had sympathized with the flames of nationalism burning in Prussia and Spain; that he had already asked that his English program should include a talk with the philosopher, Jeremy Bentham, to discuss the constitution he considered offering the Polish people.

By comparison, Castlereagh, Metternich, and Hardenberg faded into the background, gray ghosts beside the knight in shining armor. Seldom has a single individual had such an opportunity as that given to the tsar during this midsummer visit. Ceremonial occasions rarely have lasting historical importance. This one did, but only two people in all London were aware of the possibility of diplomatic disaster that lay ahead.

The Russian ambassador, Count Lieven, and his brilliant politically minded wife (they were soon to become Prince and Princess Lieven) had had the tsar's sister, the Grand Duchess Catherine of Oldenburg, on their hands since March 31. She was a widow of twenty-six, ugly, restless, and ambitious. Countess Lieven greatly disliked her, noting that she was "greedy of everything, especially of people."[2] Yet it was necessary to treat the grand duchess with deference, for her influence on the tsar was enormous. It was known in St. Petersburg, although not yet whispered in western Europe, that the tsar had been incestuously in love with her for years.

Alexander's dominating grandmother, Catherine the Great, had decided in 1792 that the fifteen-year-old boy should be married. Having looked over the field of available princesses, her choice fell on Louise of Baden, who was then thirteen. The little princess was sent across Europe with her eleven-year-old sister as companion and arrived at St. Petersburg trembling with shyness and fear of the unknown court of Russia. The last person to reassure her was the bridegroom, awkward, rebellious and unhappy. When her sister was shipped back home to Baden, Louise wrote to her mother that she felt that the only person she could talk to freely had gone and that she was desolate. Inexorably the imperial machinery ground on and the marriage took place the following year, with Louise now baptized in the Orthodox Church and rechristened with the name Elisabeth.

The years that followed were ones of bitter loneliness for her. Astonishingly intelligent and cultivated for her age, possessed of a loving and tender heart, she disliked the murky intrigues that lay below the surface of the resplendent court. Madame Vigée-Lebrun, who came from Paris to paint her, thought her ravishing, and left a description in her memoirs of the angelic sweetness of expression of the young grand duchess, with her pale skin and ash-blond hair. Her qualities appealed very little to Alexander. It was not that he was cruel; it was rather that he was himself deeply insecure and needed the reassurance that he would find later in his mistresses. Never sexually passionate, he was to be attracted throughout his life to bold, self-confident women who knew how to flatter his complex ego and feed his self-esteem. Elisabeth, with all her beauty and eager desire to help him through the troubling years that followed his grandmother's death, was unable to do so. She was too ignorant of the ways of physical love to arouse him sexually, and the bright intelligence that enraptured the rest of the court intimidated Alexander. If he wanted a serious conversation he preferred to confide in one of the liberal young men who were his boon companions.

Prince Adam Czartoryski was his closest friend. There are few more attractive figures in the history of the time than this Polish nobleman of twenty-seven, with his high courage and remarkable physical beauty. As the acknowledged leader of the movement for Polish independence, he was held in Russia as a hostage, for it was feared by Emperor Paul and his government that were he to return to Warsaw the flames of nationalism might be rekindled. He was the perfect safety valve for the heir to the throne as Paul's reign regressed from the moderate despotism with which it had opened to terrifying depths of tyranny and madness. Together the two conspirators met when it was safe to do so in order to plan the benefits that they would bring to Russia when Alexander came to power. Czartoryski was La Harpe all over again, except that instead of being a ponderous old teacher he was a charming contemporary who listened more than he talked as they shared their dreams.

Then the lonely Archduchess Elisabeth fell in love with the romantic dark-haired Pole who was her husband's best friend. He responded passionately, while the whole court held its breath. What would be the punishment inflicted on Czartoryski by the sensitive, neurotic Alexander? The couple were so violently and openly enamored of each other that it was impossible to hide the affair, yet Alexander appeared to close his eyes. His biographer, Henri Troyat, writes that "for three years he remained a complacent spectator of the liaison." [3] There is something perverse and unpleasant in the picture of the husband amused by the infidelity of his wife and his favorite.

The idyll lasted until a baby was born to Elisabeth in 1799, a little girl with dark hair and eyes, named Maria. Troyat gives us a picture of the christening.[4] Emperor Paul, regarding the baby in the arms of Countess Lieven, coldly asked: "Madame, have you ever heard of two blond parents producing a dark-haired child?" Terrified, Countess Lieven stammered out: "Sire, God is All-Powerful."

It was the end of Czartoryski's career during the reign of Paul. He left Russia for exile in far-away Sardinia, and while Elisabeth's heart was broken, so also was Alexander's. He mourned his friend and favorite until such time as he could recall him to his side. The opportunity came on his accession to the throne in 1801, and Prince Adam was made foreign minister. The intimate conversations, the sharing of liberal dreams

and aspirations began again as if they had never been interrupt-
ed. The little girl who had been born to the lovers had died
when she was a year old, bitterly lamented by her mother, and
years were to pass before the romance was resumed. The scene
for the reunion would be the Congress of Vienna, by which
time Empress Elisabeth was thirty-five and Czartoryski forty-
four.

Meanwhile, Alexander had found an endless succession of
women to assuage his vanity and bolster his male pride. At first
his mistresses were beautiful French actresses who visited St.
Petersburg on tour: Mademoiselle Phillis, Madame Chevallier
and the famous star, Mademoiselle George. There were affairs
with the wives of respectable Russians and Germans of the middle class whose husbands were more than willing to overlook
the transgressions of their spouses—Bachrach, Kremmer, Se-
verin, and Schwartz were some of their names. Frau Schwartz
was especially rewarding as a companion in bed and the tsar
was to need her comfort at the Congress of Vienna where she
joined him for a time. There were passing liaisons with the
wives of his friends, Stroganov and Kotchoubey, but only one
serious romance.

Maria Naryshkina possessed every possible quality which her
royal lover sought. Her beauty was considered to eclipse that of
any other woman at court; her own birth was noble and she had
married into a family so proud that through the centuries they
had refused to accept any titles, preferring to be known simply
as the Naryshkins. Her husband, a high dignitary of the regime,
was a direct descendant of Peter the Great. They were so rich
and luxurious that when they entertained in their palace on the
Fontanka in St. Petersburg, at their summer home on the Gulf
of Finland, or on their Italian estates, they always offered their
guests three kinds of dinner, "à la russe, à la française, à l'ita-
lienne." [5] They were accompanied on their travels by a corps of
secretaries, servants, and professional artists who were engaged
by the year to entertain them in whichever residence they happened to fancy at the moment. The fact that there was nothing

material the tsar could offer his mistress that she did not already have made her particularly attractive to him, and her warmth and exuberance gave him a sense of security he had never known before. In her arms he discovered that his natural frigidity melted and that he could be ardently aroused.

In due course the favorite became pregnant, a condition of which she could hardly wait to inform Empress Elisabeth, who had not yet been able to conceive a child by her husband. Elisabeth wrote to her mother in Germany that what she minded most was the way "the Naryshkine" chose to tell her—tossing off the news between dances at a ball. The child was a girl named Sophie, born in 1804. The next year Alexander returned briefly to his wife's bed and to the joy of all Russia a daughter, Elisabeth, was born. Sadly, she died two years later and the empress never bore an heir to the throne.

Madame Naryshkin was still *maîtresse en titre* in 1814, but for political advice the tsar turned to his plain little sister, Grand Duchess Catherine. She kept the letters which record the curious fascination she had for him.

"Goodbye, joy of my eyes, adoration of my heart . . ."

"What is that delicious nose doing that gives me such pleasure to play with and to kiss?"

"I am mad about you! And I am as excited as a maniac that I shall see you again. After all this running around how I look forward to relaxing deliciously in your arms." [6]

Countess Lieven found the feature that the tsar so admired quite hideous, calling it "a squat Kalmuck nose." But she was obliged to admit that the grand duchess had beautiful hair, sparkling eyes, a clever mind, and a vivaciousness of manner that some people found attractive. Hoping for the best, the Lievens engaged for their emperor's sister the whole of the Pulteney Hotel in Piccadilly at the price of 210 guineas a week. Catherine was delighted with this arrangement and settled down to enjoy herself, look for a second husband, and write letters to Alexander in Paris.

The prince regent came to call. She found him ill-bred and

he found her ugly. Their second meeting at an official dinner given in her honor at his magnificent residence, Carlton House, was even more unfortunate. The finest band in England had been engaged to entertain the guests. The grand duchess ordered it to be sent away, saying that music made her vomit. During dinner the prince regent employed all his charm—and he could be very charming—and she returned his effort by lecturing him on the sorest subject she could have chosen: the hard life he imposed on his only child, Princess Charlotte, whom the grand duchess had already befriended. Not only had she made friends with the heiress to the throne, but it was rumored that she was encouraging her to defy the wishes of her father and his government in regard to the marriage they wished her to make with the Prince of Orange. Already aware of her interference, the prince regent found it unbearable to be reproved at his own table.

"This is intolerable," he whispered to Countess Lieven, who wrote later that he was purple in the face. She added that from that evening on, Catherine and the regent hated each other.[7]

The grand duchess wrote to her brother that his future host in England was "obscene, disgusting, used up by dissipation." She was delighted to find how unpopular he was with the Whig Opposition party as well as with large sections of the public who took the side of his wife. That stout, outrageous figure had long been banished from royal society. The man in the street thought this wholly unfair, for while her indiscretions were scandalous, everyone knew that her husband's were equally so. Feeling ran so high that the prince regent could hardly pass through the streets of London without being hissed and booed.

This was grist to Catherine's mill. She cultivated the leaders of the Opposition and announced her intention of visiting the Princess of Wales. She would certainly have done so had not the Russian ambassador, Count Lieven, told her that he would resign on the spot if she attempted this indiscretion.

Catherine had passed on all this information to her brother in letters which he read carefully. Now, on the morning of June 7, 1814, he was in Count Lieven's carriage bowling along the roads of Kent, bound for London. He was to be the guest of a man of fifty-three whose father, King George III, was locked away at Windsor Castle, lost in his tormented dreams. The prince regent, according to the grand duchess, was not only a vain and vulgar man but a very unpopular one. Surely this English visit, while forming a pleasant interlude and an opportunity to see his sister, was not an occasion to be taken seriously.

The metaled road, the richness of the country through which he drove, the prosperity of the villages, and the glimpses of pleasant country houses set in their lush parks made the five-hour journey agreeable enough, but the tsar grew impatient at the prospect he had been told was before him. According to Lieven, since earliest morning an immense crowd had been gathering in the southeastern suburbs of London, watching the highway from Kent. The prince regent's gold and scarlet postillions, sent to meet the sovereigns, would probably be lost in the tumult of enthusiasm, for by popular demand the tsar's carriage was to be unhorsed and dragged by eager citizens all the way to St. James's Palace. The route to the palace from the outskirts of the capital was lined with wooden stands for the spectators. Those who could not afford seats would be leaning out of windows, craning their necks for a sight of the noble savior of Europe.

Surfeited with the incense of flattery, careless of the disappointment he might cause, the capricious Russian emperor ordered that his ambassador's carriage should leave the procession and proceed by another route. Outflanking the millions whose hearts were set on welcoming him, the tsar took the Surrey lanes and entered the capital by way of Camberwell and Clapham. A young man named De Quincey, who happened to be walking down Piccadilly early that afternoon, saw a plain carriage draw up before the Pulteney Hotel and a tall figure run up the steps. A moment later the tsar was in his sister's arms.[8]

He found it impossible to leave her and sent word by the distraught Lieven that he would not be using the State apartments arranged for him at St. James's Palace but would instead be staying at his sister's hotel. So much for the Lord Chamberlain, two bands, and most of the great officers of state, all of whom had been waiting since morning at the palace. Above all, so much for the prince regent who had gone all the way out to Shooter's Hill to receive his illustrious visitors.

Very soon the news that Alexander was at the hotel spread all over London and a huge crowd, making the best of a disappointing day, gathered in Piccadilly. The tsar appeared on the balcony, smiling and handsome, to receive a wild ovation. It was Paris all over again.

From Carlton House came the message that the prince regent was coming to visit the emperor immediately. The little party waited and waited, the Lievens growing more uncomfortable by the moment, the grand duchess more triumphant. After three hours another message arrived: "His Royal Highness has been threatened with annoyance in the street if he shows himself; it is therefore impossible for him to come to see the Emperor."

The regent would have been spared this humiliation had the tsar agreed to go to St. James's Palace, so close to Carlton House. As it was, the Lieven carriage was summoned once more and the emperor and his ambassador drove to call on the regent. They found him embarrassed and irritable. "A poor prince," remarked Alexander to Count Lieven as they drove back together to the Pulteney. "But one," Count Lieven answered, "who helped you win a glorious war and a peace to match."[9] This was the only private interview between the emperor and the prince regent during the whole visit.

That night and every night for three weeks, the streets of London were splendidly illuminated. The colonnaded marble screen of Carlton House was lighted by flares of scarlet and topaz interspersed between palm trees in tubs; in front of Lord Castlereagh's house at No. 18 St. James's Square there was an immense "transparency" representing a large dove with a branch of olive in its mouth.[10]

By day the tsar and the grand duchess went sightseeing—St. Paul's Cathedral, Greenwich, the British Museum, the Royal Exchange, and the many parks of the city. They went to the races at Ascot, they visited Hampton Court, always followed by admiring crowds. Someone estimated that when they walked in Hyde Park, as they did every day, as many as ten thousand citizens downed their tools and put the shutters up on their shops to follow the progress of the imperial pair. By night there were galas at the theaters, there were banquets and balls.

Whatever might be said about the prince regent—if he was, as Leigh Hunt called him in his radical weekly, the *Examiner,* "a libertine over head and ears in debt and disgrace, a despiser of domestic ties, the companion of gamblers and demireps, a man who has just closed half a century without one single claim on the gratitude of his country or the respect of posterity"[11]—no one questioned his ability to give a good party. Highly cultivated and endowed with exquisite and very original taste, he was the greatest connoisseur in Europe and his palaces were superb. He rebuilt them constantly and added to the collections: statuary, pictures (he was an early collector of Dutch masters), carpets, furniture, porcelain, ormulu—scarcely a day went by without a new purchase. Today, the British monarch's great collections owe much to her gifted, if much criticized, ancestor.

His dinner for the foreign potentates on June 8 at Carlton House was a great occasion.

> Open double doors between [vast apartments] made a continuous chamber three hundred and fifty feet long. Its ceilings were spandrelled and traceried in the "Gothick" taste, its walls panelled with golden mouldings and shields emblazoned with the quarterings of England, its windows curtained with crimson, its fairy-like chandeliers suspended from carved monastic heads . . . and at the west end a low, wide Gothic

door opened on to lawns, weeping trees, the multi-coloured fans of peacocks' tails and the setting sun.[12]

The prince regent was at his most affable, and there was much to show his guests. Perhaps the tsar preferred classic French eighteenth-century taste to neo-Gothic fantasies? If so, he might care to glance at the drawing rooms containing some of the furniture and ornaments from the palace of Versailles, which the regent had bought at a public sale after the French revolution. Or would he care to inspect the galleries of paintings? There were some new acquisitions that might interest him.

It was no good. The tsar was in a bad humor and hardly glanced at the treasures of which his host was so proud. He found the house too hot, and Queen Charlotte, the regent's mother, a very dull dinner partner. Indeed the house was very warm, as were all the prince regent's palaces, and the old queen was hardly a stimulating companion, having retained the stiff manners of the small German court in which she had been brought up many years before. But the food and wines were extraordinary—the regent had taken great trouble over them, as he did over every detail of his entertainments. Carême much enjoyed working for him when Talleyrand lent his chef to the regent for a season or two later on, and Carême was an astute judge of his masters.

It was all wasted on the Russian emperor. He played with his food and hardly spoke during the long meal. The grand duchess did nothing to help her host break the ice. Everyone was relieved when it became time to go into the Throne Room, where hundreds of very dressed-up guests were arriving to be received by Queen Charlotte and her son. The tsar stood aside watching, his bored glance on the clock. The aging but still elegant favorite of the prince regent, the Marchioness of Hertford, was brought up, eager to be introduced to "the saviour of Europe." When his host presented her, Alexander pretended not to hear. Knowing that he was a little deaf, the regent thought that he had not understood and repeated loudly: "This is my Lady Hertford." Still the tsar did not reply. Having made a deep curtsy, the royal mistress withdrew, giving him a glance that Countess Lieven never forgot. The fate of the visit, she thought, was written in that furious look.[13]

There were banquets offered by the Goldsmiths' Company and the Merchant Tailors, there were dinners and balls given by Lord Liverpool and Lord Castlereagh. There were also entertainments given by the leaders of the Whig Opposition, to which the prince regent could not possibly go. It maddened him to hear that the tsar had greatly enjoyed the hospitality of the Duke of Devonshire and Lord Grey. Relations between Carlton House and the Pulteney Hotel deteriorated day by day, and the two vain and capricious men began to behave like children. The regent kept his royal guests waiting for an hour on the occasion of a review in Hyde Park; the tsar arrived for dinner at Carlton House at 11 P.M., giving as his excuse that he had been detained by the enthralling conversation of Lord Grey, to whom he had accorded an audience.

Thinking to be cunning, the regent arranged for Alexander and his sister to make an official visit to Oxford on June 14, the night that the famous Whig hostess, Lady Jersey, was giving a ball. It seemed out of the question for the tsar to be able to return to London in time for it, but he got up in the middle of dinner in Christ Church Hall and drove through the night. Reaching Lady Jersey's at three in the morning he danced until six—the tsar was always proud of his graceful dancing.

As the ill-fated visit progressed, the popularity of Prussia and Austria increased. It was hard to make a heroic figure out of King Frederick William, but Field Marshal Blücher was a robust, impressive soldier who was warmly cheered wherever he went. Prince Hardenberg, although much handicapped by his deafness, was greatly respected by the public. Metternich behaved impeccably. Quiet, dignified, elegant, he firmly declined the invitations of the Opposition, nor did he receive Whigs at his embassy. In marked contrast to the Russians, he found the arrangements for his entertainment perfection itself, and both he and the Prussians greatly pleased the English by their genuine appreciation of all the trouble that had been taken on their behalf.

On June 18 Grand Duchess Catherine outdid herself. The occasion was an enormous banquet given at the Guildhall. As it was for men only she had not been invited, but she insisted on joining her brother as he, dressed in scarlet and gold, entered the prince regent's state coach to drive to the City of London. There were seven hundred guests at the party, which cost twenty thousand pounds. The Guildhall's gold plate was the finest in England, and a much admired feature of the menu was a huge turtle, "very handsomely presented by Samuel Turner, Esquire, a West Indian merchant." [14] There was an immense baron of beef, surmounted by the royal standard, over which presided the company of royal carvers. Musical entertainment was to be provided by stars of the Italian opera, but as they were about to begin their performance Catherine requested them to stop, making her usual remark that music nauseated her. It took considerable persuasion to have her agree that "God Save the King" might be played after the royal toast. It was following this banquet that the diarist Thomas Creevey wrote: "All agree that Prinny [the prince regent] will die or go mad; he is worn out with fuss, fatigue and *rage*." [15]

The grand duchess had gone too far. Even the usually urbane prime minister, Lord Liverpool, was furious and said to Countess Lieven: "When folks don't know how to behave, they would do better to stay at home and your Duchess has chosen against all usage to go to men's dinners." [16]

Not only the members of the government were infuriated by the behavior of the tsar and his sister. The Opposition leaders were also embarrassed. Lord Grey told Creevey that in his opinion Alexander was "a vain, silly fellow." The prince regent was unpopular, but by insulting the head of state the tsar had insulted the state itself, and for this mistake he was not to be forgiven.

A sense of anticlimax and disillusion spread among the people. Hurt and saddened that the Russian emperor should have so ill repaid their enthusiasm, the London crowds thinned perceptibly toward the end of the visit and their good-by cheers were reserved for the Prussians and Austrians. Jane Austen expressed the sentiments of many when she wrote from Chawton on June 23 that she wished the tsar well away.[17] Her opinion was echoed by the staff of the Pulteney Hotel and the state coachmen and servants who had been on duty during the imperial stay. Their tips were miserable: "A country baronet would have done better," said a contemporary observer when he heard what they had given.

The banners were furled, the illuminations which had dazzled all London were dimmed. The show was over. Alexander never again recovered the stature he had attained during those glorious spring weeks in Paris. Even allowing for the inconsistencies of his complex nature, a student of the time is still left with a feeling of mingled rage and pity at the waste of the eager mind, the charm, the power, the potential of Alexander I.

There had been no chance of doing serious diplomatic business in London as Castlereagh had intended. The tsar's petulance had come as no surprise to him or to Metternich, who well remembered his vacillations during the Campaign of France, but they had not foreseen that a whole month would be wasted. And, as Alexander insisted on returning to Russia, the opening of the congress had to be put off until October 1. Although the foreign ministers of the other three great powers (England, Prussia and Austria) agreed to foregather in Vienna before that date, it was clear that without Russia they could hardly fulfill the plan made in Paris to settle the main issues before the congress opened. Now the four powers had to face

the likelihood of the congress meeting without having first arrived at agreed positions on the principal points in dispute.

Still outwardly sanguine, the diplomats dispersed. The tsar
joined his wife, Empress Elisabeth, whom he had not seen for
eighteen months. They met in Baden where she was staying
with her parents, then proceeded to St. Petersburg accompanied by the ubiquitous Grand Duchess Catherine. Two months
later they all met in Vienna.*

---

*Since the reader will be obliged to hear about a great many new characters
in the story as the scene moves to Vienna, it might be as well to dispose of the
future of the Grand Duchess Catherine here. She did not play much of a part in
the political intrigues of the congress as she was busy pursuing the Crown
Prince of Württemberg. This unfortunate young man was in love with someone
else, but the grand duchess succeeded in becoming engaged to him and they
were married shortly after the end of the congress. She died as Queen of Württemberg in 1818, and was deeply mourned by her brother Alexander.

Vienna

THE CONGRESS was not due to open until October 1, 1814, but by the middle of September Vienna was already crowded with visitors. After twenty years during which Europe had lived in daily fear of war, upheaval, and suffering, there had come at last a relief from tension, an opportunity for carnival. The Prince de Ligne* called it "the Kings' holiday." To most of the participants, it was a great deal more than that.

The imagination of all Europe had been struck by the idea of a congress to regulate affairs. It was seen as a constituent body which would be guided by the highest principles of equity and justice. The dispossessed princes whose territories had been obliterated by Napoleon looked forward to having their stolen rights restored; the governments of the small states that still existed hoped they would be given long-coveted cities and counties. The people as a whole, however, expected more than mere settlements of frontier questions. They felt in an ill-defined way that means must be found to prevent the recurrence of the horrors of the last twenty years. In Germany and Italy the younger generation had developed a strong sense of nationalism as a result of the successful struggle against Napoleon. They longed for the creation of institutions through

* Charles Joseph de Ligne, 1735–1814. Soldier, writer, wit.

which they could realize their new dreams and hopes.

The man who played host to the giant gathering in Vienna, Emperor Francis, grew to regret having invited so many to his capital. Vienna was small in comparison with Paris or London. The heart of it was known as the inner city, in the center of which loomed the immense mass of buildings known as the Hofburg. This was the imperial residence, a town within a town. Having been built and added to over a period of many centuries, the palace was full of contrasts. A dark fifteenth-century courtyard opened through a modest archway into a startlingly wide expanse of magnificent baroque symmetry. Humidity dripped from thick stone walls and the light of day barely penetrated into the more ancient parts of the emperor's dwelling, while suites constructed in the preceding century boasted immense windows through which the sunlight poured, illuminating the gilt and white paneling, the damask walls, the laughing stucco cherubs in the corners of the gaily painted ceilings; altogether an architectural hodgepodge, but possessing considerable grandeur.

Around the Hofburg, jumbled together in a maze of narrow streets, lay the palaces of the aristocracy, the homes of the middle class, the hovels of the poor, and shops, cafés, restaurants, and theaters; the whole encompassed, as it had been since time immemorial, by ramparts. Although Vienna had ceased to be a fortress town following the expulsion of the Turks in 1683, the ramparts remained, a romantic souvenir of days long past, of hard-fought battles lost and won. No longer a defense against the invading infidels, they were now the scene of rendezvous, amorous or purely business. So small was the city these walls encompassed that an energetic man could walk their length in an hour and a half. And yet there was room for a great deal of greenery in the heart of Vienna, where even today the tiniest square is illuminated in May by the pink and white candles of the horse-chestnut trees.

The population of Vienna, which numbered 200,000 in 1814,

was augmented by half again as many people by the congress, an increase of alarming proportion to the authorities but to the people a sheer delight. The Viennese were by nature fun-loving and hospitable; they were also very proud to have their own emperor play host to the most important figures in the world. Everyone had heard stories from their grandmothers of the great days of Austria under Empress Maria Theresa; now those days would be revived and the humiliations of recent years erased. They rushed to offer their services. Sons of the nobility applied at the Hofburg to become pages and equerries, while the sons of the poor lined up for jobs as coachmen, valets, footmen—anything to be in on the show. Volunteers wishing to be employed as secret agents besieged Baron Franz Hager, chief of police, for it was known that surveillance of the distinguished foreigners would be far beyond the capacity of the regular police force.

Hager took on a large number of the citizen applicants. Some were true patriots who thought it their duty to volunteer. These were nobles with great names such as Esterházy, Palffy, and Kaunitz. Others were in it for the pay. These, mostly badly educated men and women, were infiltrated into embassies as servants. Much time was wasted in Hager's intelligence operation; one especially hardworking department spent days pasting together scraps of paper from diplomatic wastebaskets, only to find that they had put together a laundry list or a petty expense account. Another department steamed open all letters entering or leaving Vienna on which they could get their hands; the most scandalous of these went directly to the emperor. Francis I of Austria, like other heads of state before and after him, had a passion for reading secret service reports.

While Baron Hager toiled unremittingly to prepare for the congress, no one worked harder than Prince Trauttmansdorff, marshal of the court and master of the horse, who was in charge of installing the visiting sovereigns and their suites at the Hofburg. The emperor had been delighted with Trauttmansdorff's arrangements for the stables: 300 freshly painted carriages awaited the guests, their dark green varnish shining, the imperial arms emblazoned in yellow on their doors. Fourteen hundred horses and the requisite number of coachmen and grooms in yellow liveries stood ready for the great day.

The stables were a detail compared to the problems of protocol facing Trauttmansdorff. There were no precedents to guide him for no international conference on the scale of this one had ever taken place. To help him he had the advice of Metternich and the eager encouragement of Empress Maria Ludovica. This charming, delicate Italian-born princess, the third wife of the twice-widowed Emperor Francis, was ready to make any sacrifice that would assist her husband and ensure the success of the congress. Already racked by tuberculosis (she died a year later), the twenty-seven-year-old, blue-eyed, blond empress threw herself into the task of aiding the marshal of the court and hastily organized the "Festivals Committee" to plan the entertainment for the foreign guests. Naturally artistic, an enthusiastic patron of music and the theater, she looked forward to working with the French decorators Isabey and Moreau when the time came to dress up the Hofburg. Meanwhile, she struggled with Trauttmansdorff over the guest list.

They could count on having to put up in the palace itself the emperor and empress of Russia, the king and queen of Bavaria, the kings of Prussia, Denmark, and Württemberg. The size of the suites of these sovereigns came as a shock; they were prepared for the train that would follow such a potentate as Alexander of Russia, but were appalled by the numbers accompanying the lesser royalties. The distribution of apartments took many a long hour. Certainly the tsar and his entourage (which included his sister) must have the Amalia wing, a lovely series of rococo rooms overlooking the sunny Ballhausplatz. Would the king of Prussia be content with rather dark apartments built during the Renaissance, fine in their way but distinctly gloomy because of their small windows? No, that would not do at all. The empress of Austria must give up her own delightful quarters in the Schweizerhof wing to move into dank and chilly ones looking on an inner courtyard. She insisted on it. After all, the sacrifice was only for six to eight weeks, the length of time Metternich said the conference would last.

It was decided that about forty tables must be set up every night for dinner and that the knotty problems of precedence could be eased by seating sovereigns according to age. As a result, night after night poor Maria Ludovica went into dinner on the arm of the sixty-year-old king of Württemberg who, besides being the oldest of the monarchs, was easily the most unpopular. It is impossible to find a good word for him in the memoirs of the time. His girth was so enormous that a half-moon had to be cut out of the dining room table to accommodate his vast belly; yet he possessed none of the jollity commonly associated with very fat men. His manners were as coarse as his expression was grim, and he was known among the people as the "Württemberg Monster." It was a great waste of the charms of the lovely young empress with her carefree conversation and her passion for the arts: the king was a homosexual who smiled only when a handsome page approached him. His temper was not improved when, upon addressing one of the good-looking young men who stood ready to serve him in the second person singular reserved for relatives and intimates, he was reprimanded by the boy who drew himself up and informed the monarch coldly that his name was Baron Beck and that even his own sovereign used the polite form of "you" (third person singular) when addressing him.

The king of Denmark, a gentle, ugly man, who was as thin as the king of Württemberg was fat, was the most popular of the monarchs staying at the Hofburg. He wrote modestly to his wife on arrival that he was astonished and delighted by the warm welcome of the Austrian court, adding rather pathetically: "I should be quite happy if they hadn't taken Norway away from me."* He was no trouble to anyone, and the Viennese grew to

---

*Russia had promised Norway to Sweden in 1812 in order to gain Sweden's good will, and the British had underwritten the deal.

love the sight of his slight figure, dressed in a long green coat, walking the streets of the city. It was said of him that he left no beggar emptyhanded, no supplication unanswered.

Besides the crowned heads, various minor princes were squeezed into the imperial palace, but even the Hofburg could not accommodate all who came. The Germans were particularly numerous. It was as if every ancient barouche and landau from the North Sea to the Danube had been taken out of mothballs during the summer, dusted off and set on the road to Vienna. The carriages contained hopeful princes and their mates, mistresses, chamberlains, secretaries, and servants clinging to rusty iron boxes containing the family jewels that had not been worn for a generation. Princelings from more than 215 German states, many of which had been crushed out of existence when Napoleon created his Confederation of the Rhine in 1806, came to Vienna—a veritable Teutonic avalanche of deposed monarchs anxious for a piece of the new European pie that would be sliced up by the great men at the congress. Their arrivals were reported daily to the emperor by Baron Hager. A typical sampling for one day lists the following princelings from this former Germany:

> The Princes of Hesse-Philippsthal
> The Court of d'Anhalt-Bernburg
> Prince Hesse-Homburg
> Prince Reuss-Ebersdorf
> Prince Hohenzollern-Sigmaren
> Princess Hohenzollern-Sigmaren
> Prince Isenburg-Birstein
> Prince Isenburg-Budingen

On another day Hager reported a mixed bag:

The Dukes of Weimar, Oldenburg, Mecklembourg, Prince Wrede. Cardinal Consalvi [representative of the pope], the agents of the Queen of Etruria, the Hereditary Grand Duke of Hesse-Darmstadt, the Grand Master of the Duke of Weimar,

Senator von Hach of Lubeck, L. de Medici, Marquis Malaspina [deputy from Milan], the Duke of Campochiaro, Prince de la Trémoille-Tarente, Prince Wittgenstein, General Pino, etc. [The full list for September 26 covers two printed pages.]

European grandees like most of the above had relatives living in Vienna who could put them up, but other visitors were not so fortunate. Switzerland, for instance, sent a representative for each of her cantons. The Jews of Frankfurt sent a delegation, backed by Nathan Rothschild, to plead for the rights of Jews in Germany. The publishers of Europe sent representatives to ask for new laws of copyright. Besides the special interest groups, there were fashionable sightseers who came to amuse themselves and write their memoirs, like the gossipy Comte Auguste de La Garde-Chambonas. There were eccentrics like Sir Sidney Smith of England who came to induce the congress to take immediate action against the Barbary pirates. There were dancers and actresses brought from France and Italy on Metternich's orders to entertain the delegates; there were painters and decorators. Above all, there were the diplomats—the hub of the wheel of the congress. How did Vienna manage?

The Viennese managed miraculously, some for gain, many for reasons of patriotism and civic pride. Houses that had seemed crowded before now seemed to expand—whole families found they could live just as well in two rooms as in six. Such dependents as could be persuaded to leave the city were sent off to the country for the duration. And, despite the crowding, despite the frightening inflation that was already apparent in September, the atmosphere was marvelously cheerful as the congress assembled. The weather helped. It was so unusually mild an autumn that crowds strolled the streets until late at night, stopping at popular restaurants like Sperl's for a glass of wine and a look at the dancers on the parquet floor. Carl Bertuch, a bookseller and publisher from Weimar, wrote in his diary: "From here to Sperl's ... With great bonhomie, decent bourgeois women mingle with whores. The theaters stage all-night performances of comedies, ballets, and farces. All the world is in a frenzy, the servants receive liberal tips to go and have fun too, usually at the theater, so passionately beloved by the Viennese." [1]

Ever curious, the public peered into the carriages of the great as they dashed homeward through the narrow streets at night, preceded by mounted grooms carrying torches. "There goes Signora Bigottini—they say that she will open the season dancing in *Zephir and Flora*." "I wonder who the man with her was—the Grand Duke Constantine?" "It looked to me as if she was with Prince Eugène de Beauharnais—they say he's mad about her."

So the gossip flew, and nothing was too gossipy or too trivial to be picked up by Hager's agents. The Prater was a useful source for them. This lovely park on an island in the Danube was filled on warm days with a contented crowd strolling on the grass under the rich autumn foliage, swaying to and fro on the Russian swings, whirling on the merry-go-rounds, listening to the wandering minstrels. In the great allée known as the Prater promenade, the elegant world drove up and down between the lines of golden chestnut trees, while the populace watched eagerly to see who was with whom. They craned their necks to admire the turnouts and beamed with pride as they recognized members of their own popular royal family.

One of the charming characteristics of the Viennese was a lack of envy of wealth and power. Later on, when the strain of the expenses of the congress forced the government to impose a new tax on the citizens, there were complaints, but in the balmy early autumn there was nothing but applause and approval in the air. Indeed, until the end of the congress, the police reports do not show one incident of robbery, which is remarkable in a crowded city at any time and extraordinary when one contemplates the temptation offered by the influx of 100,000 strangers, many of them openly displaying the most lavish jewels, the richest of furs. Security for the monarchs was never an issue: Tsar Alexander and his fellow sovereigns strolled the streets without bodyguards.

The general good humor of the people and the warm welcome they extended to their foreign guests affected even the diplomats, by tradition touchy about their prerogatives, a slight to their person being interpreted as a slight to the country they represented. Vienna in 1814 was exceptional: the foreign missions took what they could get and made the best of it.

The Russians and the Prussians alone among the major powers had no housing problems as their entire delegations were lodged at the Hofburg. Some of the younger members of the tsar's staff found the formality of the imperial court a bit dampening to their spirits, but they soon discovered ways around the restrictions. Hager was obliged to inform the Austrian emperor that Prince Volkonsky, that gay blade, was receiving the nightly visits of Fräulein Jospehine Wolters, a nineteen-year-old opera singer from Cologne, whom he sneaked into the Hofburg dressed as a young man. There is no record of any reprimand being addressed to the prince; perhaps the story amused Francis I.

The rest of the diplomatic corps shifted for themselves. Lord and Lady Castlereagh lived at first in the street called Im Auge Gottes, but, finding their quarters too cramped for offices and staff, they moved into a magnificent twenty-two-room apartment in the Minoritzenplatz, one of the loveliest and most elegant squares in Vienna. Here they were just a stone's throw from Metternich in his Chancellery on the Ballhausplatz and around the corner from the Hofburg. Rents were very high near the Hofburg; the British government paid £500 a month to house their representative, but, as Castlereagh planned to entertain extensively, he needed this setting.

It touched and pleased the Viennese to observe the style of the foreign secretary of England and his wife during their first days. They strolled the streets arm-in-arm as any bourgeois couple might; Lady Castlereagh, fat, dowdy and benevolent, exclaiming with delight at what she saw in the shop windows, both of them unaffectedly admiring the palaces and churches on their route. This was not at all what the public expected of the haughty English. When it became known that a dancing teacher had been engaged to visit the apartment in the Minoritz-enplatz and that the Castlereaghs were earnestly learning to waltz, people were enchanted. It was said that Lord Castle-reagh, annoyed at his own ineptitude as a dancer, used to practice with a chair when his wife was out.

The British delegation consisted of two other plenipotentia-ries, Lord Clancarty* and Sir Charles Stewart; Sir Edward Cooke, the under-secretary of the Foreign Office; Joseph Planta, the private secretary; and ten young men from the For-eign Office. Clancarty was a zealous and experienced diplomat, but Stewart was a foolish choice for the mission as he was tem-peramentally unfitted for the strain that lay ahead. His bad be-havior during the congress became notorious: he was rude, domineering, and ostentatious, often appearing at ministerial dinners an hour late without excuse, insulting coachmen and other servants, on one occasion driving drunkenly down the Graben, his horse bedecked with lilies of the valley. His affairs with women were notorious even by the easy standards of the time and place. Nevertheless, Castlereagh put up with him be-cause he loved his half-brother.

Edward Cooke, the permanent civil servant who was ex-pected to carry the brunt of the work of the mission, arrived in poor health and later broke down under the pressure. The young men who were his assistants worked extremely hard, while pretending to be so infected by the carnival spirit of Vi-enna that they did no work at all. Approached by a police spy on arrival, one of them said in his lackadaisical way, "Oh, we plan to finish early at the office, drop in at some hospitable Viennese lady's salon in the evening, drink a lot of your lovely

---

* Richard Trench, 2d Earl of Clancarty, 1767–1837.

Hungarian wine and then pick up a pretty girl on the way home."

The agent wrote down the conversation and he and his colleagues looked forward to the easy target for intelligence gathering that the British embassy would present. Their annoyance was considerable when they found that there was no possible way to penetrate the operations of the English mission. The sloppy and frivolous young men were remarkably careful with their papers. A horde of King's messengers carried the dispatches back and forth to England, and it was impossible to extract information from either the servants or the scrapbaskets. The former could not be bribed and the contents of the latter were burned. As late as two in the morning smoke could be seen rising from the chimneys above the Minoritzenplatz as one of the "frivolous" secretaries of the embassy completed the day's work.

The Austrian police spies were not the only ones confused by the English style. La Garde-Chambonas, the French diarist, could never understand the reason for Castlereagh's immense prestige. His way of entertaining was anything but grand, yet people fought to be invited to the casual suppers that took place several nights a week at the British embassy. Lady Castlereagh's way of dressing was not only dowdy but sometimes ridiculous, yet her husband seemed proud of her and never looked elsewhere for feminine companionship. His conversation was not brilliant; if he ever made bons mots they were not circulated about Vienna as Talleyrand's were. Yet the tall, handsome figure had only to enter a crowded ballroom for there to be a momentary hush. An imperceptible tension hung in the air as people took in his quiet presence and watched to see to whom he would speak, drawing nearer in an attempt to overhear. To the end of the conference, it remained a mystery to La Garde-Chambonas, but, as Sir Harold Nicolson observed acidly in his admirable history of the congress, he was never asked to the Castlereaghs'.

Guileless and domestic are not the adjectives that spring to mind when referring to the atmosphere at the Kaunitz Palace in the Johannesgasse, the home of the French mission.* Talleyrand had left his tactless, unsuitable wife behind and brought as his hostess his twenty-one-year-old niece, Comtesse Edmond de Talleyrand-Périgord, daughter of the Duchess of Courland. It was hard on Madame de Talleyrand, who sobbed her heart out at the news that she was forbidden to come to Vienna, but, as the representative of the defeated power, Talleyrand needed every trump card he could get for the very difficult game he was about to play. Dorothea de Talleyrand-Périgord (better known in history by her later title, Duchesse de Dino) was ravishing, highly intelligent, and completely loyal to her uncle. His second trump was Carême.

Talleyrand had chosen his staff with care, writing in his memoirs, "In my choice I thought a good deal more about Paris, that is to say the Tuileries, than I did about Vienna, for I could count on myself for Vienna and for France."[2] He meant by this that, while he was perfectly capable of handling diplomatic affairs at the congress by himself, he was by no means confident of support from King Louis XVIII and his brother, the Comte d'Artois. Both of them had distrusted him for years and had given him the foreign affairs portfolio with the utmost reluctance and only because there was no one else with his unique ability and experience. To do the work, Talleyrand took the Comte de La Besnadière, a permanent Foreign Ministry official whom he could trust completely. As second plenipotentiary, he chose the Duc de Dalberg, who had many useful family relationships in Germany and Austria. Of Dalberg he wrote to the Duchess of Courland: "Dahlberg was chosen so that he might broadcast those of my secrets that I want everyone to know." He told her that he was also taking Count Alexis de Noailles, who was very close to the Comte d'Artois. "If one

* Not to be confused with the Chancellery, a far finer palace, built by Maria Theresa's great chancellor, Wenzel Anton von Kaunitz.

must be spied on at least it is better to choose the spy oneself."
The Marquis de la Tour du Pin was selected for his distinguished lineage and social graces. "He will do to sign pass-
ports."[3] A large professional staff from the Foreign Ministry was
included to assist La Besnadière.

The above comments were for the ear of his mistress only. To
the outer world the embassy of France presented a serene and
harmonious appearance. When Talleyrand and his niece drove
into the courtyard of their residence on September 23, everything was ready for them. Tired after a fast eight-day journey
from Paris, they must have been relieved to find Carême beam-
ing from the windows of his kitchen and the Marquis de la Tour
du Pin waiting on the steps. He and Dalberg had been sent a
month ahead to make sure that the rented palace was in order.
Instead of order, they had found the curtains in tatters, the
mattresses full of moths, the fine old carpets full of holes. It
was not the moment to bargain with the owners, for, in the
housing crisis that the congress had precipitated, it was a sell-
er's market and some other visiting dignitary would have been
only too delighted to grab the Kaunitz Palace. Instead, Talleyrand's staff set to work to repair the damage, sparing no expense, for it was tacitly understood by everyone in the embassy
down to the youngest messenger boy that on this occasion
France simply could not be outshone.

At the same time, in view of their uneasy position, it would
not have done to be flamboyant. The house suited Talleyrand
perfectly. It was in the Johannesgasse, a quiet little street not
far from St. Stephen's Cathedral and about twenty minutes on
foot from the Hofburg. While large, the Kaunitz Palace was
nothing like so fine as the superb Dietrichstein or Liechtenstein Palaces in the Minoritzenplatz where the British lived, but
it had been built in the early eighteenth century, probably by
Lukas von Hildebrandt, who with his great contemporaries, the
Fischer von Erlachs, created the style known as Viennese baroque. This style is not the colorful, exuberant baroque of pro-

vincial Austria, but it has a restrained elegance that is sophisticated in its sobriety. The Kaunitz Palace, with its plain pale
yellow plaster street front wore an air of discretion. The stucco
decorations above the eighteen tall windows that looked down
on the Johannesgasse were luxuriantly carved, but there were
no other touches of fantasy and the noble limestone staircase
that led up to the first or entertaining floor was the one grand
feature of the interior. A series of damask-hung drawing rooms,
paneled in gold and white, ran the length of the house. One
high-ceilinged room led into another, some heated by fireplaces, but most by tall porcelain stoves built into a corner of
the room and fed from behind by a special servant known as
the fire tender. These stoves were often ravishing works of art,
as pretty as or prettier than the finest furniture in the room.

Of all the many remarkable women who were present at the
congress, it was perhaps Dorothea de Talleyrand-Périgord who
enjoyed it the most and was herself most changed by it. Later
she was to write: "Vienna. The whole of my destiny is contained in the name of this city."[4]

She had never known happiness. Born in 1793, she was the
youngest of the four daughters of the Duke of Courland, whose
grim northern duchy lay on the Baltic Sea. Nominally the king
of Poland had been his feudal overlord until the year before
Dorothea was born, when Courland became an appanage of
Russia. Immensely rich, the ducal family moved with the seasons from one of their vast estates to another. Mittau was the
ducal palace in Courland itself, but they spent more time at
Sagan, a grandiose and extremely uncomfortable castle in Prussian Silesia, one hundred miles southeast of Berlin. Life was
run on royal lines at Sagan. There was a resident troupe of
actors to entertain the huge house parties that came for the
shooting; musicians were brought from Berlin and singers from
Italy; the banquets were superb and very heavy.

As a little girl Dorothea often spent her summers at Löbikau,
a family estate in Saxony, alone with her mother and her moth-

er's lover, Count Alexander Batowski, a slender, dark-haired Pole. She was to write thirty years later: "Seven centuries of noble lineage, an attractive face and a reputation for goodness established from her youth, distinguished my mother. . . ."[5] This is a generous and loyal description, and not entirely untrue. The Duchess of Courland was unquestionably beautiful and intelligent; she might well have retained the reputation for goodness of which her daughter wrote had she not married at the age of nineteen the impossible old Peter Biren, Duke of Courland. Arrogant and spiteful, he was loathed by his subjects, and his young third wife was obliged to take on her shoulders all the responsibilities involved with keeping the duchy afloat in the complicated maelstrom of eighteenth-century power politics. It was she who went to Warsaw to defend the family rights against the Poles and Russians, it was she who was to make the tsar into a sort of family counselor and friend. In the course of her struggles, she was aided by the young and romantic, Batowski who was almost certainly the father of Dorothea.[6]

Duke Peter of Courland died in 1800 and, while to the seven-year-old girl this meant only that a shadowy, little-known and seldom seen figure had disappeared, it also meant that she and her sisters were now among the greatest heiresses in Europe. Her share included a magnificent palace on the Unter den Linden in Berlin.

Dorothea was a lonely little girl, far too thin, with immense dark eyes and sallow skin. Her older sisters were not close to her, and her mother's life was a hectic one. Batowski disappeared after the duke's death, and a new lover, Baron Gustav Armfelt, a Swedish officer, replaced him. "My whole family," Dorothea wrote bitterly years afterward, "was under the spell of Baron Armfelt; so fatal to the tranquillity of all those whom he called his friends. He ruled our domestic life despotically. . . ."[7]

Dorothea had forgotten, if she ever knew it, that the hated Armfelt had done her one important good turn. He discovered that her English governess was not only cruel but was teaching her charge nothing, and he insisted that she should be dismissed by the duchess. Shocked, the duchess not only did so but flung herself into the task of finding a replacement who would make something out of her shy, moody child. In her enthusiasm she engaged not just one, but two instructors—the Abbé Piattoli and a Miss Regina Hoffmann. Both were excellent teachers, both were devoted to their pupil, and provided her with the first affection she had known. In those days, a young girl of the cosmopolitan aristocracy of Europe was considered sufficiently educated if she knew several languages well, and Dorothea's sister Wilhelmina bemoaned all her life the fact that she had been given no further teaching. Dorothea was far more fortunate. The excellent duo of Piattoli and Hoffmann encouraged her voracious reading on every subject in every language and, when she developed a passion for mathematics and astronomy, they encouraged that.

Fearing that her thirst for learning was making her too serious, Abbé Piattoli sought to distract Dorothea with tales of people he had known in other countries, among them his brilliant pupil, Prince Adam Czartoryski, the Polish resistance hero who had become the close friend and foreign minister of the young and idealistic Tsar Alexander. Dorothea adored the stories about Prince Adam and made her tutor tell over and over again every detail he could remember about the legendary figure. At the age of twelve, she was thoroughly in love with the romantic hero she had never met and she determined to marry him.

The childish fantasy became a serious matter. Instead of forgetting Prince Adam, she grew up stubbornly refusing to consider any other suitor. The good abbé saw nothing impractical in the plan. He built up Dorothea to Czartoryski and persuaded him to come to Mittau to have a look at the young girl. His visit lasted three weeks, during which he hardly spoke to the gangling fifteen-year-old, who nevertheless was ecstatically happy and confident that only shyness prevented him from opening his heart to her. In fact, Prince Adam could not make up his mind. It was certainly time he got married and, although twenty-three years his junior, Dorothea was an excellent match.

The duchess, while anxious to get her daughter off her hands, was looking for a better bet than the charming Pole. Granted he was a statesman of international standing, as well as gallant, brave, and handsome, but he had fallen out of favor with the tsar and had just left the Russian service. To be unpopular with the tsar of Russia spelled disaster for any ambitious man in eastern Europe. She was delighted when Prince Adam prolonged his hesitation and she lost no chance to torture poor Dorothea with the humiliation inflicted on the family by the reluctance of the arrogant Pole whose birth and wealth were so inferior to the Courlands'.

Desperately, Dorothea invented excuses for Prince Adam and remained constant to him while her mother flung suitor after suitor at her. A procession of grand names arrived at Löbikau and Mittau to beg for her hand: Prince Augustus of Prussia, the Duke of Coburg, the Duke of Gotha, Prince Florentin of Salm. Dorothea eyed them coldly, certain that they were only interested in her money and her lineage. "Thin, even skinny with drawn features and murky skin," she wrote of herself sadly.

Her mother then did something truly wicked. It happened that Talleyrand was looking for a wife for his nephew and heir, Comte Edmond de Talleyrand-Périgord. It also happened that the tsar owed him a favor. Alexander, who was devoted to the duchess, was delighted to enter into an intrigue which would please her and repay his friend Talleyrand at the same time. He went to Löbikau himself in October 1808, taking Edmond with him. The trap was set. Alexander made it very clear that he desired the match and to oppose the wishes of the tsar was next to impossible for any of his subjects. Still Dorothea might have resisted had not the duchess, alarmed by the rumor that Prince Adam had at last made up his mind to propose, descended to the lowest of tactics. She forced old Abbé Piattoli, who was dying, to deny to Dorothea what he knew to be true: Prince

Adam now wished to marry her. She even made him write the unhappy girl a lying letter saying that the prince had just married a Miss Matuschewitz in Warsaw.[8] To ensure that the story was believed, she invited a Polish lady to stay at Löbikau, Countess Oguinska, who repeated the fable of the marriage most convincingly.[9] Later, Dorothea was to learn from Prince Adam himself that he had decided to marry her, but by then it was too late.

She was married to Edmond in Berlin the following year, 1809, and went to live in Paris. This was the Duchess of Courland's idea of paradise; she followed the young couple as soon as she could and settled down happily. She had always been an admirer of Napoleon; Dorothea loathed Napoleon. Passionately pro-Prussian and an active sympathizer with the liberation movement, she greatly disliked the thought of the French court and all the emperor stood for. When he married the Archduchess Marie Louise, she was obliged to serve as lady-in-waiting to the new empress, an honor she did not enjoy.

Edmond Talleyrand-Périgord was a good army officer, respected by his colleagues and his men. As a husband, he appears to have been neither kind nor unkind; a stupid man, he probably found his clever, moody wife as alarming as she found him unattractive. It seems likely he disliked being bullied into marriage as much as Dorothea did. The totally loveless couple produced three children: a son in 1811, a daughter in 1812, and another son in 1814. After that, their duty done, they rarely lived under the same roof, and were formally separated in 1818.

When, during the Campaign of France, Talleyrand had sent the Duchess of Courland to the safety of the château of Rosny, Dorothea and her children accompanied her. When Paris fell to the Allies, they returned and almost immediately tragedy struck. Little Charlotte-Dorothea, a baby of two, fell ill with the measles, which was a dangerous illness in those days. Dorothea adored the child, and when the little girl died she was desolate. Who was it who came forward to give her the tenderness and affection that she needed at such a moment? Talleyrand. It was a critical period for him, but he managed to find time to drop affairs of state every day that spring in order to come to comfort the bereaved mother. She was deeply grateful, and they grew very close as an uncle and niece might. To cheer her up, he persuaded her that it was her duty to come to Vienna to help him.

By now she had grown very lovely. When she first arrived in Paris, the often critical Madame de Boigne had written: "Although still a child, she was exceedingly pretty, engaging and gracious; already the distinction of her intelligence shone through brilliantly."[10] The skinny schoolgirl became a slim, but alluring figure toward which men's heads would turn when she entered a room. Her face filled out, the great dark eyes were now in proportion with their frame. And inevitably she gained self-confidence as she realized that she was thought beautiful. In the four years with Edmond, the world would hardly have guessed how empty the marriage was. The fashionable young couple went everywhere and, despite Dorothea's dislike of the Napoleonic regime, she had to admit that Paris society was highly entertaining in comparison with provincial Berlin. She was flattered to find that people found her witty as well as charming, and she learned to conceal the deep seriousness of her nature, to laugh and joke when it was appropriate to do so, to please men by being silent when they wished to talk. She was never close to women—indeed, until she went to Vienna she was not close to anyone.

It was there that she flowered and developed the full potential that Talleyrand had seen. Politically shrewd by nature, intensely loyal to her husband's uncle, she was to be the ideal hostess for him. There is no record of what the Duchess of Courland felt about the arrangement. She was now fifty-three and to have her sixty-year-old lover go off with her twenty-one-year-old daughter must have been a bitter blow. Yet she made no attempt to follow immediately, which was odd in view of the fact that all four daughters would be living in Vienna that autumn. Perhaps she had perfect confidence in the innocence of the relationship between Talleyrand and his niece. If so, her instinct would have been justified, for while there was a good deal of scurrilous gossip in Paris about the ménage, there was nothing improper about their relationship then.

While the diplomats and their staffs were occupied settling in during the last days of September, the ladies of the Viennese aristocracy were also busy completing plans for the entertainment of their visitors. It was decided that there would be a ball at the Hofburg once a week and that Princess Metternich would receive on Mondays, that Saturdays were reserved for Princess Trauttmansdorff, that there would be entertaiments at the imperial residence of Schönbrunn just outside Vienna, shooting parties at the emperor's country estate of Laxenburg, theater galas, concerts, a great fete in the Augarten, and another in the Imperial Riding School. These would be important occasions, but the Viennese hostesses prepared to fill in every empty moment with dinners and receptions in their lovely palaces. Princess Thürn und Taxis, Princess Fürstenberg, the Countess Zichy, Princess Esterházy, Princess Liechtenstein, and Countess Fuchs-Gallenberg were just some of the hostesses whose names recur constantly in the memoirs. The monarchs and the ministers were soon on dropping-in terms with these charming women, and when the official parties were over what could have been more agreeable than to meet each other informally in the hospitable houses that were always open to them? It was all very pleasant, all very easy, and as no one ever seemed to need to sleep during the congress, the candles burned late in the drawing rooms while below in the courtyards the tired coachmen dozed on the boxes of the waiting carriages.

Almost immediately the first romances of the congress were picked up by the secret police. The Duc de Dalberg began a long affair with his own cousin, the Countess Schönborn. The king of Prussia, who had not looked to right or left since the death of Queen Louise in 1810, became besotted overnight with love for Countess Julie Zichy and took to following her around with an earnest devotion that bored the spectacularly beautiful young woman considerably. Like every other lady in Vienna, she was far more pleased by the attentions of the tsar. Alexander, at thirty-seven, was at his most engaging. He was a different man from the churlish despot who had so offended the English during his visit three months before. Perhaps he was less dominated by his sister, the Grand Duchess Catherine, than he had been in London. Even that hard heart had succumbed to the magic in the air of Vienna; she had fallen in love with the crown prince of Württemberg and spent her time pursuing him. In any case, Alexander was in the sunniest of moods at the beginning of his stay. "Every morning he rubbed his face with a block of ice to tighten up his skin. He was at every reception, he attended every salon, and put himself out to be charming to every pretty woman."[11] He adored dancing.

> Tightly buttoned into his military tunic with a stiff, high collar, his thighs encased in the tightest of white kid breeches, his high boots gleaming and shining, he leapt up at the first sound of dance music. . . . Talking to women he was so flattering that some of them began to wonder if his compliments could be sincere. Some of them found him "too charming." One by one, or simultaneously, he claimed to have fallen in love with Princess Gabrielle Auersperg, Countess Caroline Szechenyi, the Countess Sophie Zichy, Countess Julie Zichy, Countess Esterházy and Countess Saaran.[12]

It is unlikely that any of these attractive Viennese ladies took him seriously, but to have a flirtation with the glamorous Alexander was part of the fun of that intoxicating autumn. Far more important to the story of the congress were the erotic intrigues conducted by two foreign ladies of high rank, the Duchess of Sagan and the Princess Catherine Bagration. In fact, it is impossible to describe the political situation without describing them, for they affected it through their relationships with the leading players in the drama.

Wilhelmina Sagan was the oldest of the four Courland sisters. The favorite of her dour father, she inherited great estates from him, one of which was the castle of Sagan in Silesia with which went the title she was to use during most of her turbulent life. At the age of eighteen, she was seduced by her mother's lover, Baron Armfelt, the Swedish adventurer whom Dorothea hated. Two months pregnant with Armfelt's child, Wilhelmina was hastily married off to the younger son of a noble French house: Prince Louis Rohan-Guémenée. He was penniless and accepted his bride's condition philosophically in view of her munificent dowry. The baby, a girl called Gustava, was taken off to Sweden to be brought up by Armfelt's family, a decision which Wilhelmina later regretted bitterly. At the time she was too young and shaken to fight to keep her child.

The Rohans traveled about Europe luxuriously on her money—London, Paris, Dresden, Prague—an easy, carefree life. However, by 1804, after four years of this nomadic existence, Wilhelmina had grown weary of it and of her husband. They were divorced, and the following year she wed a handsome, gloomy Russian named Prince Wassily Troubetskoi. This marriage barely lasted until 1806 when Wilhelmina obtained her second divorce. Having paid heavily to be free, Wilhelmina decided then and there that husbands were too expensive. From now on, she told her friends, she would only take lovers.

The year 1813 found her in Vienna, having just turned thirty-two. Like all the Courland girls, she was beautiful, with brown eyes and blond hair and her father's high coloring. She was highly intelligent without being as serious-minded as her youngest sister, and she was surprisingly modest and unself-conscious considering her great name, wealth, and power. Her best biographer, Dorothy Gies McGuigan, has painted a vivid picture of her receiving visitors in the morning in her old wadded dressing gown, her hair in a black sleeping cap, with two slices of lemon bound to her temples. She was very generous, always ready to take in a poor exile, lend her jewels, empty her purse.[13]

Highly sexed and very attractive to men, she had no difficulty in finding lovers; in 1810, she fell deeply in love with a brave young Austrian officer, Prince Alfred Windischgraetz. They were sublimely happy together, and she would have remained simply a great lady who was the mistress of an attractive soldier, and thus merely a background figure at the Congress of Vienna, had it not been for the dramatic events on the international scene during the summer of 1813.

During the spring of that year Prince Metternich, while the most important man in Austria, was also a very unpopular one. It was the period already described during which he was playing a lone hand as he slowly led his country into war with Napoleon. The emperor, trembling for fear he would once again be brought down to disastrous defeat by his foreign minister's rashness, stubbornly resisted any move that might be provocative. There was, however, a strong war party opposed to Metternich's devious tactics led by his rival, Count Philip Stadion, and the members of this party deplored what seemed to them the foreign minister's lack of determination. There were also young idealists who, inspired by the Prussian model, wished to rise in arms to fight for the liberation of the Tyrol and other occupied provinces; Archduke Johannes, brother to the emperor, was their leader, and they considered Metternich a rank coward.

For once he was a lonely man. His admirable wife, born Countess Eleonore (Laure) Kaunitz, was a loving woman who was also a shrewd and understanding partner. The granddaughter of Maria-Theresa's great chancellor, she had been married for her money and position, and she was well aware that she was too plain to attract the sophisticated young diplomat who became her husband and the father of her children. In Dresden, his first post, she had been obliged to look on as Clemens enjoyed a wild love affair with a beautiful young Russian, Princess Catherine Bagration, who bore him a child she had the gall to name Clementine.

In Paris there had been the affair with the French emperor's sister, Caroline Murat, and another one with Laure Junot, the wife of one of Napoleon's generals. This might have ended in tragedy had it not been for the quick wits and valor of Countess Metternich. General Junot, returning from a campaign, discovered some compromising letters in his wife's desk. Mad with rage, he sent for Laure Metternich to watch him kill his wife and then kill the Metternich children, following which he planned to challenge the guilty lover to a duel.

"Oh, no you won't," said Laure Metternich shortly, "you will be hanged for it, and meanwhile I shall put my children under the protection of the Emperor." [14]

General Junot was so taken aback by her calm that he put down the sewing shears with which he had been about to attack his wife and the matter ended there. Napoleon packed the Junots off to Spain within a day or two and Paris rang with the tale of Laure's courage.

By 1813, Metternich had known the Duchess of Sagan for several years, and their relationship was a pleasant one, faintly flirtatious but not more than that. However, during the tense spring of that year when he felt unpopular and alone he began to see more of her. It was a delightful short walk from the Chancellery to the Palm Palace in the Schenkenstrasse where she lived, and he found her an intelligent and sympathetic listener. Her sharp political mind astonished him; besides which, she was very seductive. The fashion of the day was a nearly transparent dress which followed the lines of the body, slit to the thigh, with only the lightest of clinging shifts underneath it. Hair was worn in ringlets which in all the portraits of the day make the wearer look delightfully natural and casual, although hours must have gone into achieving the effect.

In June, Wilhelmina left for what she thought would be a quiet summer on one of her estates in what was then Bohemia, today Czechoslovakia. She owned two, very close to each other: the huge castle of Nachod and another much simpler establishment which she greatly preferred called Ratiborzitz. This was a simple yellow manor house of no particular style, lying in an unpretentious park landscaped in the English fashion. There were no formal parterres or allées; instead the woods of chestnut and linden grew naturally and casually to the edge of the meadow that bordered the house. The other side of the manor looked down over a modest garden to the little river Aupa. The house was full of sun; the colors were pastel and the furniture of walnut and fruitwoods was totally free of the heaviness that characterized palace furniture of the day. Books lay about on occasional tables; a piano and a harp in the corner of the central room invited the musician; the dining room painted palest pink and gray was one of the lightest rooms in this very bright house.

Wilhelmina was always content to return to Ratiborzitz where her habit was to wear peasant dresses, work in the garden, oversee the farm, and enjoy a romantic idyll with her current lover. In that summer, 1813, the pace changed with astounding rapidity. Napoleon was at Dresden, having entered into an armistice with the Allies in order to give his war-weary armies a rest. To plan their next steps, the tsar, Nesselrode, the emperor of Austria, and Metternich, plus the Prussians headed by Hardenberg, moved into Bohemia. Gitschin, very near Ratiborzitz, was the headquarters of the Austrians; the tsar stayed not far away at Opocno. Thus Wilhelmina found herself entertaining the most important men in Europe during the month of June. It was a continual house party, for the sovereigns and statesmen found it infinitely pleasanter to come over for a few nights to the cheerful country house among its fragrant woods than to remain in the magnificent but chilly castles that had been assigned to them as headquarters.

It was during this month that Metternich fell wildly and hopelessly in love with his hostess—in love as he had never been before. His letters to her from this time on are quite different in tone from any of his other love letters. They are indiscreet, heartfelt, and quite unpretentious—astonishing letters for the vain Metternich to address to anyone. What Wilhelmina felt is hard to determine. She was still in love with Prince Alfred Windischgraetz, but it was flattering to have the most important man in Austria besieging her like a lovesick schoolboy, and she liked the excitement of it all. When he was there, couriers dashed up the country road to Ratiborzitz bringing the latest news from all over Europe; there were conferences with Nesselrode and Hardenberg; the omnipresent Friedrich von Gentz sat like a spider at his master's side and when Metternich was obliged to leave for Prague, remained with her as a sort of companion-watchdog.

She moved to Prague herself during the fruitless peace conference in July—more to see her gallant soldier-lover, Prince Alfred, than to meet Metternich, but during her stay she permitted Clemens to arrange a secret rendezvous at a small place called Laun. There they spent the night together for the first time, and he was to write to her months later that even if he lived to be very old, this would be the sweetest of all his memories.[15]

During the winter of 1813–1814, she remained in Vienna. Metternich, far away in Germany and France, suffered agonies as he heard rumors of her infidelities. Prince Alfred was with his regiment in the thick of the Campaign of France, but Laure slyly wrote to her husband that the duchess was said to be carrying on an affair with Frederick Lamb, the English diplomat. There was said to be another Englishman called George Charles Vernon and a young wounded Russian officer called Obreskov who had also taken her fancy.

It was odd that Metternich should have expected anything else, as he had known for years that Wilhelmina had a well-established reputation for promiscuity. Yet in his passion the worldly statesman seemed to have become naive, and the relationship was marred throughout its course by the violence of his jealousy.

However, there were periods of intense rapture to make up

for the pain she caused him. They met in Paris after the abdication of Napoleon, and there was a real reunion when at last he returned to Vienna for good in July. They made love whenever he could get away from his duties, snatching a few hours in the Chancellery while Laure and the children were away, an afternoon in the villa he had built in the Rennweg outside the city walls, a night in the Palm Palace.

This big palace in which the duchess lived was divided into two. The right-hand staircase led to her apartments and the left-hand one to the apartments of Princess Bagration. The two ladies were not friends and their close juxtaposition amused Viennese society as much as it tormented Baron Hager's agents, whose job it was to be accurate in their reports of which staircase was taken by the very important gentlemen who visited the Palm Palace during the congress.

Catherine Bagration was related to the tsar. On her father's side she was the great-niece of the Empress Catherine, on her mother's side the great-niece of Potemkin. Her husband, a young general and the hero of Borodino, fell at that battle in 1812. She had been faithless to him as early as 1802 when she had the love affair with Metternich in Dresden which led to the birth of the baby she named Clementine.

Known as the "naked angel" because of her deep décolletés, the pretty little blond princess possessed nearly as shrewd a political mind as her neighbor the duchess, and she was generally thought to be in the pay of the tsar. Certainly her house was to be useful to him during the congress, for she entertained frequently and well and everyone went to her parties despite her scandalous reputation. Compared with Catherine Bagration, Wilhelmina led the sexual life of a nun. The police frankly called the left-hand side of the Palm Palace a "b——." They noted that Catherine's affairs with Prince Charles of Bavaria, Count Schulenberg, and Count Schoenfeld were not enough to satisfy her and that she had added to the list of her lovers the crown prince of Württemberg and the crown prince of Bavaria, often receiving several of them on the same day in what one agent discreetly referred to as "intimate audience." After the tsar himself first spent the night with her in September, she told a friend that she did not just love him, she adored him, but it is unlikely that she truly loved any of the men she saw during the congress, except the crown prince of Württemberg whom she genuinely mourned when he left Vienna to marry the tsar's sister.

While there have been many international conferences since the one at Vienna, in none of them have women played such major roles behind the scenes as did the three beautiful foreigners just described. Dorothea de Talleyrand-Périgord, her sister Wilhemina Sagan, and Catherine Bragation were to influence important matters in the year 1814.

The Grande Armée: the retreat from Russia. (*Bettmann Archive.*)

Pulling down the statue of Napoleon in the Place Vendôme. (*Bibliothèque Nationale, Paris.*)

Metternich, by Lawrence. (*Royal Collection. By gracious permission of Her Majesty the Queen.*)

Talleyrand, by Prud'hon.
(*Bibliothèque Nationale, Paris.*)

Castlereagh, by Lawrence.
(*Royal Collection. By gracious permission of Her Majesty the Queen.*)

Alexander I of Russia, by Gérard. (*Giraudon, Paris.*)

Francis II of Austria, by Lawrence. (*Bettmann Archive.*)

Frederick William III of Prussia, by Lawrence. (*Royal Collection. By gracious permission of Her Majesty the Queen.*)

Prince Adam Czartoryski, by Olechkevitch. (*Bibliothèque Nationale, Paris.*)

Arthur Wellesley, Duke of Wellington, by Lawrence. (*Wellington Museum, London.*)

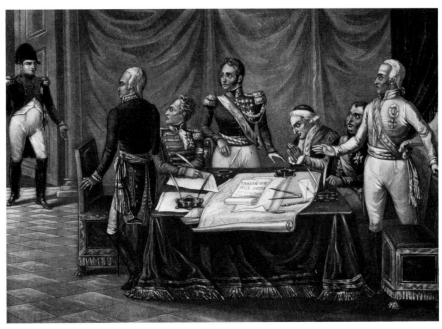

"Good God! Here he is!" a contemporary cartoon. (*Bibliothèque Nationale, Paris.*)

Mr. All-things-to-all-men: Talleyrand at Vienna, a contemporary cartoon. (*Bibliothèque Nationale, Paris.*)

Princess Bagration, by Isabey.
(*Giraudon, Paris.*)

Wilhelmine, Duchess of Sagan.
(*Charmet-Plon, Paris.*)

Laure, Metternich's wife.
(*Charmet-Plon, Paris.*)

The Duchess of Courland.
(*Plon, Paris.*)

Dorothea, Duchess of Dino, by Prud'hon (*Bibliothèque Nationale, Paris.*)

The Congress Opens

B Y SEPTEMBER 13, 1814, the foreign ministers of the four principal powers—Austria, Russia, England, and Prussia—were assembled in Vienna. We have seen that there had been no time
in either Paris or London for more than the most fragmentary
discussions of their plans. They seem to have failed to realize
how complex and difficult it would be to establish the rules for
organization and procedure. "Not even the English," wrote Talleyrand to Louis XVIII, "whom I thought to be more methodi-
cal than the others, have done any preparatory work on this
subject." [1]

When they did realize, to their dismay, that they had less
than two weeks to prepare for the opening of the congress, they
set to work in a flurry of confusion and discord, making proposals and counterproposals that were often as illogical as they
were controversial.

At that time the distinction between "great powers" and
"small powers" was nonexistent, and the modern term "super-
power" would have been unthinkable. It was assumed to be a
cardinal, if unwritten, principle of international law that all sovereign states were equal. Thus it had been highly imprudent to
use the word congress when issuing the invitation contained in
Article XXXII of the Treaty of Paris. The secret article of that
treaty, in which the four members of the Quadruple Alliance

reserved for themselves all decisions on important matters, was known only to Talleyrand. It had not occurred to the smaller countries that their envoys to Vienna were to be considered merely as a decorative background to the real proceedings and that their views would be largely ignored. Morally, the secret article was indefensible, and when Talleyrand arrived on September 23 he was more than delighted by the embarrassing position in which the "Big Four" had placed themselves. He was to write in his memoirs:

> The role of France was singularly difficult. It was very tempting and very easy for the Governments which had so long been hostile to keep her excluded from the major questions affecting Europe. By the Treaty of Paris France had escaped destruction, but she had not regained the position that she ought to occupy in the general political system. Trained eyes could easily detect in several of the principal plenipotentiaries the secret desire to reduce France to a secondary role.[2]

His first task to be accomplished at Vienna, therefore, was to assure beyond any possible doubt France's place as one of the world's great powers. To achieve this aim, he adopted a most singular and ambiguous form of attack. He had learned that the representatives of the four great powers had been in conference together since their arrival, excluding the counsels of the smaller nations. This was exactly what he had expected, and, as the exclusion of France was what he was determined to prevent, he set about stirring up the resentment of the smaller powers and promising them his backing. France alone the great powers could risk ignoring, but France leading the rest of Europe became at once a dangerous enemy.

There were few secrets in Vienna and, although Talleyrand was careful not to complain or seem to seek admittance, the uneasy ministers who were completing their program for the opening of the congress got wind of his design. They thought it wise to invite him and his Spanish colleague, with whom he had been collaborating, to join them for a conference on the afternoon of Friday, September 30, at Metternich's Chancellery in the Ballhausplatz. It was a magnificent five-sided baroque palace, the first floor, or piano nobile, of which had been completely done over that summer on the minister's instructions. It shone with its new curtains and carpets and sparkling chandeliers. There were many fine state rooms in which to entertain guests or conduct diplomatic business; of them all Metternich appears to have preferred a sunny chamber which looked out on the horse-chestnut trees below. It was pentagon shaped, like the house itself, and decorated in the style of the day, which in France would have been called Empire. He himself lived on the same floor next to the state apartments, while Laure and the four children were upstairs.

Although Talleyrand arrived punctually at the Chancellery, the others were already in their places around the long table in the middle of the curiously shaped room. Castlereagh sat at the head and presided. The first question was asked by Talleyrand. Why had he been summoned alone and not with the other French plenipotentiaries? Because it was thought best to have only the heads of missions at the preliminary conference. Then why were there two Prussian representatives, Humboldt as well as Hardenberg? Because of Prince Hardenberg's infirmity. (He was nearly stone deaf.) "Oh, if it's a question of infirmities we can all have our own, and make the most of them." [3] To soothe him it was agreed that in future there would be no objection to having two delegates attend from each mission. A tiny point, but Talleyrand had won it.

"The object of today's conference," said Castlereagh, "is to acquaint you with what the four powers have done since we have been here," and the protocol was passed to Talleyrand. Glancing at it, he saw the word "allies" and sprang on it immediately. Where were they? Were they still at Chaumont, or at Laon during the Campaign of France? Had no peace been made? If they were still at war, whom was it against? "Let us speak frankly, gentlemen; if there are still any allied powers this is no place for me." [4]

The other ministers disclaimed any ugly motive behind the

use of a word which they had adopted only for convenience and brevity. "Brevity," snapped Talleyrand, "should not be purchased at the price of accuracy." His further objections to the document were so vehement that his colleagues gave up the fight and agreed to tear it up immediately. They proposed to show him a much more important paper. This was produced, and the thunderstorm that followed staggered everyone.

Talleyrand argued that the Quadruple Alliance had ceased to have any meaning the day the Peace of Paris was signed. The assumption of control by the Big Four possessed no historical, legal, logical, or moral justification, he said; if they had pledged themselves to anything, they had pledged themselves to summon the whole congress on October 1: there was no escape from that position.

When Talleyrand had finished his tirade, the men around the table sat stunned for a moment. Gentz, who had been present as secretary-general of the congress, wrote in his diary:

"The intervention of Talleyrand and Labrador [the Spanish representative, Don Pedro Gomez Labrador] has hopelessly upset all our plans. Talleyrand protested against the procedure we have adopted and soundly rated us for two hours. It was a scene I shall never forget."[5]

The first to speak was Hardenberg, who protested strongly that Prussia did not want to see tiny states the size of Leiden and Liechtenstein meddling in great territorial questions. Fearing another torrent of French eloquence in reply, Castlereagh hastily adjourned the meeting.

It had been a most cynical performance. Talleyrand cared not at all about the small powers whose ardent champion he had become. Duff Cooper succinctly described his maneuver in his classic biography of Talleyrand: "He had succeeded in getting his foot in the door of the European Council Chamber. . . . Very soon those who were already ensconced there were glad enough that he should come in and shut the door behind him, leaving his former partners in the passage."[6]

Unable to find an answer to the unexpected attack, the Big Four were forced to agree to destroy the results of two weeks' work and start all over again, this time with the help of Talleyrand. Gentz was ordered to draft a communiqué to be issued in the names, not of the four, but of all the signatories of the Treaty of Paris—England, Russia, Prussia, Austria, Spain, Sweden, and Portugal—announcing the postponement of all plenary sessions of the congress in order to give time for reflection. It concluded sententiously by expressing the hope that the questions at issue would "mature in harmony with the public law, the provisions of the present Peace and the expectations of the age." Later it was agreed to postpone the plenary sessions indefinitely.

There never was a *congress* of Vienna, as Gentz was to observe in the following year. It was eventually convoked to sign the Final Act in June 1815, but that act had been written almost entirely by the great powers. The small countries might just as well never have come to Vienna; their representatives were occasionally called in as time went on to serve on various committees when it was convenient for the four to have them there, but they were powerless to affect major decisions. Thus they remained as expensive guests of the Emperor Francis, with little to do. The staffs of the great powers, on the contrary, were overworked; small wonder that Castlereagh's principal assistant, Edward Cooke, broke down during the winter.

As for Talleyrand, he had not achieved his aim by his sarcastic intervention. He had sought immediate inclusion in the inner councils of the Big Four, but for this he had to wait until the end of December when they were driven to accept him by the dangerous turn the conference proceedings had taken. By this time Europe was once again on the brink of general war, and the weight of France was badly needed on the diplomatic scales. Until then Talleyrand had to bide his time, certain that he would not be excluded indefinitely. The only well-prepared foreign minister, he never deviated from the instructions that he had written for himself months before in Paris. His vision had been so clear that there was nothing to change in the ably drafted thirty pages as the months went by, for he had long foreseen the various contingencies that might arise. Meanwhile, not displeased by the results of the first round of the negotiations, in which he had made his colleagues feel both guilty and foolish, he was content to drift for a time as the situation crystallized, making his influence felt with the assistance of his three trumps: his own immense prestige, his beautiful niece, and his admirable chef.

It seems inconceivable today that after such a violently contentious meeting, the statesmen involved should have continued their daily round of festivities as though nothing had happened. But in 1814 there were no eager reporters on the scene to track down the story of Talleyrand's disruption of the plans of the Big Four, there were no press conferences, no television cameras. All the same, Metternich's calm was extraordinary. Gentz was struck by it and wrote that "the Prince does not feel as I do all there is of embarrassment and even of dreadfulness in our position."[7]

Prince Metternich was anything but a frivolous man. To all Europe he was known as the smooth, often devious, but generally successful manipulator whose efforts had been crowned by his present role as host, after the emperor, to the brilliant assemblage gathered in his own capital to create a new and durable settlement of the affairs of the Continent. He was also known for his pride and his vanity. Now, thanks to Talleyrand, the organization of the congress was in disarray, and, because neither he nor Castlereagh had succeeded in pinning down the tsar on the most vital issues before them during the preceding months, the negotiations that followed were bound to be thorny. It might be assumed that a foreign minister in such a situation would have stayed in his office, summoned his assistants for advice, taken counsel with his friends, called off his engagements, dined with his wife and family, and gone to bed early in order to be prepared for the next hard day.

But Metternich, apparently unaware of the "dreadfulness of our position," went off cheerfully to the Hofburg to attend an imperial reception for a short time, then wound his way down the Schenkenstrasse to the Palm Palace. Wilhelmina had already received him that morning at eleven o'clock, which he called "my hour," but he was full of the news of the afternoon with Talleyrand and anxious for her opinion. He had come to depend increasingly on the soundness of her judgment, besides which he had never been more in love with her. The tempests of jealousy which had disturbed the affair during its first year had been wholly dispelled by a rapturous reunion in Vienna on July 25, during which Wilhelmina promised him that she was his and his alone and that he must no longer fear Prince Alfred Windischgraetz or any other man on earth. It was heaven to hear her say it, and Clemens believed and trusted her wholly. Never had he been so content.

Finding her that Friday evening entertaining various guests who, like himself, had dropped in after the Hofburg reception, he waited until they had taken their departure and stayed on. He did not return to the Ballhausplatz until the next afternoon. A few days later he wrote to her:

> My friend, I have been crying like a child—but since July 25 and October 1 I only cry tears of happiness; and it is to *you* I owe this happiness—*the greatest of my life!*[8]

It is not hard to imagine his reception at the Chancellery when he at last returned home: Gentz bent with pursed lips over a mountain of accumulated messages and letters, Laure's martyred expression as she greeted him, the anxious faces of the children, the masklike impassivity of his valet, Giroux.

There is no trace of this romantic adventure in the police reports, which were devoted to another rendezvous at the Palm Palace that same night. Two agents had been on duty in the courtyard of the palace. One reported simply that the tsar had paid Princess Bagration a visit following the Hofburg party.

The porter rang four times to announce him, and the princess, who had refused to see visitors all day on the grounds
that she was ill, came out on the staircase dressed en négligé.
She took Alexander into her boudoir where he at once noticed a man's hat. The princess gave an explanation which
amused the Tsar: "The hat belongs to the decorator Moreau,
he has been doing up my apartment for my party tomorrow."
The Tsar stayed for two and a half hours. HONI SOIT QUI
MAL Y PENSE![9]

The second agent was much more gossipy and long-winded!

October 2
No one in the city is talking of anything else . . . the princess is beside herself with delight over having had such a
triumph over the Queen of Ratiborzitz [the Duchess of Sagan]
who is her rival vis-à-vis Prince Metternich. Now she is the
first to receive the distinction of being singled out by Emperor
Alexander. These two powerful foreign women, rivals in taste as
in ambition, are living by chance under the same roof. . . .
It seems likely to me in view of the partiality that Metternich is showing to the duchess and the frequent visits Talleyrand makes her, that the Austrian party will be established in
her apartment and the Russian party at the Bagration's. It isn't
the first time that women's intrigues have influenced affairs of
state. So much for men!

Metternich's enemies are overjoyed by this development.
They are all for the Russian Andromeda and against the Courland Cleopatra. They hope that the Tsar will often take the left-
hand staircase. We shall see. The bets are taken, the armies are
on the field, and the firing has begun.[10]
The triumphant Princess Bagration confided the whole story,
including the episode of the hat, to an indiscreet woman friend
and it was then that she said, speaking of Alexander: "I don't
just love him, I adore him."[11] She probably did adore him at
that moment. Her jealousy of the duchess for having stolen the

lover by whom she, Catherine, had had a child in Dresden years ago had been mounting for months. During the previous winter she had discovered that Wilhelmina was writing letters to Metternich in Germany and had bribed their mutual porter to watch the mail closely. Now she had a splendid chance to revenge herself.

Alexander was suspicious of the Duchess of Sagan during the early part of his Vienna stay. True, she was a Russian subject and her mother was an old friend of his. Also she was charming and beautiful and in every way fitted to receive him. Yet she was known to be the mistress of Metternich, the man whom he had loathed since their first awkward dealings in Switzerland and France. Surely, it seemed to the tsar, it would be safer and more comfortable to allow Princess Bagration to establish a Russian salon in which he would be as much the host as if it were his own embassy.

That very night, Saturday, October 1, the salon opened with a brilliant ball for two hundred people given by the princess. All the actors in the play of the preceding twenty-four hours came, and the tsar danced first with the princess and then with the duchess. After that he crossed the room to speak to Prince Hardenberg. The deafness of the Prussian chancellor made it impossible to have a conversation without shouting for all to hear, so Alexander drew him off for a talk in the princess's boudoir. The diplomats present watched them go suspiciously. A solid Russo-Prussian front was the last thing that the English, Austrians, and French wanted. It was also noticed that the tsar hardly addressed a word to Prince Adam Czartoryski, who had arrived in Vienna that day to join Alexander's staff as Polish adviser. This, too, was ominous, for Prince Adam embodied the aspirations of all those who still hoped for the creation of a free and independent Poland.

The inexhaustible tsar, having danced until four in the morning at Princess Bagration's, was up early to attend a clerical-military fete just outside the city walls. Cavalry from the most dashing Austrian regiments paraded before the assembled monarchs and then formed a double square in the autumn sunshine, in the middle of which Mass was sung before a tented altar.

In the evening there was a masked ball at the Hofburg attended by ten thousand people. The enthusiastic Comte de La Garde-Chambonas has left us his memories of that first great palace ball:

> The continuous music, the mystery of the disguises, the intrigues with which I was surrounded, the general incognito, the unbridled gaiety, the combination of circumstances and of seductions, in a word the magic of the whole vast tableau, turned my head, older and stronger heads than mine found it equally irresistible. [12]

La Garde's superlatives were fully justified, for the Hofburg balls were indeed dizzy-making, intoxicating occasions. The decorations were never the same at any of them; on October 2 the theme was red and gold and the tapestries and hangings accorded to it. The guests wore dominoes or costumes and the women were masked until midnight, at which hour they tossed aside their disguises. There were the sovereigns and their ministers, whose passing through the rooms caused the others to hush and stare, then to crowd closer. La Garde described the tsar opening the ball with the empress of Austria, then leading the long line of dancers in the ritual, slow polonaise across the first vast ballroom, the Redoutensalle, up the grand staircase, across several more rooms and finally into the huge Audience Chamber, with its golden pillars and red velvet hangings.

The stately polonaise was a tradition, but it was the waltz that the guests enjoyed. There were the heavy German princesses whirling in the tight skirts that so ill became them, the Hohenzollern-Sigmarens in the arms of the Hesse-Homburgs, the family jewels blazing on their bursting bodices. There were the beautiful young people, seventeen-year-old Marie Metternich and the handsome Prince Charles of Bavaria, the ravishing Countess Julie Zichy and the debonair Prince Eugène de Beauharnais. There were the delegates of the smaller states, happy to be jostling with the highest in the land, there were merchants and bankers and their sober overheated wives, there were the slim elegant dancers from the Paris ballet. This already vast assemblage was augmented by several thousand cheerful gate-crashers who had bribed the doorkeepers to let them in to gorge on the food and drink from the buffets that stood in every room and leave at dawn with a fine haul of imperial silver spoons in their pockets—three thousand spoons were stolen at the first ball.

La Garde has also given us a picture of the quieter scenes that were taking place in the smaller drawing rooms that led off from the turbulent ballrooms. It was an art to catch the attention of one of the great men present and to engage him in political conversation. He describes Talleyrand sitting in his chair talking about Murat to Prince Leopold of Naples and the pope's representative, Cardinal Consalvi, and on the other side of the room Lord Castlereagh leaning against the chimney discussing Poland with a minor sovereign: "The words treaty, indemnity, borders could be heard—the King was very heated." [13]

When the last waltz had been played and the guttering candles put out by the tired servants, Empress Maria Ludovica was carried fainting to her rooms, there to be put to bed by her worried ladies. For her the state balls were a dreaded ordeal, as indeed they were for the emperor. He was heard to gasp in early October, "If this goes on I shall abdicate. I can't stand this life much longer." [14]

Francis I was to be obliged to put up with "this life" for a good deal longer. On the morning of October 3, the ministers of the Big Four got down to the key issue of the congress, the future of Poland. Once that was settled the other territorial problems would fall into place, but not until then.

During the eighteenth century the Polish nation had been unable to maintain its independence in the face of the expansionist ambitions of her three greedy and powerful neighbors—Russia, Prussia, and Austria. Three times she was torn apart, the first partition occurring in 1772, the second in 1793. While her population was greatly reduced on both occasions, she was still an entity on the map of Europe until the third and final partition of 1795–1796 when she was totally absorbed by her neighbors; the proud country that had been Poland ceased to exist.

After his defeat of Prussia in 1807, Napoleon recreated a small part of Poland, calling it the Grand Duchy of Warsaw, and two years later he added to its territory on the defeat of Austria. Although the French emperor was devoted to his beautiful Polish mistress, Marie Walewska, it was not for love of her that he reconstituted the nation that had suffered extinction a few years earlier. He took this step for purely political reasons, seeing in the rump duchy dependent on himself a useful new ally in the east, which could provide him with fifty thousand first-class soldiers for his armies.

Emperor Alexander, as we have seen, was far more sentimental about the Poles than Napoleon. Still influenced by the teachings of Prince Czartoryski, he at times saw himself as the humane liberator who would restore Poland's independence. At other moments he envisaged an enlarged kingdom of Poland under Russian control. This would have had the agreeable result of extending his empire to the banks of the river Oder. As the congress gathered in September, it was still unclear to the other members of the Big Four what the tsar's ultimate attitude would be. His generals and the great Russian landowners were bitterly opposed to the policy of offering the Poles a constitution. The very thought of this democratic experiment made them shudder as they contemplated the contagious effect on Russia itself. The tsar, whose complex nature contained a strain of caution, listened carefully to these conservative advisers. Yet he could not forget the pleas of Czartoryski and the views of Jeremy Bentham, the English liberal philosopher he had consulted so earnestly in London two months before. Meanwhile, a vast Russian army of occupation remained in Poland.

The future of the important German country of Saxony was tangled with Poland's fate. If it were to be decided to create an independent kingdom of Poland, then the countries which had seized Polish provinces at the time of the partitions would have to be compensated elsewhere for their loss. Austria would be satisfied with the return of her former territories in Illyria and further compensation in Italy, but Prussia was the stumbling block. She was certain to demand the whole of Saxony, which would considerably disturb the balance of Continental power.

It seems to have been taken for granted by all powers concerned that the kingdom of Saxony was up for grabs, fair game because its ruler had clung with fatal tenacity to the cause of Napoleon until the very end. For this, King Frederick Augustus of Saxony was in disgrace with his fellow monarchs. To punish him he was not allowed to come to Vienna, where his interests were informally represented by Count Friedrich von Schulenberg.

Castlereagh represented a country that had no territorial ambitions in 1814. With Britain's mastery of the seas unquestioned and the vital port of Antwerp and the mouth of the river Scheldt in friendly hands, the security of the island kingdom had been attained. Having spent untold numbers of lives and an immense amount of money on a long war of attrition, the very last thing the British people wanted was to become involved in murky Continental quarrels. Production and trade had risen steadily throughout the war, and when peace came the English understandably felt that they had a right to settle down to enjoy their prosperity in tranquillity. If Castlereagh had been a lesser man it would have been easy for him to have attended the Congress of Vienna as a handsome figurehead, ratifying by his presence the decisions of the European powers. What possible good could be served by entering the complicated row over the future of Poland? Eastern Europe seemed very far away to the Cabinet in London, and, if they thought about it at all, the other members of the government remembered Alexander's pious platitudes about granting a constitution to an independent Poland. Despite the personal unpopularity he had acquired during his June visit, they naively believed that he had meant what he promised.

On one point both the Tory party and the Whig Opposition were in accord. This was that Castlereagh must bring home from Vienna an international agreement for the abolition of the slave trade. The Duke of Wellington used strong terms to warn his friend, the foreign secretary, of "the indescribable degree of frenzy existing here about the Slave Trade." The missionary spirit of the British was fully aroused, and the country at large cared far more about achieving this humane end than they did about the future borders of Prussia and Austria.

Castlereagh was to give this fine ideal his full support, but he could not envisage the abolition of the unholy commerce as the only trophy he would bring back from Vienna. He saw further than the government he served, and the essence of his policy was to assure that no one nation should again rise to dominate Europe. He clung to his steady belief that England's safety depended on a stable and tranquil Continent. The instructions that he must have drafted for himself have never been found, but it is easy enough to trace his principles.[15]

Very much on his own in Vienna, Castlereagh received few replies to the long and detailed letters he wrote to the Cabinet describing the progress of events, and the advice that did reach him from home was generally out of date by the time he received it. It took two weeks for the most hard-riding king's messenger to arrive from London and the same time to return.

As Castlereagh wrote to the prime minister in November, his main aim was to establish a "just equilibrium" in Europe.[16] By this he meant the strengthening of the center of Europe against the east and west. Accordingly he desired the creation of a strong Prussia allied to Austria. In the tradition of his master, William Pitt, he envisaged this central bloc as what he called "an intermediary system between France and Russia."[17] It never occurred to him that Prussia, an ally in the preceding century, could pose a future threat, and he supported her wish to establish herself in the Rhineland. As he saw it, a strong Prussia on the Rhine would eliminate the possibility of a French attempt to regain possession of Antwerp. Regarding Poland, he determined to fight for a free and independent nation.

One cloud on the horizon could not have been anticipated by Pitt. For some time now the Foreign Office had been concerned by reports from British diplomats and agents all over the world of Russian intrigues, expansionist in nature. They were too consistent to be ignored or dismissed as the products of a few suspicious minds. From the British ambassador in Madrid to remote agents of the East India Company on the subcontinent came similar warnings against the designs of the giant whose armies were flushed with their heady victories in the recent conflict. It was clear that if Poland was to be saved from becoming a Russian satellite, she would have to be made larger and stronger than the territory and population contained in Napoleon's small duchy of Warsaw. But in order to create a larger Poland, Prussia and Russia would have to surrender their annexed Polish provinces, receiving compensation elsewhere. Austria could be generously satisfied in Italy and what is now Yugoslavia, Prussia in the Rhineland and Saxony. It seemed to Castlereagh that on the whole this neat plan would be beneficial to all concerned. It depended on persuading the tsar to resist the temptation a subjugated Poland offered him. Despite the warnings that rained in on Castlereagh from his sources throughout the world, despite a singularly unsuccessful meeting with Alexander immediately after the latter's arrival in Vienna, despite the open boasts of Nesselrode that a country with

600,000 men under arms had no need to negotiate, he still appeared to hope at the end of September that he could bring the tsar to see reason.

Talleyrand's views were far more realistic than those of his English counterpart. He wrote that in order to accomplish his primary task of re-establishing France as one of the great powers: "It is necessary above all that the French representative should understand, and should make it understood, that France wanted nothing more than she possessed, that she had sincerely repudiated the heritage of conquest, that she considered herself strong enough within her ancient frontiers, that she had no thought of extending them, and, finally, that she now took pride in her own moderation." [18]

In his succinct instructions to himself, he had laid down the position of France on every matter of substance that would be discussed at Vienna, from the future equilibrium of Europe to the slave trade, and had then enumerated the four main goals: [19]

1. That Austria should be prevented from making one of her princes king of Sardinia.

2. That Naples should be restored to her former ruler.

3. That the whole of Poland should not pass to Russia.

4. That Prussia should not acquire the whole of Saxony.

He had long insisted that the partition of Poland was a crime and that its reconstruction was desirable. He again affirmed this view in his instructions.

> The re-establishment of the Kingdom of Poland would be a benefit and a very great benefit; but only on the three following conditions:
>
> 1. That it should be independent.
> 2. That it should have a strong constitution.
> 3. That it should not be necessary to compensate Prussia and Austria for the parts they would lose. [20]

Having thus stated his ideal solution to the pivotal Polish question, he proceeded to shoot it down. Before the Vienna negotiations had even started, he predicted the impossibility of fulfilling the above conditions. His written conclusion was that it would be necessary to accept a continuation of the old partition plan in view of the stubborn resistance he foresaw on the part of Russia, Austria, and Prussia to a free Poland. He wrote this reluctantly, adding that a partitioned Poland would not be destroyed forever.

> The Poles although not forming a political entity will always form a family. They will no longer have a common country, but they will have a common language. They will, therefore, remain united by the strongest and most lasting of all bonds. They will, under foreign domination, reach the age of manhood which they have not attained in nine centuries of independence, and the moment when they reach it will not be far distant from the moment when, having won their freedom, they will all rally around one center.[21]

Like Castlereagh, Talleyrand believed that the powers must strive for a just equilibrium of Europe. But he very much doubted that an ideal balance could be achieved. The most he expected was a compromise solution, and he differed sharply from Castlereagh on one important issue: the future of Prussia. Far from seeing a strong Prussia as the buffer state of Europe, he saw it as a menace to the balance of power, a Sparta-like state built around its army. Should Prussia receive all of Saxony and most of the Rhineland, Talleyrand envisioned an expansionist power fully as dangerous as Russia, perhaps ultimately more dangerous to France. On this point he was determined not to give in.

The future of the kingdom of Naples was another question on which he was obdurate. The legitimate Bourbon rulers of Naples had been ejected by Napoleon and replaced by the former Marshal Murat and his wife, the emperor's sister Caroline. Talleyrand made much of the principle of legitimacy at Vienna; one of his objects was to assure the return of the former Neapolitan king.

While the issue was of far greater importance to France than it was to the other powers, it was all the same to be an awkward one to solve, for Austria backed the retention of Joachim Murat on the throne of Naples, and England supported her.

The Austrian position was somewhat uncertain at the beginning of the conference. In their discussions in London during the summer, Metternich had supported Castlereagh's plan, but an important body of Austrian opinion led by his influential rival, Count Stadion, and the military leader, Prince Schwarzenberg, was less concerned with the fate of Poland than the prospect of a Prussia strengthened by the acquisition of Saxony. To them it seemed of primary importance that Austria should retain her dominance in the Germanic body. This, they asserted, could only be assured by keeping Prussia small and weak. Castlereagh's pro-Prussian stance seemed as dangerous to them as it did to Talleyrand, although for different reasons. Metternich himself, possessed as he was with a passionate distrust of the tsar, cared above all that Russia should not obtain Poland. He also inclined toward cooperation with Prussia, believing, as did Castlereagh, that a strong central German bloc was greatly in the interests of European stability. Thus, at the end of September, Austria's policy was not yet clearly formed on the key questions confronting her. It was to harden rapidly during the terrible confrontations between Metternich and the tsar during the following two months.

The Prussian position was complicated by an important treaty made in 1813 between Russia and Prussia, known as the Convention of Kalisch. By its terms the king of Prussia had promised his Polish provinces to the tsar in return for a commitment from the Russians that the kingdom of Prussia would be restored to the position of power which she had held before her overthrow by Napoleon in 1806. Implicit in the agreement was the understanding that Prussia would be repaid for her concessions in Poland with compensation in Saxony and the Rhineland.

The attitude of the Prussian general staff was one of unabashed greed. What they wanted was Saxony, the whole of that rich German country which was their neighbor. And they wanted the Rhineland, including the fortress of Mainz. The king was a puppet in the hands of the tsar, and the danger of a Prussian-Russian alliance was obvious to Castlereagh and Metternich. They put their hopes in Chancellor Hardenberg, who was known to be less opportunistic than his generals and wise enough to see the dangers of Russian expansion to the west. There was every reason to think that if a willingness to compromise could be displayed on all sides the problems before them could be resolved according to Metternich's original schedule and they could all be on their way home before Christmas. On this optimistic note, they settled down to work.

The Approaching Crisis

As the congress never sat in plenary session, the machinery for consultation that developed was an ad hoc arrangement arising out of the necessities of the situation. The ministers of the Big Four, Austria, England, Russia, and Prussia, rose early and spent their mornings receiving official visitors or working on their papers. They generally met as a directing committee at 2 P.M., usually at Metternich's Chancellery, occasionally at Castlereagh's residence across the way in the Minoritzenplatz. Dinner, the main meal of the day, was taken between 5 and 7 P.M. and was followed by visits to a popular hostess to hear the gossip of the town and exchange ideas, then came the theater or a concert and a reception or ball. This was not a fixed schedule and could vary widely—during the first week in October, Talleyrand wrote to his king that for two days in a row there had been no meetings at all, as sovereigns and ministers alike had left Vienna for an immense shooting party at Laxenburg, the Austrian emperor's estate outside the capital. Here thousands of pieces of game were killed, huge and heavy meals were consumed and politics were temporarily put aside. On other days the diplomats worked very hard indeed: the agent in charge of the surveillance of Hardenberg sent in the following report of his day at the end of that same week:

On Saturday, October 8, the prince worked from 9 A.M. to 2
P.M. General Knesebeck, General Schoeler and Prince Hohenzollern all came to call on him but he was too busy to see any
of them and only Gentz [Secretary of the Congress] was admitted about noon.

At 2 P.M. he went to Metternich's for a conference where
there were Nesselrode, Castlereagh and Humboldt. This
lasted until 4 P.M. Then Prince Hardenberg came home for
dinner and had as guests Radziwill, Saint-Marsan, Baron Mar-
tens, Arnstein, Humboldt, and his secretary. After dinner he
received visits from Count Stephen Zichy, Prince Hohenzollern, Baron Binder and Prince Adam Czartoryski. After the others left Czartoryski and Radziwill stayed behind. When all the
visitors had left the private secretary Jordan burned quantities
of papers.

At 8:30 P.M. the Prince went to see Metternich where a second conference took place lasting until 11 P.M. Talleyrand,
Castlereagh, Nesselrode and Humboldt were there.[1]

This was a long day for a man in his sixties, and Hardenberg
did not go on to a ball that night. It is worth noting that although he had been too busy to receive three important Prussians in the morning he had found time for the two Poles,
Radziwill and Czartoryski, later in his crowded day. The Poles
needed his advice badly, for the tsar was no longer listening to
Adam Czartoryski and it was beginning to be whispered
throughout Vienna that he was now irrevocably determined to
annex all of Poland. Not only would this mean the end of Polish dreams and hopes but also that the Polish-Saxony imbro-
glio was likely to lead to general war.

The tsar, in fact, was not listening to any of his advisers. The
Russian delegation was a large and strong one, with three
plenipotentiaries: Count Andrei Kirillovich Razumovsky, Count
Gustav von Stackelberg and Count Nesselrode, the foreign minister. There was Baron Stein for German affairs, assisted by the
competent Alsatian Johann Anstett, Czartoryski for Polish affairs

and the able diplomats Pozzo di Borgo and Capo d'Istria for general matters. On the military side there were the Generals Ouvaroff, Kisselev, and Ojarowski, besides Volkonsky and half a dozen more aides-de-camp. Yet, despite the team of experts beside him, Alexander now insisted on acting as his own negotiator, thus immensely delaying the work of the conference. He appeared to trust no one, least of all his own foreign minister. The other ministers would obtain Nesselrode's agreement on a point at issue at their daily conference, only to have the tsar reverse the decision that very evening. To have a head of state double as his own ambassador immensely complicates diplomatic procedure, as was vividly illustrated just over a hundred years later when President Woodrow Wilson adopted the same tactics at the Versailles peace conference following World War I.

It was obvious that all other matters must be held in abeyance or put in the hands of subsidiary committees until settlement was reached on the Polish-Saxony problem, and it was with this issue that the directing committee was to wrestle through the months of October, November, and December, while the Prince de Ligne's famous bon mot, "Le congrès ne marche pas, il danse" (the Congress doesn't advance, it dances), seemed all too pertinent.

As the festivities grew more scintillating every day, the Viennese dressmakers and their apprentices labored under the strain of supplying the requisite number of dresses as the season progressed: blue and silver gowns on Sunday night for the ladies attending the Hofburg ball at the Imperial Riding School, ethnic costumes for the Metternichs' next Monday affair, etc. The frivolities fill pages of Hager's agents' reports:

> The Tsar had sent a courier dashing to St. Petersburg because he was not satisfied with the fit of the hussar's trousers that he had worn at the Zichys'. . . . Lady Castlereagh has been much criticized for wearing her husband's Order of the Garter as a decoration for her hair. . . . The jewels worn that night by the

ladies were worth uncounted millions, no one dared estimate
their value. . . . The British Ambassador Lord Stewart has taken
up Princess Bagration and the Crown Prince of Württemberg is
extremely jealous of his attentions to the Russian beauty. . . .
The King of Denmark has taken a mistress and has established
her in rooms he has rented from Princess Paar.[2] *

Many of the reports of a political nature referred to the growing unpopularity of the Russians, who were thought to be increasingly arrogant: "They consider themselves already the
masters of the world." Word filtered out from the Hofburg of
the dislike the Russian emperor's staff inspired among the Austrian servants because of their overbearing ways, their vanity,
and their bad manners toward inferiors. Princess Bagration's
salon continued to be a fashionable Russian headquarters, but
the reputation of its beautiful hostess became a little too frayed
when a respectable Austrian couple of the nobility took their
young daughter to the Palm Palace. The innocent girl was led
off by a dashing Russian hussar officer to visit the salons at the
end of the huge apartment. Half an hour later the father went in
search of his daughter and heard screams coming from behind
a locked door; he was obliged to break down the door in order
to rescue his shaken and disheveled child. Viennese society
blamed the parents more than they did Princess Bagration, saying that even a pair of fools ought to have known better than to
take an unsophisticated virgin to that house.

There was one Russian host at the congress on whom the tsar
could absolutely rely for the distinction of his entertainments.
Count Razumovsky, a veteran diplomat who had already served
several times as his country's ambassador to Austria, was again
established in his magnificent embassy as the tsar's chief plenipotentiary. This remarkable man was the grandson of an illiter-

---

* The king of Denmark's friend was a pretty Austrian working girl with whom
he was very happy until she lost her head and began calling herself the queen
of Denmark. This was too much for Princess Paar, who threw her out, thereby
depriving the king of the one solace of his simple and lonely existence.

ate Cossack peasant. His uncle, Alexsei, who had been taught to read and write by the village priest, became the lover of the Empress Elisabeth and probably married her (secretly and morganatically) in 1742. A huge fortune and great estates were bestowed on him and on his brother Kyrill and these were inherited by Kyrill's sons.

A great patron of the arts, Count Andrei used his inheritance to form a fabulous collection of pictures and furniture which he housed in the palace he had bought and presented to his government to serve as the Russian embassy. A good amateur musician, he was a patron of Haydn, Mozart, and Beethoven, the last of whom dedicated the three Opus 59 quartets to him. Devoted to the tsar, he felt it an honor and a privilege that the emperor and empress should entertain in his residence during the congress.

The entertainments were very grand indeed. At one supper for 360 people the menu included sterlets from the Volga, oysters from Brittany and Belgium, truffles from Périgord, oranges from Sicily, pineapples from the imperial hothouses in Moscow, and strawberries from England. "Besides which, each guest had in front of him a plate of cherries, which had been brought in from St. Petersburg through the intense cold, which cost the Russian government one rouble per cherry."[3] A troupe of Russian dancers entertained the party before and following the meal, after which the emperor led the party in a triumphant series of waltzes. "As for the Emperor of Russia, he dances while Rome is burning," wrote Sir Edward Cooke, Castlereagh's right-hand man. The overworked civil servant may not have been as good a reporter at the fête as the ineffable Comte La Garde, who wrote: "I really cannot believe my own memories of the splendor of this occasion."[4]

La Garde's superlatives are wearily repetitious, but in the case of Razumovsky's superb receptions he did not exaggerate. Later in his memoirs there is a vivid description of the terrible night of December 31, when the Russian embassy burned down due to a malfunction of the elaborate central heating system which Razumovsky had installed—the first of its kind in Vienna. The whole of the city rushed to the scene, to find the ambassador sitting cool and unperturbed among the scorched ruins of his treasures. He received the monarchs who came to sympathize as calmly as if he had been expecting them to drop by for tea to admire one of his new acquisitions, and seems not to have known self-pity. He was long remembered in Vienna after he returned to Russia, less perhaps for his material splendors than for his patronage of the great composers of the day. He had been largely responsible for the historic concert of November 29 at which Beethoven, by then totally deaf, conducted his Seventh Symphony, followed by a piece he had just written in honor of Wellington's victory over the French at Vitoria.

La Garde's description of the tsarina is another that rings true.

> Blessed with a lovely face, her eyes reflected the purity of her soul. She had beautiful thick ash-blond hair which she usually let float loosely over her shoulders. Her figure was elegant, supple and flexible and her way of walking so particular that she could be recognized at once, even when she was wearing a mask. Besides having a charming character she had a quick and cultivated intelligence, a love of the arts and a generosity without limits.[5]

Everyone seems to have loved Elisabeth of Russia. The police agents employed to watch her wrote angrily in their reports of the insults to which she was subjected by her husband:

> Last Friday Alexander forced his poor wife to go to a ball at the Bagrations'. The Empress agreed reluctantly but when she arrived she was put on a sofa that was in such bad shape that it collapsed under her. The next night there was a family dinner at which Alexander was so rude to the Empress and to her brother [the Grand Duke of Baden] and her sister [the Queen of Bavaria] that they say that the Empress will not go back to

Russia but will return to her brother at Karlsruhe. . . . The Empress of Russia, whose marriage is so unhappy, never dines
with the Emperor or with his sisters, the Grand Duchesses. If
it is true that she will not return to Moscow this will cause a
sensation there, for she is much loved in that capital.[6]

The above notes are quoted from policy reports of January
and February 1815. In a much earlier report, October 3, 1814,
the agent mentions briefly: "Czartoryski continues to be very
much in favor with Empress Elizabeth." Continues? He had just
arrived in Vienna, and the passionate love affair between the
gallant Pole and the beautiful young empress had broken up
years before. Did it burst into flame again in the aphrodisiac
atmosphere of the Vienna congress? She was now in her mid-
thirties and he in his midforties—both renowned international
personages whose every move and gesture were followed and
remarked upon. Secret rendezvous would have been difficult to
achieve and none of the gossipy memoirs even hint at a liaison.
Yet it is impossible to believe that nothing happened. There is a
significant passage in Czartoryski's diary referring to the tsarina:
"I see her here, very much changed, but to me she is always the
same and so are her feelings and my own. . . . Her letter . . .
Exchange of rings . . . I wish her happiness and am jealous of
this happiness; I love her hopelessly and yet . . ."[7]

What did "and yet" mean? We will never know, and can only
hope that Elisabeth was able to snatch some moments of joy in
the arms of her lover during the months in Vienna. They would
have been rare, for it would have been too dangerous for the
leader of the Poles to risk the everlasting displeasure of Alexander. As has been seen, Adam was already treading on very thin
ice. It seems probable that the tsar was eventually made aware
by some informer that the flame had been rekindled and that
this time, unlike the previous occasion, he was not indifferent.
His harshness to his wife as the winter wore on might have
been the result, but this can only be conjecture.

The police reports are full of poignant descriptions of the

little salons in Vienna where the Poles met nightly to compare notes. They had no means of knowing exactly what was happening as the great men of the congress discussed their fate, and their hopes rose and fell as the rumors flew. It was a dreadfully difficult winter for Prince Czartoryski, and he must have badly needed the comfort that the lovely empress could give him. For her, it would have been the second and last time in her sad life that she had known what it was to be a fulfilled and happy woman.

The man who finally took on the tsar was Castlereagh. It was singular that it should have been he who elected to lead a direct attack on Alexander, rather than one of the ministers whose country was directly concerned, but perhaps he felt that just for that reason he had a better chance of success than Metternich or Hardenberg. He therefore embarked on a series of interviews during October that were all the more painful because they were so polite. The tsar permitted himself to be outrageously rude to the other ministers, but to Castlereagh he was invariably courteous. The struggle went back and forth, with Castlereagh fighting for his conception of "a just equilibrium" and the tsar insisting that he planned to bestow a liberal constitution on Poland which would enable that country to thrive under his kindly tutelage. There was an icy exchange on October 13 when Castlereagh told the tsar: "It depends exclusively upon the temper of your Imperial Majesty . . . whether the present Congress shall prove a blessing to mankind or only exhibit . . . a lawless scramble for power."[8] To this the tsar answered that the Polish question could only end in one way since he was in possession.[9]

In other words, might was right, and Russia would not budge. Castlereagh, having failed in his unilateral attempt to influence Alexander, threw himself into the task of forming a united front consisting of the ministers of Austria, Prussia, and England. This was not easy to achieve. Both Hardenberg and

Metternich were appalled by the implications of the tsar's stubbornness regarding Poland, but as Hardenberg frankly explained to Castlereagh he dared not openly attack Russian policy until he was given assurances regarding the future of Saxony. He promised, however, that "if Austria and Great Britain would guarantee Saxony to Prussia he would unite with them to oppose such resistance as prudence must justify to Russian encroachments." [10] He then put Prussia's demand for the incorporation of Saxony within her territory, plus the Rhineland fortress town of Mainz, into written form and sent the letters to his Austrian and English colleagues. Castlereagh accepted the terms immediately; Metternich hesitated, visibly unhappy. It was a cruel decision for him to have to make. If he accepted Hardenberg's ultimatum he would enrage Stadion, Schwarzenberg, and the other powerful anti-Prussian forces in Vienna, which included the several hundred German princelings assembled there for the congress. Yet was this not a lesser evil than permitting the tsar to set up a Polish state under his own sovereignty, thus bringing Russia dangerously far to the west? Metternich procrastinated—from October 10 to October 22—while Castlereagh waited impatiently and Hardenberg insisted that he must have an answer. The sovereigns and their retinues were soon to set off for a ceremonial visit to Budapest and time was running out.

The circumstances under which Metternich at last produced his reply could only have occurred at the Congress of Vienna, where pleasure and business were so astonishingly intermixed. On Saturday night, October 22, he attended a ball at Count Zichy's where he encountered the Prussian chancellor, as he knew he would. Taking a paper from his pocket he handed it to Hardenberg. It was a memorandum in which he stated that Austria would not object to Prussia obtaining control of Saxony, provided that Bavaria would have Mainz, and that Prussia would support Austria on Poland. Presumably Hardenberg read this very important document on the spot and went at once to

Castlereagh, who was also at the ball, for by early the next morning, a Sunday, all three ministers had agreed to meet secretly that day at Castlereagh's apartment to discuss the terms that Metternich had offered.

They were extraordinarily generous terms, considering Metternich's position, and Castlereagh persuaded Hardenberg to waive the question of Mainz for the moment in view of the tremendous concession Metternich had made regarding Saxony. He then drew up a plan for immediate action: the tsar was to be presented with a firm refusal by the new alliance of England, Austria, and Prussia to recognize Russia's claim to Poland. If Alexander made difficulties, the whole congress was to be summoned. The purpose of this would be "to declare to the Emperor of Russia to what extent and upon what conditions Europe in Congress can or cannot admit His Imperial Majesty's pretensions to an aggrandizement in Poland."[11]

The solution to be proposed was for an independent Poland, including all the territory that had belonged to her before the first partition, but by now even Castlereagh had abandoned hope for the creation of such a state. The best alternative was a new partition whereby Prussia, Russia, and Austria would each be given some territory but would nonetheless accept the creation of a free Polish entity within the old borders. This arrangement was far from satisfactory but infinitely preferable to Russian annexation of the whole country. Above all, in that secret meeting at his residence, Castlereagh had established that entente between Prussia and Austria, the formation of which was the keystone of his policy.

His satisfaction was to be short-lived. Alexander lost his temper badly on hearing the news of the joint *démarche* and castigated both the Prussian and Austrian ministers in front of their masters. Emperor Francis of Austria stood firmly by Metternich, but Frederick William of Prussia quailed. Castlereagh had badly underestimated the extent of the king's subservience to the emperor of Russia. On November 6, just after the return of the monarchs from Hungary, the tsar invited Frederick William to dinner and all but ordered him to tell Hardenberg that he must cut off negotiations with his English and Austrian colleagues. The king complied immediately and, when Hardenberg failed to keep his part of the bargain, it was inevitable that Metternich's attitude would change. Very soon the united front that Castlereagh had worked so hard to build up had collapsed, and the resulting detriment to his prestige and his own confidence was enormous. Talleyrand was to note in November that he seemed "like a man who has lost his way." [12]

In England the Whig Opposition lost no time in attacking Lord Liverpool and his Tory government. What was Castlereagh doing? He had been sent out to reach an international agreement on the abolition of the slave trade and to assist in the peaceful settlement of other matters. Now it appeared that he had been locked for weeks in unsuccessful and possibly dangerous combat with the tsar of Russia, during which he had promised Prussia all of Saxony in return for her stand against Russia, and had offered as a bonus the important southern fortress of Mainz. Why was he against the tsar's plan for a free and independent Poland? Everyone remembered how eagerly the emperor had consulted Jeremy Bentham about a liberal constitution for the Poles during his summer visit to England. What about the "good old king of Saxony"? In the debate on November 8 in the House of Commons, Samuel Whitbread expressed the view that "the annexation of Saxony by Prussia would be as unprincipled a partition as the world ever saw." [13]

It appeared to the public as though Lord Castlereagh had decided for peculiar reasons of his own to make an enemy of the tsar of Russia as well as to despoil the king of Saxony. Weeks later in Vienna he would read one of Whitbread's flights of oratory: "The rumours are that the Emperor Alexander has strenuously contended for the independence of Poland and that he has been opposed in his noble views by the British Ministers. We now live in an age when free nations are not to be sold or transferred like beasts of burthen, and if any attempt of the kind is made the result will be a bloody and revengeful war." [14]

The attitude of the Cabinet itself was not helpful to the beleaguered foreign secretary. Lord Liverpool was never interested in foreign policy and Nicholas Vansittart, the chancellor, was an advocate of appeasement. In a memorandum circulated among his colleagues he attacked Castlereagh's policy as too bold, and suggested that "we ought to avoid irritating Russia by a pertinacious opposition which is unlikely to be successful." [15]

Castlereagh did his best to persuade Liverpool that Vansittart was wrong and that the danger of Russian expansion was a very real one. Writing to the prime minister on November 11 he spoke of the tsar: "You must make up your mind to watch him and resist him as another Bonaparte. You may rely upon it—my friend Van's philosophy is untrue as applied to him. Acquiescence will not keep him back, nor will opposition accelerate his march." [16]

In London the Cabinet remained jittery. The peace negotiations taking place in Ghent to end the American War (known to Americans as the War of 1812) were protracted and unfinished, and the news from Vienna was hardly reassuring. Accordingly, the only important instruction he was to receive during his entire stay at the congress went out to Castlereagh on November 27, 1814, drafted by Lord Bathurst on behalf of the Cabinet:

"*It is unnecessary for me to point out to you the impossibility of His Royal Highness consenting to involve this country in hostilities at this time for any objects which have hitherto been under discussion at Vienna.*" [17]

Three weeks after receiving this categoric instruction, Castlereagh signed a treaty which made definite provision for war on the part of Great Britain. It was a courageous act and a thoroughly successful one for which he was ultimately applauded by his government. But in the preceding period when his earlier policy had failed as a result of the weakness of the king of

Prussia, it hardly helped his position in Vienna to receive so little support from London. It was soon known that he was being hotly criticized in the House of Commons and that his own party was barely lukewarm in its backing of him. While Castlereagh never "lost his way," as Talleyrand had cruelly suggested, his failure with the tsar was a serious setback and he was obliged for a time to drift, letting events take their course.

Metternich should have been the natural choice to replace him as mediator, but for personal reasons he had no chance to succeed. Alexander and he had disliked each other from the moment they met and in Vienna the relationship had deteriorated further.

October 1814 was a terrible month for Metternich. It had started brilliantly for him, with the euphoric day and night with Wilhelmina Sagan after the stormy meeting with Talleyrand. He was to continue to call October 1 the day on which he had known the greatest happiness of his life, and there seemed every reason to expect the rest of the month to be equally felicitous. At the age of forty-one, he was the most powerful statesman in Austria and was presiding over the most imposing conclave the world had ever seen. As he walked through the sunny streets of his capital in that golden autumn, heads turned to watch his elegant progress with admiration and respect, and he smiled back at all the world with the benevolence of one who is certain of his position and of himself. Above all he was certain of the mistress he loved so passionately; he trusted her completely and even the difficult political problems confronting him seemed manageable in his happy mood. He was at the height of his career—immensely strong physically and mentally.

This was Clemens Metternich as October opened. By the tenth of that month he was an all but broken man, looking years older than his age. On that day he happened to receive two Swiss visitors, and one of them, Jean-Gabriel Eynard of Geneva, left an account of his visit. He and his companion found the minister's anteroom jammed with other suppliants when they arrived at one o'clock, among them important men such as the Pope's envoy, Cardinal Consalvi. There was nothing unusual about that, for every delegate in Vienna had something to talk to Metternich about and his waiting room was always crowded. Famous for his beautiful manners, he would give his complete attention to the problems presented to him, and this made visitors feel that the great man had nothing to do but listen to their stories. The Swiss waited patiently; they had come to discuss a piece of territory that Geneva claimed should be part of Switzerland rather than France. At last Eynard and his companion were ushered in and, although Metternich received them with his usual graciousness, the two men were immediately shocked by his appearance and manner. Eynard wrote in his diary that night that he seemed "overwhelmed with exhaustion."[18] His face was haggard and drawn, his eyelids drooped, he could barely suppress yawns as they talked.

The transformation was the result of a series of sleepless nights following a little dinner given on October 5 by the dashing young officer, Prince Alfred Windischgraetz, Wilhelmina's former lover, who, she had sworn to Metternich, no longer mattered to her. Windischgraetz had just returned to Vienna as colonel of a famous regiment of cuirassiers which had been renamed for its titular commander, the Grand Duke Constantine. The dinner guests had consisted of Wilhelmina, Talleyrand, Dorothea de Tallyrand-Périgord, Gentz, and a handful of others. There was nothing unusual about such a gathering—Wilhelmina had probably asked Alfred to invite Talleyrand and her sister Dorothea whom he might not yet have met, and the remaining guests were old friends. What was startling and important was the atmosphere of the evening. Clearly Wilhelmina and Alfred were newly enraptured with each other, so much in love that everyone at the party noticed it. By the next day the gossip was all over Vienna that the affair was on again. Gentz, the malicious troublemaker, lost no time in rushing to Metternich with the story. The effect was devastating, and there then commenced a chapter in the unhappy lover's life that Dorothy Gies McGuigan has correctly called "six weeks of hell" in her admirable account of it.

It was a time of acute political crisis when Metternich needed to have his mind at its sharpest, yet on October 12, the day after Hardenberg had presented Castlereagh and Metternich with his crucial memorandum containing the Prussian terms for a settlement on the Saxony question, Gentz had arrived at the Chancellery at nine in the morning to find his master slumped in his chair after a sleepless night spent writing a letter to Wilhelmina. When Gentz raised the subject of Saxony, Metternich turned aside with a weary shrug, announcing that he had no time to discuss it; he was on his way to the Palm Palace to carry his letter to the duchess himself, and to see her if possible. Night after night he poured his heart out in long letters of reproach, of tormented jealousy, of protestations of eternal love. He never accused her directly of infidelity, for he had promised to trust her always, but they are letters of a tortured soul. Sometimes they are rambling; a short one dashed off on October 9 during a meeting of the ministers of the Big Four is almost incoherent.[19] To have written a love letter at all during a ministerial meeting was an act of frivolity very unlike the Metternich that the world knew, but during these weeks he was a man obsessed.

The letters hardly moved Wilhelmina. She was annoyed and irritated by them, writing back as briefly as possible. It was not that she did not appreciate Metternich. She had certainly been flattered by his attentions and probably she did love him after her fashion, but it was not in her nature to love any man with the consuming passion that he demanded of her. They continued to see each other at nightly balls and receptions and occasionally she permitted him to resume his old habit of dropping in at what he called "my hour" (11 A.M.), but this was small comfort to him for since October 1 she had refused to receive him intimately and he generally found other people in her salon when he arrived.

As if it were not enough to be haunted by the thought of handsome young Windischgraetz receiving the favors of the fickle duchess, the wretched Metternich soon had another cause for anguish in the blossoming friendship between his beloved and the tsar.

At the beginning of his visit to Vienna, Alexander had devoted himself to Princess Bagration and had delighted that lady by speaking disparagingly of the duchess to her, but by the end of October the police spies were reporting that on his visits to the Palm Palace, the Russian emperor now took the right-hand staircase as often or more often than he did the left-hand one. Wilhelmina had a strong reason to wish to please the tsar and a most important favor to ask of him. As we have seen, her only child, Gustava, her illegitimate daughter by her mother's former lover, Baron Armfelt, had been taken away soon after birth to be brought up by the Armfelt family in Sweden. Now Wilhelmina longed to get the young girl back, and it was well within the power of the tsar to arrange this. She had asked Metternich to intercede on her behalf, but, much as he wished to please her, his relations with Alexander were such that he would have been a hopeless choice as intermediary. Therefore Wilhelmina flung herself upon the tsar, using all her charm, and Metternich was obliged to be an observer of her first successful onslaught. The occasion was a ball at Count Stackelberg's house. Metternich was standing nearby when the emperor approached the duchess. Sinking to the ground in a demure but graceful curtsy, she asked if he would deign to grant her an audience, as she had a special reason for wanting to talk to him. The tsar was at his most charming: "My dear Wilhelmine, there is no question of an audience. Of course I shall come to see *you!* Only name the day and hour—shall it be tomorrow at eleven?" [20]

She accepted most gratefully and flew home to prepare for the important meeting. Preoccupied as she was by the question of her child's future, it is unlikely that she gave a thought to Metternich that night. He, on the other hand, went back to the Chancellery and sat down to write a letter to her which is dated

October 21, 4 A.M. In it he poured out all the agony she had made him suffer:

> I am punished for having given up my soul and existence to a charm which was only too seductive. You have done me greater harm than can ever be compensated by the whole universe—you have broken the springs of my soul, you have compromised my existence at a moment when my destiny is linked to questions which will decide the fate of whole generations to come—my friend, I forgive you everything. You would have acted differently had your heart served you better. . . .[21]

It was a terrible letter, so long that it occupies two very large and closely printed pages in the collected Metternich-Sagan correspondence. He meant it to be a letter of rupture and intended her to take it as such, but there could be no clean break in this tortured relationship.

He would never have written it had he not been a very tired man, wounded to the quick by the sight of his mistress groveling to the tsar, his mortal enemy, just as the bitter dispute over Saxony and Poland was coming to a head. His rather pompous reference to the future of unborn generations quoted above shows one side of his wounded pride. Then, without a thought for his feelings, she had instantly acquiesced in surrendering to the emperor his sacred hour—eleven in the morning. Imbued with a loathing of the tsar that was by now pathological, he surely supposed that the chosen hour had been intended by the emperor to be a direct slight—another instance of Russian arrogance.

Gentz found him at his desk at 10 A.M. brooding over the letter. There were irrevocable phrases in it, should Wilhemina choose to take them at face value: "In this moment which resembles death and I have lost my last illusion . . ." He was through, through, through with happiness, and would live on in "a world without color and a life without charm." It was farewell.

The next day, October 22, Metternich at last prepared the memorandum for Hardenberg which he was to present to him at Count Zichy's ball that night and which was followed by the secret meeting at Castlereagh's apartment on the afternoon of Sunday, October 23.

The question now arises of how much Metternich's professional performance was affected during these days and weeks by his passion for the duchess, his physical exhaustion, and his bitterness toward Windischgraetz and the tsar. Certainly, as he fell into deep depression, his friends and colleagues became increasingly uneasy. Gentz's diaries are full of references to his own exasperation: he wrote on October 14 that on returning to the Chancellery to report on an important conversation with Castlereagh, he found Metternich unable to talk of anything except "alas!—the unhappy liaison with Windischgraetz, which appears to interest him more even than the affairs of the world." [22]

Gentz's indiscretions could be very mischievous, as when in November he wailed to Talleyrand and the Danish envoy, Baron Niels Rosenkrantz, about his difficulty in persuading Metternich to concentrate on the work in hand. To the king of Denmark he said that Metternich "had not had his head about him for the past several weeks, so much had the thwarted love affair with the Duchess of Sagan absorbed him, and it was for that reason that affairs had not moved ahead and had been so badly handled." [23]

The indiscreet Gentz was not alone in his opinion. It was at this time that Edward Cooke, Castlereagh's senior adviser, wrote acidly that Metternich was "most intolerably loose and giddy with women." [24] The fashionable salons buzzed with gossip concerning the affair. In some quarters it was stated categorically that Metternich had broken with the duchess, but this was denied by equally well-informed sources. In fact there was no real rupture, but the police reports record the damage to Metternich's prestige that the gossip created. The Prussians laughed about his being "crazy with love, wounded pride and vanity, idling away all his forenoons—not rising until ten, then running to the Duchess of Sagan and spending the rest of the morning sighing at her feet. . . ."[25] The Russians sneered that Metternich was "laughable with regard to his womanizing."[26]

These accusations were exaggerated and unfair. Metternich continued to hold the ministerial meetings daily, and his load of responsibility was far heavier than that carried by his colleagues. There were long consultations with the emperor about the clouds on the domestic horizon as the expenses of the congress threatened to bankrupt the state. Inflation was rampant by early autumn, and the expenses of the royal tables at the Hofburg were never less than 50,000 florins a day, which was roughly what was budgeted for the daily expenses of the entire Ministry for Foreign Affairs. In November both the Russian and English governments offered to compensate the emperor for at least part of the crippling outlay, but Francis I was too proud to accept. Austria would continue to play host to the congress, play host magnificently, and it was the duty of the emperor's chief minister to do his part.

From the beginning of the congress until the end, the Metternichs entertained 250 people or so at supper at the Chancellery every Monday night—elegant parties to which invitations were eagerly sought. But these were minor occasions compared with the great ball on October 18 that they gave at the villa in the Rennweg. It was to be a Peace Ball, celebrating the first anniversary of the Battle of Leipzig, and Metternich had been planning the arrangements for months.

It was another of those summerlike days that characterized the weather during that extraordinary autumn and began with an immense victory parade of the Austrian army in the Prater. This was attended by the sovereigns and was followed by a banquet for the veterans of the recent war, twenty thousand strong. In the evening eighteen hundred guests proceeded to the Metternich villa to dance until dawn in a classical pillared pavilion that had been built for the occasion. There were the usual polonaises, followed by waltzes and Russian dances in honor of the tsar. There were hidden orchestras in the gardens for those who cared to wander off from the brilliantly lighted ballroom and explore the newly erected miniature temples of Apollo and Minerva, half lost in the shrubbery. There were ballets and *tableaux vivants,* there were balloons which released splendid fireworks representing the arms of the sovereigns. The ladies wore the symbolic colors of peace, blue and silver, with olive wreaths in their hair. Always perfect hosts, famous for their exquisite attentions to their guests, Laure and Clemens Metternich drifted gracefully from group to group, and it was unlikely that anyone present could have guessed that they had hardly been on speaking terms since the Sagan affair had poisoned their domestic relationship. Usually the best of fathers, Metternich now noticed only the existence of his favorite child, seventeen-year-old Marie, whose prattle about dresses and parties and compliments from admirers could still bring a smile to his tired face.

The Peace Ball occurs in the memoirs again and again as a particularly beautiful fete, perhaps the most beautiful of all the congress occasions. Countess Elisa von Bernstorff wrote:

> The crush for carriages was so great that we had to wait hours for them. . . . I shall never forget the original and beautiful appearance of the scene. [Imagine] a flight of stairs almost as high as a house, carpeted in red, canopied with Turkish tents and lighted by bright pitch torches, on which camped a large part of the company, wrapped in cloaks. . . . I waited until early dawn for the arrival of my carriage.[27]

Toward the end of the triumphant night, unnoticed by Countess Bernstorff and nearly all the rest of the company present, a curious little scene took place between the tsar and his host. The tsar, surrounded by a circle of listeners, said sarcastically to Metternich: "You diplomats make decisions and then we soldiers have to let ourselves be shot up into cripples for you." When the tsar noticed that Archduke Johann was listening, he repeated his remark.[28]

It was a cruel and unfair accusation, coming from Alexander. He himself was hardly in a position to speak for "we soldiers," for during the terrible French assault on Russia in 1812 he had been far away in St. Petersburg, while the ancient city of Moscow lay at the mercy of Napoleon. Metternich was unable to reply to the attack and could only wonder at the significance of it; the next morning Gentz found him brooding unhappily. He noted in his diary: "Sad morning after. Very black scene." [29]

The following Monday, October 24, the tsar sent for Metternich. If his remark at the end of the Peace Ball had been offensive, his words and his conduct during this interview were savage. For two hours he attacked Metternich on the subject of Poland, blaming Austria for the deadlock that the congress had reached. Talleyrand was to report later that the tsar had used words that he would not have dared to use in scolding a servant. At moments he seemed to lose control of his movements as well as his words, seizing his sword and waving it in a menacing manner. Metternich ended the violent scene by saying that he would offer his resignation to his own sovereign and leave it to him to decide the rights of the tsar's accusations. He returned home in a condition of rage and despair that alarmed his whole household.

All Vienna heard the story, and Metternich's prestige, already shaky, reached its nadir in the next two weeks. When the tsar returned from Budapest, it became known that he had ordered the king of Prussia to tell Hardenberg to cut off negotiations with the English and Austrian ministers. This grim ukase was blamed on Metternich, and it appeared likely that he would be replaced by Stadion. Not only did his Austrian critics attack him for what they considered his stumbling diplomacy, but the German princes were equally bitter. These former rulers of small states which had been destroyed by Napoleon had come to Vienna hoping to regain their former independent princedoms.

Now Metternich had joined with Castlereagh in attempting to form another Germany—a loose federation of larger states dominated by Austria and Prussia. They felt let down, abandoned, betrayed. What was more, it was now apparent that the policy had failed and that, thanks to Metternich's blunders, the tsar had become an implacable and dangerous enemy.

The loyalty of Emperor Francis saved Metternich. Stubbornly, he still believed in his minister, although he was sorrowfully aware of the Sagan scandal. When the police reports informed him that the affair had ended he said gratefully that he was glad to learn it, for now Metternich would be able to devote himself entirely to affairs of state. Metternich himself wrote to Wilhelmina at the beginning of November that he was ill, exhausted, and despondent, but her casual reply gave him little comfort. Despite the letter of rupture, the correspondence had continued. It was impossible in that small society that they should not meet constantly at social occasions, and on his part the pain continued, to diminish only gradually. It was December before Gentz and the other observers could report that he had returned to his old self. Again the question arises, how much were public events influenced by his personal tragedy?

The facts were these. The first phase of the negotiations of the congress had ended in a severe defeat for Castlereagh. The plan had been his, and it was destroyed by the subservience of the king of Prussia to the tsar. The united front once broken, Prussia now relied on Russia to obtain the whole of Saxony. The two German powers had become irreconcilable rivals, due to the failure to check Russia, and in the new and embittered situation the conduct of diplomacy was all but impossible. By late November the danger of war was very great, and all the great powers except for England began military preparations.

Despite the criticism that rained in on him from every side, it is impossible to blame Metternich for the impasse. In following Castlereagh's lead, he was simply reasserting the policy he had described in his first diplomatic dispatch, written long ago in

Dresden: "Austria and Prussia must forget their recent past . . . not competition but cooperation is their natural policy. An equilibrium is possible only through a strong central Europe backed by England." He failed in his attempt, but it was a courageous act of statesmanship all the same. What is remarkable is that he survived the attacks of his enemies and the heartbreak of his love affair without suffering complete collapse, for the strain of the double crisis was very great.

It was assumed in the anti-Metternich salons that the minister, sunk in idleness and apathy, would cancel the costume ball that he had planned for November 8, two days after the fatal dinner during which the tsar had given the king of Prussia his orders. On the contrary, the party took place as scheduled and was as great a success as the Peace Ball had been. Once more the scene was the Rennweg villa, illuminated in a manner that was described as fairylike by the breathless memoir writers. The ladies wore ethnic costumes, with the Austrian ladies in the peasant dress of the different provinces of the empire. Wilhemina Sagan was especially admired and poor Lady Castlereagh especially ridiculed, as her idea of ethnic dress was to twist her husband's Order of the Garter through her disheveled hair. It was an immense crowd, with every crowned head and diplomat in Vienna present, including the tsar and the king of Prussia. Sharp-tongued Gentz had to admit that despite the strained circumstances the Metternichs had pulled off another social triumph.

Crisis Surmounted

TALLEYRAND and his beautiful niece had of course attended the Metternich ball, and as usual there was something theatrical about their entrance. There was no diplomat remotely like him among the galaxy assembled at Vienna: with his carefully arranged powdered hair, dressed in the manner of the 1780s, his high-collared pale gray or mauve velvet coat and his ruffled cravat, his chest blazing with diamond-encrusted decorations, and the Order of the Golden Fleece about his neck. He invariably wore black silk stockings, black pumps with red heels and diamond buckles. It was the *ancien régime* come alive again, and while people gathered around him to hear what he would say they were a little afraid. He spoke so little, knew so much and had seen so much, was he truly as inhuman and sphinxlike as he appeared? Dorothea was the perfect complement to him—the nineteenth century incarnate. Slim, tall, perfectly made to wear the body-clinging fashions of the day that less beautiful women found so difficult to carry off, she had lost the serious manner that had sometimes intimidated people who had known her earlier. As she was to write later, "Vienna, all my destiny is in that name." Twenty-one years old, she was radiant with a happiness that she had not known could exist. Her mother had lent her her finest jewels to wear at the congress—a singularly unselfish act on the part of the mistress whom Talleyrand had left behind—but Dorothea hardly needed the glitter of the Courland millions around her slender neck, for she had thrown herself into the intoxicating amusements of Viennese society with an enthusiasm that neither she nor anyone else had guessed was in her.

At the beginning of their stay Talleyrand had needed her badly. The outcome of the scene he had made on September 30 with the ministers of the Big Four was a Pyrrhic victory. He was excluded from the informal but vital meetings they held, and the exclusion rankled. In a letter from the Duc de Dalberg to his wife in Paris written at this time and intercepted by Baron Hager's police, Dalberg wrote that he was glad that the duchess had not accompanied him to Vienna as the position of the French embassy was a sorry one. Only second-rate diplomats and minor members of the Austrian aristocracy attended the parties given by the representative of the former enemy. This letter can be taken with a large grain of salt, for Dalberg had instantly plunged into an affair with one of his Viennese cousins, Countess Schönborn, and the last thing he wanted was to have his wife join him while he was engaged in dalliance with pretty Sophie Schönborn. Nevertheless, it certainly helped Talleyrand to have his hostess and niece related to half the grandest names in the city.

Besides her innumerable German and Austrian cousins, Dorothea could claim three sisters in Vienna. Pauline, second of the Courland daughters, had married Frederick Hermann, Prince of Hohenzollern-Hechingen. Dorothea had written of him: "a great nobleman, no doubt, of whom the only criticism I can make is that there was absolutely nothing in him which one could find to praise except the distinction of his birth."[1] Jeanne, the next sister, had married an Italian, Francis Pignatelli, Duke of Acerenza, from whom she was separated. Dorothea deplored both the marriages as indeed she had those of her oldest sister Wilhelmina Sagan, but the beauty and the fortunes of the three older Courlands gave them positions which could not be denied except by the most prudish, and there was very little prudery in the highest circles of Viennese society in 1814. The salon of the Duchness of Sagan was particularly important to Talleyrand, both politically and for pure enjoyment. Not only did he meet everyone he wished to meet there, but he delighted in the company of the hostess. It was to him that she confided the terrible scenes of which she had been the cause between Metternich and the tsar. He was grateful for her confidences, amused by her lack of hypocrisy and absence of embarrassment. In return he talked freely to her, for they spoke the same language. One day he said to her: "Only this morning I was reproached for changing my mind. But is there anything which proves my loyalty more than my faithfulness to my natural fickleness?"[2]

Curiously, he took an instant dislike to the Duchess of Sagan's rival, Princess Bagration. She made a gigantic effort to make an intimate of him, but, although she might have become a useful ally as the mistress of the tsar, he could not bring himself to submit to what he scornfully referred to as "her Cossack charms." She revenged herself by saying that he revolted her "with his eyes like a dead fish and his heavy eyelids which go down like the shutters on a shop-window."[3]

Within a very few weeks after the opening of the congress, it was not necessary for Talleyrand to seek either diversion or political gossip outside his own house, for already the whole of Vienna was honored to be invited to come to him. As was his lifelong habit he rose late, and the ceremony of dressing was as much of an occasion as it had been in the rue St. Florentin. Comte de La Garde has left us an awed souvenir of attending the "lever" at the Kaunitz Palace at 1 P.M., with the visitors in attendance while the valet Courtiade sprayed on the famous orange blossom toilet water and whisked the last traces of powder off the shoulders of the prince's coat.

Dinner, Talleyrand's one meal of the day, took place at 5 P.M.

His chef, Antonin Carême, was an interesting man. Completely self-educated, he became a prolific and literate writer and a keen amateur architect. He was to die before he was fifty from breathing inordinate amounts of carbon monoxide in the badly ventilated kitchens in which he worked, but his had been a proud career. His specialty was cold foods, a very recent innovation, but he also invented 299 soups![4] It was Talleyrand who gave him the idea of putting grated cheese on top of onion soup while they were in Vienna together. Carême liked Vienna, writing in his memoirs that after Paris it was the most agreeable capital in which he had practiced his profession. He delighted in the baroque architecture, and from the professional point of view he criticized only the butchers with whom he dealt. Their meat was of deplorable quality, whereas the supply of game was superb, especially partridge and quail. Nor could he find fault with the trout, salmon, and sturgeon from the Danube. He regretted the absence of French truffles and had nothing but scorn for those imported from Italy, which he found flavorless. Fruit and vegetables were abundant, and he fancied the white asparagus which were in the market all winter long. All in all, he concluded: "Vienna has many advantages although it cannot be compared to Paris."[5]

There were nearly always guests for dinner at the Kaunitz Palace, and other visitors dropped in afterward. La Garde described Talleyrand and his niece sitting side by side on a sofa, the visitors in a circle of chairs facing them, engrossed by the brilliance of their host's conversation. The accuracy of this scene, like much of La Garde's reporting, can be doubted. Talleyrand rarely held forth in public and reserved his wit for tête-à-tête conversation with people who amused him. He especially disliked reminiscing in company. On one occasion young Archduke Johann, eager to learn the history of the complex negotiations that had led to the abdication of Napoleon and the restoration of the Bourbons, asked him what he had done during the Campaign of France. Talleyrand answered in two words: "J'ai boité" (I limped).

The police agents in charge of surveillance of the French diplomats were as frustrated as those whose job it was to penetrate the secrets of the British. It was impossible to intercept the long letters to King Louis XVIII which Talleyrand sent to Paris by special courier, and when once a piece of paper written by him during a meeting was retrieved from a wastebasket and laboriously pieced together it turned out to contain a dissertation in excellent Latin on the subject of the revolution of the planets.[6] The staff and the servants of the Kaunitz Palace were incorruptible, and only one member of the household appeared to offer an interesting lead. This was an Austrian composer, Sigismund von Neukomm, who had accompanied Talleyrand from Paris. He appeared to go out rarely and was known to take his meals on a small table in the ambassador's own apartments. What could he be doing? What was his role? To further confuse the police the sounds of piano music could be heard throughout the night coming from the prince's rooms. They could only conclude that the music was intended to drown the voices of conspirators, of whom the chief must be the mysterious Neukomm.[7]

It took several weeks and the assistance of Metternich himself to track down the truth. Neukomm was in Talleyrand's employ, as he had been for the preceding six years, to help his master get through his long sleepless nights. La Tour du Pin had installed a comfortable armchair in Talleyrand's study near which he could place the papers his chief wished to peruse while the house was quiet. In an inconspicuous corner of the room Neukomm sat at the piano and played while his master read or pondered. Haydn and Mozart were Talleyrand's favorite composers. Soothed and distracted by the music, Talleyrand often read until dawn broke and the moment had come at last for him to put his work away and go to bed. It was hard for the police to accept such a simple explanation.

These nights in Vienna during the autumn of the congress must have been lonely ones for Talleyrand, even with the accompaniment of his beloved music. His professional abilities were not being used to their full extent, and his personal life was in an unwonted state of confusion. He had brought Dorothea to Vienna because she charmed him, and he needed her as his hostess. She had played her part perfectly, but there was a new complication—he had fallen love with her. For the first time in his long life he trusted someone completely, depended on the presence of another being. It was upsetting to know that he could not do without her and that she was twenty-one years old to his sixty-one. Her success in Vienna had not surprised him. He had been amused, rather than disturbed, by a light affair she had been conducting with Prince Trauttmansdorff, the good-looking marshal of the court. He was a charming flirt and just the person to accompany Dorothea to the balls when her uncle preferred a quiet evening.

Much more serious was Dorothea's romance with Count Karl Clam-Martinitz, for whom she deserted Trauttmansdorff. Clam was a major in the Austrian cavalry, aide-de-camp to Prince Schwarzenberg. Just a year older than Dorothea, he was already considered one of the most brilliant young officers in the service and destined for a great career. He was handsome, ambitious, and clever; she found him irresistible and fell in love with him as she had never been in love since her childhood infatuation with prince Adam Czartoryski. He returned her affection and their liaison was soon accepted by all Viennese society. It seemed appropriate to everyone, for it was known that Dorothea's marriage had been a failure, and for the promising young officer, a mistress as beautiful and admired as the Comtesse de Talleyrand-Périgord could only be an asset. What did Talleyrand feel? He had never known the sentiment of jealousy and perhaps he did not feel it now, but he surely must have suffered from the fear that he might lose the one person who had ever become indispensable to him.

Politically he could not be optimistic for, as he wrote on November 17, "The Tsar is another person from what he was in Paris."[8] Talleyrand, too, had had his scene with Alexander, nearly as disagreeable as the one Metternich had undergone. He described it in his memoirs: "I will keep what I have conquered," said the tsar. "Your Majesty can only desire to hold what belongs to him legitimately." The conversation continued along these futile lines until Talleyrand, according to himself, burst out: "Europe! Europe! Unhappy Europe! Will it be said that it is you who have destroyed her?" The tsar only replied: "Better that it should be war than that I should renounce what I occupy."

Greatly disturbed, Talleyrand then began a series of conversations with Metternich and with Castlereagh that were to bear important fruit. Normally he would have taken Dorothea into his confidence, and together they would have discussed each move he made, but during the month of November she was totally engrossed in preparations for an event that was to take place on the twenty-third of that month. This was the Carrousel, the most elaborate and spectacular festival of the congress. A medieval tournament was to be reenacted in Fisher von Erlach's Imperial Riding Hall, and for weeks it had been the talk of the town. "Saxony and the Carrousel," commented La Garde, "are the only subjects we discuss."

It seems almost inconceivable that so politically minded and intelligent a young woman as Dorothea could have taken a charade like the Carrousel seriously at such a moment. She knew very well that Europe hung between peace and war and that the masquerade for which she and the other members of her set were rehearsing was a ridiculous extravaganza. Yet the fascination of the Congress of Vienna is partly due to the bizarre interplay of the serious and the frivolous. We have seen Metternich set off for Countess Zichy's ball carrying a crucial state paper which he was to hand to Prince Hardenberg between dances; it would not have occurred to him to miss the party any more than it would have seemed possible for the golden youth of Viennese society to resist the fun of preparing for the elaborate medieval tournament.

When the great night came, every seat was occupied long

before a fanfare of trumpets announced the entry of the knights on their coal black Hungarian horses. These were twenty-four of the best riders among the young aristocrats of Vienna; Prince Windischgraetz was one and Prince Trauttmansdorff another. On they came in single file, first at a brisk trot, then a canter, and finally a pounding gallop which shook the vast hall. Then they reined in abruptly in front of the box in which sat the ladies of the tournament and paused in salute, while the crowd stood and cheered in delirious applause.

The ladies had arrived heavily veiled to take their places. Now they cast their veils aside and leaned forward to greet their knights. Their dresses were interpretations of the costumes of the days of chivalry, dazzling in their richness of color and material. Dorothea wore a long tunic of black velvet with slashed sleeves and a white satin underskirt, while Wilhelmina Sagan was in emerald green velvet. Both wore every jewel that they possessed and some that they had borrowed from relatives and friends. Then the tournament began—a magnificent exhibition of horsemanship even for Vienna, where every young nobleman had been trained to the sport since infancy. The audience held its breath as the knights charged, thundering forward, the pennants on their lances waving. The jousting was so realistic that one young noble was knocked from his saddle by his opponent and carried off while the crowd groaned.

When the drama had been played out, the company moved to the ballroom to feast and dance; the twenty-four ladies of the tournament opened the ball with a quadrille. The evening was considered a triumphant success and fills pages in the memoirs of the day. It is also mentioned in the police reports, for even the rich women who had taken part were alarmed by the huge cost of their frivolities. One agent wrote: "Ladies cannot manage on their ordinary budgets, and husbands are already reduced to adding another sizable deficit to their accounts."[9]

The tsar had fallen ill on November 17 and was unable to attend the great occasion. For several weeks he could be approached only by his intimates. "A very black scene," Gentz commented at the beginning of December, the third month of the congress. Diplomatic negotiations appeared to have reached a complete impasse. Prussia stubbornly insisted on her right to all Saxony and a large part of the Rhineland; the tsar's last word to Castlereagh in reply to his suggestion that the Polish question should be laid before the whole congress had been an inflexible refusal. Castlereagh's hope for a balanced Europe centered on a common front between Austria and Prussia lay shattered, and the situation was not only back to where it had been when the diplomats had started in September, but more dangerous in view of the warlike mood in Vienna and Berlin.

Lord Castlereagh therefore wrote a warning letter to Lord Liverpool on December 5, in which he informed him that "in the present extremely tangled state of affairs" a sudden outbreak of war was possible and he did not think that Britain could keep out of it.[10] At about the same time Talleyrand, who shared his views, requested and obtained from King Louis XVIII partial mobilization of the French army. It was thanks to the resolution of the Englishman, assisted by the intervention of the Frenchman, that war was averted.

Castlereagh had been drifting unhappily since the failure of his original policy. He now reasserted himself forcefully, altering course as the situation demanded. France, aligned beside Great Britain and Austria, formed the new coalition that he devised. It required the coolest of nerves to change the structure of the alliance when affairs were at crisis point, but Castlereagh did not hesitate to throw the weight of France upon the scales.

Talleyrand seized his opportunity immediately. In order to please the British, he now sacrificed the interests of the French West Indian planters and accepted the proposal of the Liverpool government that the slave trade should be abolished at once, north of Cape Formosa, and he further suggested that a committee of the congress should consider its universal abolition.[11] This gesture toward winning British good will was instantly followed by one calculated to please Austria: he opposed the proposal of the Spanish delegate that the future of Italy should be decided by a European committee and instead insisted that Austria alone should deal with the Italian peninsula. Talleyrand's move indeed helped Metternich, and the relationship between the two ministers was excellent as Talleyrand prepared to fire his heaviest volleys. These were two notes, dated December 19 and 26, in which he stated that the annexation of Saxony by Prussia and the dethronement of its lawful monarch were insupportable violations of the principle of legitimacy. Simultaneously, he let it be known that he had persuaded all the minor German states to address a formal and collective note to the congress protesting Prussia's aggressive policy.

The result of Talleyrand's *démarche* was just what he had expected. The Prussians, enraged by his interference, went a step too far. Hardenberg announced that if Prussia's claim to Saxony was denied he would regard it as a declaration of war. Castlereagh replied to what he called "this most alarming and unheard-of menace" that if such a temper really prevailed it would be better to break up the congress immediately. Then, dismissing from his mind any scruples he may have had about flouting his instructions, he drew up with his own hand a secret treaty which he presented to Metternich and Talleyrand. They accepted the draft immediately and the treaty was signed by the three powers on January 3, 1815. By its terms, Austria and France pledged themselves to provide 150,000 men each and Great Britain the equivalent either in subsidies or mercenary troops. The alliance was to be defensive in character, but meant war if Prussia did not give way over Saxony.

As a result of this decisive action, the Prussians backed down and their Russian allies accepted the situation with reasonable composure. For some time the tsar's generals had been alarmed by the open bellicosity of their greedy Prussian colleagues, and neither power liked the thought of facing the mighty force that would now be created by Castlereagh's treaty. By a lucky chance the negotiations between the British and Americans that had been dragging on at Ghent now drew to their close with the signing of a peace treaty. Castlereagh's position at Vienna was considerably fortified by the news that Britain had a free hand and, as early as January 5, he was able to write to Liverpool: "The alarm of war is over."[12]

Talleyrand was ecstatic. He wrote exuberantly to the king: "The coalition is dissolved. . . . France is no longer isolated in Europe. . . . So great and fortunate a change can only be attributed to that protection of Providence which has been so clearly visible in the restoration of Your Majesty."[13] He could not resist adding:

> After God the main causes of this change have been:
> My letters to M. de Metternich and Lord Castlereagh and the effect produced by them.
> The suggestions that I made to Lord Castlereagh concerning an agreement with France, which I reported in my last letter.
> The pain that I took to calm his suspicions by showing complete disinterestedness on the part of France.
> The peace with America.[14]

The avoidance of war had been a very near thing and, due to lack of accurate information from Vienna, all Europe seethed with terrifying rumors. It was said in London that the Grand Alliance established at Chaumont had foundered and that Russian and Prussian armies were even now on their way to occupy Hanover as well as Saxony. Castlereagh had been the author of the Treaty of Chaumont, and it was he who had called the bluff of Prussia and Russia when the machinery of his Quadruple Alliance threatened to fail. Nevertheless, unlike Talleyrand, he did not feel impelled to boast to his sovereign of his part in the achievement. "The climate of Russia," he wrote with his usual equanimity, "is often more serene after a good squall."[15] He permitted the news of his secret treaty to be leaked discreetly and awaited the results with composure. The speed of the climb down was remarkable. Metternich proposed on January 28 that negotiations on the Polish-Saxony question should recommence; his offer was accepted and by early February agreement was reached.

It was a compromise solution. Both Alexander and Frederick William of Prussia obtained less than they had wanted, but the fate of the Poles was to be much as Talleyrand had envisaged it in the instructions he had drawn up for his own guidance. Austria remained in possession of her share of the last partition except for the important town of Cracow, which became a free city. Russia was given Warsaw and most of Napoleon's grand duchy, which contained about three million people. Prussia received Posen and, in return for handing over her former possession of Warsaw to the Russians, was amply compensated by receiving two thirds of Saxony and territory in the Rhineland. The remainder of Saxony was to be returned to its legitimate king. To sweeten the blow of renewed partition, the Poles were offered and accepted the project of a new constitution to be drawn up by Adam Czartoryski for what was left of the former grand duchy of Warsaw, now to be known as the kingdom of Poland.

Metternich, without whose loyal support Castlereagh would never have succeeded in fashioning the treaty which had halted the Prussian-Russian threat of aggression, was bitterly criticized by his countrymen for the agreement. Stadion, Schwarzenberg and the archdukes accused him of having surrendered so much territory to Prussia that she would soon replace Austria as the dominant German power. Metternich remained blind to this danger. His intricate design was to form a balance of legitimate sovereigns, no one of whom would grow strong enough to achieve hegemony. Never interested in economic factors, he found it impossible to imagine that Prussia could grow dangerously strong. He answered his critics by pointing out that Austria had obtained Salzburg, the Tyrol, the Illyrian provinces on the Adriatic, Venice, and Lombardy. An Austrian archduke, brother to the emperor, would replace Napoleon's sister Elisa on the throne of Tuscany. Genoa was to become part of Piedmont under the rule of the king of Sardinia, who was to be "protected" by Austria. Later Naples was taken from Napoleon's unreliable brother-in-law Joachim Murat and returned to the Spanish Bourbon monarchy, to whom it was made clear that their orders would come from Vienna, not Madrid.

On February 6, Castlereagh wrote to inform Lord Liverpool that "the territorial arrangements on this side of the Alps are settled in all their essential features." [16] The adjustment of frontiers would be undertaken by two important committees, the German Committee and the Statistical Committee. The latter body would establish the populations of the territories to be transferred. The former was to draft a new constitution for the German states and would consist of representatives of Austria, Prussia, Bavaria, Württemberg, and Hanover.

When news of the Vienna agreement reached London, there was an outburst of party recrimination such as had seldom been seen. The anger was partly due to rancor on the Whig side. It was intolerable to the Opposition that the Tory government should not only have won the war, but also succeeded in making a peace settlement. But the intense ferocity displayed on the floor of the House was not caused by political frustration alone. The Whigs took their liberal principles seriously, and Samuel Whitbread had spoken for all his party in November when he had attacked the government for having betrayed the cause of freedom for which the people of Great Britain had fought so long and hard. Later on another member, John Lambton, took up the cudgels. He condemned "the acts of rapine and aggression of the club of confederated monarchs at Vienna, who appear to have met, not to watch over the interests of Europe, but as contemners of public faith and justice, as the spoilators of Saxony and the oppressors of Norway." [17] He was followed by the golden-voiced Irishman, Richard Brinsley Sheridan, who rose to decry the "crowned scoundrels cutting up Europe like carcass-butchers."[18] The speech was the more telling as it was known that Sheridan did not have long to live.

It was not only in Parliament that the government was attacked. The great poet Wordsworth was up in arms when news came of the Italian settlement. He raged at the thought that Italians should be "transferred to Austria, to the King of Sardinia and the rest of those vile tyrants."[19] Lord Byron was equally savage: "Here we are, retrograding to the full, stupid old system—balance of Europe—posing straws upon Kings' noses, instead of wringing them off."[20]

It was time, and more than time, for Lord Castlereagh to come home to defend his policies. He was replaced in Vienna by the Duke of Wellington and left for England on February 14. Just before leaving he succeeded in carrying off an important prize: a joint declaration by the eight convening powers represented at the congress that the slave trade was repugnant to the principles of civilization and morality and calling for its universal abolition at the earliest possible moment. For this achievement he was heartily applauded on his return by the champions of the antislavery cause, but their plaudits were all but lost in the clamor of hostile voices.

He rose in the House of Commons to answer Samuel Whitbread, who had earlier insisted that "for condoning public brigandage Lord Castlereagh should be arraigned before the tribunal of the world." Although Castlereagh was always an awkward speaker, even his enemies were forced to admire the imperturbable, handsome figure whose lack of oratorical skill mattered little in that debate. Instead of disclaiming responsibility for his actions in Vienna he accepted it. He rebuked the House for having embarrassed His Majesty's Government in the midst of crucial negotiations; he had been obliged to take action even without reference to his own Cabinet since, had he delayed his decision, the "whole machine of Europe would have been arrested. Mr. Whitbread's habit of broadcasting accusations based upon insufficient information was both dangerous and indecent."[21] Finally, he added, "The Congress of Vienna was not assembled for the discussion of moral principles, but for great practical purposes, to establish effectual provisions for the general security."[22]

The controversy then moved from the House of Commons to the House of Lords, ultimately to die away as other events overtook it, but it is interesting to reflect on the implications of the last sentence in the above paragraph. Castlereagh's words must have sounded dry and unfeeling to the idealists in England who either heard them in the House or read them in the newspapers the next day. Yet he was not ignorant, cynical, or stupid. "It is impossible," he wrote, "not to perceive a great moral change coming on in Europe, and that the principles of freedom are in full operation."[23] The fallacy of his policy was that he underestimated, as did his fellow statesmen at Vienna, the strength of the wave of patriotic fervor that had swept through Spain and Prussia and was soon to inspire the Greeks. It was hard for leaders born in the eighteenth century who had lived through the excesses of the French Revolution to realize that for silent millions the ideals of the Revolution were very much alive. Still inarticulate, they clung to the hope that the statesmen at Vienna had not forgotten the great words, liberty, equality, and fraternity, and that out of the deliberations of the congress would come a better world. Vaguely they groped toward what was later called self-determination; above all they longed for a democratic order in which, as under the French Republic, able men of humble background could achieve positions of importance. Had not Murat, the son of an innkeeper, risen to become a marshal of France? The principle of the legitimate rights of kings of which so much had been made at the congress meant nothing to the voiceless millions.

It was inevitable that Metternich should have been the most hostile of the leaders at Vienna to what Henry Kissinger has, in

a fine phrase, called "the great dreams of an impatient generation."[24] His static policy was largely dictated by the position of
his country. Francis I ruled over an extraordinarily mixed empire consisting of Germans in Austria, Magyars in Hungary,
Czechs in Bohemia, Italians in Lombardy, Serbs and Croats in
Illyria, and Poles and Ruthenes in Galicia. This fragile structure
was highly vulnerable to constitutional ideas and nationalistic
aspirations. Even had Castlereagh been farsighted enough to
realize that an alliance frozen in its desire to maintain the existing order would not last in a dynamic world, he could never
have persuaded Metternich, Alexander, or Talleyrand that it
was not enough to have given stability and repose to a Europe
that had been shaken for twenty years. Alexander was no longer
the young ruler who had hung on the words of La Harpe and
Czartoryski; he was to turn even further away from their liberal
precepts as the years of his reign went on.

Final Acts

As the war clouds lifted during the month of January, Vienna knew the anticlimax that often follows release from tension. Several causes aggravated the mood of discontent. The currency inflation that had been disturbing enough in the autumn had gravely increased in the new year. The citizens suffered further from a 50 per cent income tax that the government had been obliged to impose in order to defray the mounting expenses of the congress. It is remarkable that the emperor and empress retained their popularity as the luxurious entertainments of the court continued with monotonous regularity until the beginning of Lent, but the poor appear to have been grateful for permission to stand outside the Hofburg when the balls were over to be given the remains of the food that had been served at the palace. The imperial servants put out trestle tables carrying every leftover, from orange peels to half-eaten rolls, and the people carried them away murmuring words of thanks to "Papa Franz," as they called Francis I. Heavy snow enveloped the city during January and the price of firewood soared to a degree that alarmed even the rich.

All Vienna had mourned the death of the Prince de Ligne in December. This cosmopolitan aristocrat had been born an Austrian subject in 1735, in what was then called the Brabant (now

Belgium), and all who knew him during his long life appear to have adored him, men and women alike. To the younger generation in Vienna he was as fascinating a figure as Talleyrand, and far less intimidating. It was considered a great honor to be invited to the modest apartment in which he had lived since the loss of his great estates and fortune during the French Revolution. His bons mots were famous, and he died calmly after remarking to those around his bed that he was happy to be able to offer the visitors to the congress one more fine show: the funeral of a field marshal of both the Russian and Austrian empires. The cause of his death in his eightieth year was pneumonia—the result of a cold caught on the windy ramparts as he waited for a midnight assignation with a lady.

Alas, it is hard today to read his two-volume autobiography. Time has tarnished the silver arrows of his wit and few of his jokes seem amusing. Nevertheless, some of his less well-known remarks are memorable: for example, when his son and his friends implored him to lead a Belgian revolution against Napoleon, he replied with his usual exquisite politeness that he was much flattered by the invitation but must decline it "because I never lead revolutions in the winter." Unquestionably he was a charming man and, moreover, he was a kind one. Through the summer and autumn of 1814 he appears to have been one of the few people who took the trouble to go out to the palace of Schönbrunn to visit Marie Louise, ex-empress of France. She had been living there with her three-year-old son since their arrival in Austria following Napoleon's abdication. It was a secluded life in which her only companions were her child and the French household that had accompanied her. Count Neipperg, the Austrian general who had become her lover on the journey to Vienna, visited her as often as he could and she was later to marry him and live with him in Parma, but during the winter of 1814–1815 her future was undetermined. Under the Treaty of Fontainebleau it had been agreed that she would rule over the duchy of Parma, which would pass on her death to her son, but this settlement was contested by Labrador, the Spanish representative at the congress, and by Talleyrand, both of whom advanced the claims of other candidates. King Louis XVIII had thoughtfully sent on to the handsome little king of Rome all his toys, which had been left in the Tuileries Palace in the haste of departure, and the child played happily with his pony cart and his battalions of miniature soldiers. But his mother found the days long as she waited to know what fate would be decided for her. Letters arrived from her imprisoned husband on Elba, but she did not reply to them.

While the Prince de Ligne pitied Marie Louise for her ambiguous position, neither he nor anyone else could pity her for the splendid residence in which her father, Emperor Francis, had housed her. Schönbrunn, today only a few minutes drive from the heart of Vienna, is the finest of the Habsburg palaces. Conceived by the great baroque architect Fischer von Erlach for Empress Maria Theresa, it was to the Austrian imperial family what Versailles was to the French royal family. Versailles is far larger and its sublime magnificence is incomparable, but it is hard to imagine children playing in its galleries, whereas even today a visitor can easily envisage Maria Theresa's brood of eleven boys and girls racing down the corridors of Schönbrunn or dashing out through the open doors for a game of hide-and-seek in the chestnut-laden park. The palace is painted a warm color known as imperial yellow, and the western façade on the garden glows like antique gold in the late afternoon light. In the exact center of this façade, separated by a long gallery, are two small but exquisite rooms: the round Chinese room and the oval Chinese room. They epitomize the eclectic, bewitching style known as Austrian rococo. Black and gold lacquer panels are set into white woodwork and above and around these gleaming panels float vases of blue and white porcelain placed on gilt brackets in a seemingly haphazard design. Mirrors are ornamented with delicate gilt tendrils of flowers and branches, and their pattern is repeated in a narrow frieze at the base of the ceiling. In the round room there are two fireplaces built to warm the empress when she held her private conferences, or settled down for a game of cards when the day's work was done. No rooms in all Europe are more intimate in feeling or more lovely than the Chinese rooms at Schönbrunn.

The palace was in its full winter glory on January 22, 1815, when, after many postponements, a much-heralded event took place. This was a sleigh ride planned to convey the emperor's guests from the Josephplatz in the center of Vienna to beautiful Schönbrunn for a day of festivities. To Empress Maria Ludovica and Prince Trauttmansdorff, this had seemed a delightful plan when they arranged it. They had not foreseen the problems that would arise. The weather was tricky that month—whenever a cold spell promised the hard, smooth surface suitable for sleigh riding, a thaw would set in, turning the snow into slush, and the date of the party would have to be changed again.

At last a thick snowfall was followed by a severe frost and the illustrious guests received word that the rendezvous was definitely fixed for the morning of the twenty-second in the Josephplatz. Even then things did not go smoothly. Some of the ladies, fearful of the cold, demanded at the last moment that carriages should convey them instead of the richly decorated sleighs that had been prepared. Sir Charles Stewart, apparently in a state of high intoxication, arrived late and drove himself into the middle of the waiting procession thereby causing considerable confusion. At last thirty sleighs set off, led by the emperor of Austria with the tsarina beside him. She was dressed in a white ermine coat and wore a cap of vivid green silk that was topped by a high plume and decorated with diamonds that had belonged to Catherine the Great. Twenty-four pages in medieval dress and a squadron of the Imperial Guard escorted the sovereigns, and the horses that pulled the brightly colored sleighs were bedecked in tiger skins. Bright ribbons and bows were braided into their handsome manes. At first they were kept at a walk so that the crowds on the streets could admire the splendid sight, but once out of the heart of Vienna they were allowed free rein to dash along the road to Schönbrunn. A huge six-horse sled lumbered along in the rear, carrying an orchestra in Turkish costume which bravely continued playing martial airs even as it fell behind the fast-moving imperial train.

The banquet that was waiting for the party when it arrived at the palace was followed by a display of skating in which a young member of Castlereagh's staff, identified only as "Sir Edward W., member of London's Skaters Club and accustomed to charming Hyde Park strollers on the Serpentine,"[1] performed whirls, loops, and figure eights. "He then drew with his blades the initials of the Queens and the other highborn ladies, who had left their sleighs to watch and applaud his skilled performance."[2] After this dazzling exhibition the party went inside to hear the opera *Cinderella* sung by the imperial opera troupe and to watch a ballet that had been specially written for the occasion. Schönbrunn was filled with orange and myrtle trees in blossom and every room was lighted by great gold candelabra which had been brought from the imperial treasury in the Hofburg. Outside the cold had grown intense, and the guests reluctantly left the glowing palace to regain their sleighs for the return to the city by torchlight. Despite the late hour and the bitterness of the night air, there were still enthusiastic crowds waiting on the streets to see them pass.

Ten days after this stirring event the Duke of Wellington arrived in Vienna. The coming of the great man caused the hearts of even the most jaded hostesses in the city to beat faster. There were other celebrated soldiers in Europe in 1815, but none had the prestige of the man whom the French called "Le Vainqueur du Vainqueur du monde." We last saw the duke arriving in Paris to receive the plaudits that were due him as victor of the long struggle against Napoleon in Portugal and Spain. He then took up his post as British ambassador to France and, in September 1814, wrote cheerfully: "I think everything goes well here."[3] Two weeks later he reported: "I think we are getting a little unpopular in the town but I don't think that circumstance is of much importance."[4] On October 4 he was obliged to admit that the situation was in a state of "constant uneasiness."[5] This was the result of a combination of two factors. One was the ineptness of the restored monarchy. The government of Louis XVIII wallowed along, unadmired even by the eager royalists who had welcomed the return of the Bourbons. Wellington wrote to Castlereagh: "There are Ministers but no Ministry."[6]

The other factor was the bitterness of the officers and men of Napoleon's Grande Armée, who had been put on half pay or sent home to starve in the towns and villages from which they had set out in glory. A British artillery officer, passing with his guns through a provincial town, tested the sincerity of the obsequious cries of "Vive le Roi!" by murmuring "Vivé l'Empereur." Immediately men began to look at one another with delighted expressions. "Mais oui, Monsieur," they cried, slapping their thighs, "Vive l'Empereur, vive Napoléon!"[7] While the army in Paris wore the Bourbon white cockade, they sang the Marseillaise when they huddled together in the cafés before returning to their barracks, and they drank to "his" health, meaning Napoleon's. When they spoke of the king they called him "le cochon."

In November Wellington narrowly escaped an assassin's bullet as he attended a review, and the British government became haunted by a vision of the new French government being overturned by a mob of Bonapartist ex-servicemen. In this case, the British ambassador would certainly be seized. Lord Liverpool and his colleagues racked their brains as to how they could best get Wellington out of Paris in a face-saving manner. Perhaps he would agree to go to America as commander in chief? No, he would not, unless expressly ordered to do so. He had little sympathy with the American war and preferred to remain where he was, going about his business, entertaining luxuriously in the fine house he had bought for his government, and presenting his usual imperturbable face to the world: "I entertain a strong opinion that I *must* not be lost . . . but I don't like to be frightened away," he wrote.[8] Lord Liverpool replied by sending him a copy of the report of a secret agent: "Unless Duke Wellington [*sic*] is instantly recalled from France, and in as private a manner as possible, he will be assassinated: a plott [*sic*] is forming to complete the horrid deed."[9]

Eventually an excuse was found that would not reflect on the duke's personal courage and would seem plausible to the French. Because it was necessary to recall Castlereagh to London so that he might defend his actions at the congress before the House of Commons, the complex negotiations in which he had been engaged could only be continued by an ambassador with great authority. Wellington accepted the assignment and arrived in Vienna on February 3. He was at first a sad disappointment to the eager hostesses who had been looking forward to his arrival, for he declared that their drawing rooms were much too hot and that as a result he had caught a severe cold which prevented him from dining out. Later he was to enjoy himself enormously at the congress, for the company of women delighted him throughout his life. He avoided Viennese intrigue and scandal himself, but was not unamused by the gossip that swirled about his distinguished colleagues.

Castlereagh was to leave for England ten days after the duke's arrival, and the two old friends settled down to some very hard work during that short period. Wellington had gained much administrative and diplomatic experience during his years in India, besides which he had a natural ability to go straight to the heart of any problem that confronted him. He also possessed a wide knowledge of human nature. Thus it was not hard for him to grasp the problems that Castlereagh laid before him, and a solution was found to all of them by the time the Final Act was signed in June. The Duke of Wellington was called away on urgent business before his task was accomplished, but a strong British delegation under Lord Clancarty had a representative on every one of the important committees that finished the job. These committees, composed of representatives from the convening powers, had been sitting intermittently since October. Once a settlement was reached on the Poland-Saxony question, the ambassadors of the major powers were free to concentrate on the other matters awaiting their attention and the committees worked hard and well.

Among the general subjects dealt with at Vienna was the rights of the German Jews. To get this matter on the agenda of the German Committee it had been necessary for the Jews to bribe Gentz, but eventually a rather vague statement confirming the rights of the Jewish community was inserted in the Final Act. This was nothing like so strong a declaration as Nathan Rothschild and the other Jewish leaders would have liked. Nevertheless, the emancipation of the Jewish people from the iniquities under which they suffered was recommended by the congress. The delegates probably felt more at home dealing with practical matters, such as the navigation of international rivers, than they did with matters concerning the rights of man. The committee assigned to the waterways worked constructively and efficiently and its decisions were to be the basis for similar international agreements in the future.

Another matter to which much time was devoted was that of diplomatic precedence. The recommendations laid down at Vienna are still valid today. Rules drawn up by the pope in the Middle Ages had been codified in 1504, and many an unseemly row had been caused by them in later times. Spain, for example, held a lower place than France, and a violent street row had occurred in London in 1661 when the Spanish ambassador's coach tried to push in front of the coach of the French ambassador. Diplomatic relations between the two countries were severed and there was even a threat of war. The Congress of Vienna sensibly decided to put an end to the bickerings between sensitive plenipotentiaries by establishing the rule that seniority should determine the precedence of diplomatic representatives: their position would be classed by the date of the official notification of their arrival at their post. It was also agreed that the order in which diplomats should sign treaties would be decided by lot. Later, at Aix-la-Chapelle, this agreement was amended to the more practical method still employed whereby the signatures are affixed in alphabetical order. A further arrangement divided diplomatic representatives into four classes: "Ambassadors and papal legates, Ministers plenipotentiary, Ministers resident, and Chargés d'Affaires." [10]

Switzerland had sent delegates from each of its nineteen cantons and the Swiss Committee wrestled for months with the differing interests represented by them. At last a confederation of twenty-two cantons was formed, the directorate of which was to rotate among Berne, Lucerne, and Zurich. More importantly, the perpetual neutrality of Switzerland was recognized by the five great powers.

The Italian territorial questions, as described earlier, were settled largely to the advantage of Austria, which attained what amounted to dominance over the peninsula. The matter of the former Dutch colonies was negotiated by Castlereagh before he left Vienna. It was too early for any British statesman to conceive of the British empire as the Victorians were to know it, and there appears to have been no clamor in the House of Commons over the remarkably generous terms Castlereagh gave the Dutch. Great Britain retained the Cape of Good Hope, which had been in her hands since 1806, but returned to the king of Holland the fabulously rich Dutch East Indies, which had been conquered by England during the Napoleonic Wars.

It was June before the German Committee, consisting of Austria, Prussia, Bavaria, Württemberg, and Hanover, completed its work. Of all the Germans in Vienna, only Freiherr vom Stein wanted a unitary German Reich. The German princes refused to surrender so much as a crumb of their independent sovereignties, and the liberals, who wanted some sort of federal union, were divided among themselves how this was to be achieved. Many solutions were proposed and discarded; the German Committee was enlarged to include Saxony, Hesse-Darmstadt, the Netherlands (for Luxembourg), and Denmark (for Holstein). The princes and free cities were also admitted. A final scheme was adopted on June 9, 1815, and by its terms a federal diet was to be established at Frankfurt, which was to draft the laws of a confederation of Germany; each sovereign was to grant a separate constitution to his subjects. Thus no central body would possess authority. This was the weakest and would turn out to be the most dangerous decision of the Congress of Vienna. Talleyrand had been alone among his colleagues in predicting the unchecked rise of a powerful and militaristic Prussia. While we can criticize this and other parts of the settlement of 1815, in fact there was not another general conflagration in Europe for just under a hundred years. Can so much be said for the next great peace conference, in 1919? And the peacemakers of 1946 have not left us a tranquil or stable world. Considering the turmoil into which the Napoleonic Wars had thrown the Continent, the work of the Congress of Vienna was a tremendous achievement.

One subject must surely have arisen in the talks between Castlereagh and Wellington: the future of Napoleon Bonaparte. It may be remembered that Castlereagh had refused to sign the clause of the Treaty of Fontainebleau which designated Elba as the former emperor's place of exile. Metternich had opposed the plan with equal vehemence, saying that to send Napoleon to an island so dangerously close to the Italian and French mainlands would mean war within two years. They had been overruled by Alexander, who was in one of his most magnanimous moods at the time.

A great deal of news about Napoleon's first nine months on Elba had reached Vienna. At first he had attempted to turn his tiny kingdom into a miniature version of the Tuileries. The citizens of his capital, Porto Ferrajo, were outfitted with state uniforms of blue embroidered with silver and were transformed into court chamberlains. Awkwardly, the notaries and shop-keepers of the town assembled at the royal villa accompanied by their wives. These uneasy women all but tripped over the court trains of violet and yellow that they had been commanded to wear. When the grand marshal flung open the doors of the Salle des Pyramides to announce the emperor, they either gaped in awestruck silence or burst into nervous twitters.

After a month or two even Napoleon saw the pointlessness of the pathetic charade and abandoned it, but he still retained a large household of French and Elban officials, a vast number of servants, a stable of his favorite horses which had been sent over from France, and a small army of twelve hundred soldiers. Visitors came and went—his Polish mistress Marie Walewska arrived secretly and he publicly received any visitors of note who requested audiences. His mother joined him and his sister Pauline Borghese was a regular and faithful visitor. It was no-ticed that he was growing increasingly corpulent and spent hours a day luxuriating in the hot waters of the pretentious Pompeian bath he had had installed for himself. To the observ-ers who studied him, he seemed to have become a lazy, indo-lent figure, satisfied to pass his evenings playing dominoes with his mother for very low stakes. At precisely nine o'clock he would retire for the night.

The British commissioner charged with Napoleon's security was Colonel Sir Neil Campbell. His reports went to Vienna and London via the British minister to Tuscany, Lord Burghersh, who had resided in Florence since October with his pretty wife, Priscilla.* Burghersh was to grow increasingly disturbed by Campbell's sloppiness as the winter wore on, and relations

---

*The Burghershes remained in Florence for many years and raised their growing family there. Priscilla continued to be close to her uncle Wellington and corresponded with him until his death.

between the two men became strained. What worried Burghersh was that, although he had positively refused to grant a
request from Sir Neil to settle in Tuscany and confine his duties
to brief visits to Porto Ferrajo, Campbell gave the impression
that Burghersh had agreed to his residing on the mainland.
Campbell's routine calls on Napoleon became more and more
infrequent; his visits to his mistress in Leghorn longer and
longer. Moreover, he found the Florentine society that Priscilla
Burghersh had collected around the British legation extremely
congenial. To excuse himself he wrote: "Napoleon has gradually
estranged himself from me, and various means are taken to
show me that my presence is disagreeable . . . for the purpose
of inducing me to quit Elba entirely." [11]

Nothing would have suited Napoleon more than to have got
rid of Neil Campbell, and his snubs to him were surely inten-
tional. Three main reasons were to persuade Napoleon to fulfill
the promise he had made before leaving France in April 1814
that he would be back before the violets bloomed again. One
was his fear of being transferred to some more distant place.
His sources in Paris had informed him that Talleyrand had been
pressing for his removal to the Azores, or even St. Helena, and
that Metternich had been in correspondence with the government of Louis XVIII on the same subject. Bored as he was on
Elba, Napoleon could hardly bear to contemplate what his existence would be like on a barren rock in the South Atlantic.

Finances were a major preoccupation. By the Treaty of Fontainebleau he had been promised a liberal annual allowance,
but this had never been paid by the French government. He
could not possibly continue to live in the semiroyal style to
which he was accustomed, nor could the proud former master
of the world imagine living in any other way. The allied ministers at Vienna saw the danger of humiliating Napoleon and suggested to Talleyrand that he protest to Louis XVIII. He did so,
only to receive a letter from the king in which he said that he
would be delighted to pay the pension "if the excellent idea of

the Azores were put into execution."[12] It was the failure of
Louis XVIII to carry out the provisions of the Treaty of Fontainebleau that convinced Napoleon that he was no longer
committed to observe the terms of the document he had
signed.

A third factor in Napoleon's decision was the news pouring
in from France of the growing unpopularity of the Bourbons.
An old soldier had made his way to Elba in November and been
received at the royal villa. He described his month-long journey during which he had sampled opinion in every town he
came through. "They are waiting for you," he told Napoleon,
"the present state of affairs can't last another six months. Everyone was complaining about something and nobody was satisfied with anything."[13] He was not the only messenger to bring
such tidings to Elba.

Sir Neil Campbell said good-by to Napoleon on February 16
before leaving on a visit to Leghorn and Florence "for the sake
of my health." Napoleon wished him a safe journey and added
politely that he hoped Sir Neil would be back by the twenty-
eighth of the month as his sister Pauline Borghese was giving a
ball that night. Campbell said that he would be happy to accept
so delightful an invitation. Arriving a few days later in Florence,
he went to the British legation in order to hand in his latest
dispatch for transmission to Lord Castlereagh. Instead of the
warm and friendly reception usually accorded visitors to that
hospitable house, Sir Neil was greeted coldly by Lord Burghersh, whose patience by now was at an end. He told Campbell
that he had been carrying out his duties in an improper manner
and ordered him to remain "more constantly at his post."[14]
Much worried by the reprimand, for he knew that if anything
went wrong on Elba he would be blamed, Campbell returned
to the island, arriving, as he had promised Napoleon he would,
on February 28 in time for Princess Borghese's ball. He was
greeted with the news that two nights before Napoleon had sailed
aboard the brig *Inconstant* for an unknown destination, accom-

panied by six smaller vessels carrying the contingent of twelve hundred soldiers that had been allotted him under the Treaty of Fontainebleau for his protection. He also bore with him all his sister's jewels, which she had handed to him as a last token of her loyalty.

Thus opened the chapter of French history known as the Hundred Days, marking the period between Napoleon's escape from Elba and his defeat at Waterloo. In Vienna, Metternich had gone to bed late on the night of March 6. The story of what happened when he awoke is best told in his own words:*

There had been a meeting in my rooms of the plenipotentiaries of the Five Powers. This meeting had lasted until three in the morning. I had forbidden my valet to disturb my rest if couriers arrived at a late hour of the night. In spite of this prohibition, the man brought me, about six in the morning, an express despatch market URGENT. Upon the envelope I read the words, "From the Imperial and Royal Consulate at Genoa." As I had only been in bed for about two hours I laid the despatch, without opening it, upon the table beside my bed. I tried to go to asleep. But having once been disturbed I was unable to rest again. At about 7.30 I decided to open the envelope. It contained only the following six lines: "The English commissioner Campbell has just entered the harbor enquiring whether anyone had seen Napoleon at Genoa, in view of the fact that he had disappeared from the island of Elba. The answer being in the negative, the English frigate without further delay put to sea."

I dressed myself in a flash and before 8 A.M. I was with my Emperor. He read the above mentioned despatch; he then, with the perfect calm that never deserts him on great occasions, said to me: "Napoleon appears anxious to run great risks; that is his business. Our business is to give the world

---

* There are many descriptions in the memoirs of how the news came to Vienna. I have chosen Metternich's because no other account reports the incredible line: "Has anyone seen Napoleon?" which evidently was the anguished cry of Sir Neil Campbell as he sailed into the harbor of Genoa.

that repose which he has troubled all these years. Go at once
and find the Emperor of Russia and the King of Prussia; tell
them that I am prepared to order my armies once again to take
the road to France. I have no doubt that the two Sovereigns
will join me on my march." At 8.15 I was with the Emperor
Alexander who used the same language as the Emperor Francis. At 8.30 King Frederick William III gave me a similar assurance. By 9 o'clock I had returned home. I had already summoned Field Marshal Prince Schwarzenberg to come to my
house. At 10 the Ministers of the Four Powers had gathered at
my invitation in my study. At the same hour aides-de-camp
were flying in all directions carrying to the several army corps,
who were retiring, the order to halt. In this way war was decided in less than an hour.[15]

On landing in France Napoleon had immediately announced: "The Congress is dissolved." This was an incorrect
judgment. The various committees continued to fulfill their duties and the Final Act was signed nine days before Waterloo.
Furthermore, on March 13, the eight convening powers, Austria, France, Great Britain, Prussia, Russia, Spain, Portugal, and
Sweden, signed a declaration in which they undertook to fur-
nish their assistance to the king of France and the French nation, proclaiming that Napoleon Bonaparte had placed himself
outside the pale of civil and social relations. This strong show
of unity was succeeded by a treaty which reaffirmed the Grand
Alliance formed at Chaumont. Castlereagh had already written
to Wellington: "Your Grace can judge where your personal
presence is likely to be of the most use to the public service.
The Prince Regent, relying entirely upon Your Grace's zeal and
judgment, leaves it to you, without further orders, either to remain at Vienna or to put yourself at the head of the army in
Flanders"[16] "I am going," wrote the Duke of Wellington, with
his unusual unsentimental brevity, to Lord Burghersh on March
22, "into the Low Countries to take command of the army."[17]
Thus the Congress of Vienna entered upon its own Hundred

Days. It was soon learned that Napoleon had landed in the South of France on March 1 but few people thought that he would reach Paris; he would be assassinated on the way, or taken prisoner by those loyal royalist troops Talleyrand was always talking about. It was in this optimistic spirit that the agreement of March 13 had been signed in which Bonaparte was declared an outlaw. Yet below the surface of resolution and unison, behind the impassive masks that the allied ministers and sovereigns showed to the world, lay a growing sense of foreboding as week followed week. Lord Clancarty, who was to succeed Wellington as head of the British delegation, wrote: "It was not difficult to perceive that fear was predominant in all the Imperial and Royal personages."[18] La Garde found a singularly felicitous phrase: "A thousand candles seemed to have been extinguished in a single moment."[19]

On March 19 Gentz gave a dinner attended by Metternich, Talleyrand, and all four Courland princesses: Wilhemina Sagan, Pauline Hohenzollern, Jeanne d'Acerenza, and Dorothea Talleyrand-Périgord. Charming as the company was the party was not a success, according to the host, due to the ominous reports from France. Napoleon had reached Grenoble and men were flocking to his standard by the thousands. Worse still was the defection of Marshal Ney, who had been sent out by the king with six thousand men to block the road to Paris. After reading the proclamation that Napoleon had published on landing in France, the marshal had cried out: "Nobody writes like that any more! The King should write like that!"[20] Deeply moved by the stirring words of his former commander, Ney embraced Napoleon when they met and, instead of bringing him back in an iron cage as he had promised Louis XVIII he would do, he joined his forces to those of "the outlaw" and soon the tricolor was flying above an army of twenty thousand men.

In faraway Schönbrunn, Marie Louise had retired to her bedroom when her excited French ladies brought her the news of the escape from Elba. Her howls and sobs penetrated the thick walls during the night, alarming her household. When at last she grew calmer she went to talk to her father in order to obtain his assurance that she need never return to France. Soothed by his guaranty and comforted by his understanding, she went back to Schönbrunn to give the order that her suite were to remove the Napoleonic uniforms they had been wearing since they left France and to replace them with Austrian imperial liveries. Napoleon's arms, which had been painted on her carriage doors, were now to be painted out. She would neither receive messengers from her husband nor reply to the frantic letters he addressed to her during the Hundred Days imploring her to return with their son.

Although it would be a week before the news reached Vienna, on the dark night of Sunday, March 19, Louis XVIII dragged his heavy body to a discreet side door of the Tuileries Palace and disappeared into the rain bound for a second exile. The following evening a fast-driving cabriolet, escorted by cavalry, dashed into the courtyard of the palace and the people who had been awaiting its occupant carried him triumphantly up the stairs on their shoulders. Napoleon had returned.

It was Holy Week in Vienna, for Easter fell very early that year—March 26. These days are still observed in the Catholic country of Austria as a time when theaters, places of entertainment, and even museums close; only the churches are filled. In 1815 the devout quiet of Good Friday was undisturbed by fresh news from France, and the servants at the French embassy were about to go to bed when a muddy carriage drew up to the Kaunitz Palace bearing a most unexpected visitor. Out tottered the Duchess of Courland, who had driven from Paris in the record time of five days to seek refuge with Talleyrand and her daughter Dorothea. She reported that when she left the city on Palm Sunday Napoleon had been approaching rapidly and that the king and his government were about to run. Exhausted as she was by her journey, unnerved as Talleyrand must have been by the dreadful news his former mistress brought, appearances were observed. Carême produced a magnificent Easter dinner attended by all the Courland daughters in honor of their mother.

It was a beautiful, springlike weekend, and the Prater was crowded with families in their Easter finery strolling along the promenades while the bands played, but the staff of the French embassy had little heart for celebration. After Talleyrand, it was La Besnadière who was the most despairing. This permanent official of the Foreign Ministry had been the linch pin of the mission, and he was justly proud of the feat that his master and he had accomplished. Only four months earlier France had been isolated, unwanted at the council table of the great powers. With remarkable skill Talleyrand had brought her back to a position of the first importance; now the structure that he had erected with such effort was to be blown away like a house of cards if what the duchess reported was true. La Besnadière was the only man in the mission who had no need to worry about his own future; as a high civil servant his position would be secure, but as a professional diplomat and a patriotic Frenchman he was in anguish.

Talleyrand had written the king urging him not to leave France. If he was forced to vacate Paris, let him take the two chambers of government and his loyal troops with him to some town in the north or east of the country and make his stand there. Had the advice been accepted? It would be days before the government's destination would be known in Vienna, but in their heart of hearts even the two royalists on Talleyrand's staff, la Tour du Pin and Noailles, doubted that Louis XVIII would have the stomach to fight. Dalberg was positive that once more the king would slip across the frontier to safety in Ostend or Ghent, both so conveniently situated for a second flight to England.

It was the bleakest Easter weekend the occupants of the Kaunitz Palace had ever known. Personal tensions aggravated the political ones, for Dorothea could hardly conceal her rage that her mother should have abandoned the two small Périgord boys who had been left in her charge. It would have been easy enough to find a corner for them in the duchess's carriage; instead of which she had forgotten them in her selfish desire to get out of Paris. As for the duchess, within twenty-four hours of her arrival she became aware, in her shrewd way, that there was a new factor in the family equation. Her daughter's infatuation with Count Clam came as no surprise; rumors had reached Paris of the affair between Dorothea and the Austrian officer. What was new was the change in Talleyrand's relationship with her daughter. That the eager lover who had written most passionate letters to her only a year before should now be besotted with love for her own daughter must have come as a cruel shock to the duchess. While still handsome in her mid-fifties and very elegant, she was well aware that she had lost Talleyrand forever. Nevertheless, there is not the slightest intimation of displeasure in her subsequent behavior. She did not move, as she easily might have done, to the home of one of her other daughters; in fact, she remained at the Kaunitz Palace for more than two months.

On the Tuesday after Easter, Wilhelmina Sagan gave a large farewell party for the Duke of Wellington, who was to leave Vienna the following day. He had been much diverted by the company of the Courland sisters during his stay in the city and had become truly fond of Wilhelmina. Resplendent in his field marshal's uniform of red and gold, he was kissed by all the ladies when they said good-by and promises were exchanged that they would all meet in Paris. The tsar was more solemn: placing his hand on Wellington's shoulder he said, "It is for you to save the world again." [21]

April and May were months of waiting for news from the north. Talleyrand received a letter from the king in Ostend, explaining that it had been impossible for him to make a stand, for he had had no loyal troops left. From Paris came a not unexpected blow: Talleyrand's properties had been sequestered and his funds frozen. He was now *persona non grata,* one of the handful of men to whom Napoleon refused the amnesty he freely granted to those who had served the Bourbon government. Talleyrand could only cut down his household, borrow money to keep going, and await events.

Dorothea worried as the sixty-one-year-old statesman withdrew increasingly into his thoughts, seeming hardly to hear the bright, brittle chatter of the Duchess of Courland which had amused him so much in the old days. Knowing that he was unhappy, Dorothea began to see less of her lover Clam and sought in every possible way to entertain the uncle who had been so kind to her. Visitors to the French embassy found it as brilliant as ever, with faithful Carême still in the kitchen performing miracles on a strictly curtailed budget.

There were other unhappy people in Vienna that spring. Catherine Bagration had been obliged to say farewell to the one man she had ever truly loved: the crown prince of Württemberg. He left in April on his journey homeward, destined to become the husband of the intolerable Grand Duchess Catherine. Poor Princess Bagration accompanied him on his road as far as the first relay station and then returned, sobbing so pitifully that the police spies reported that even her creditors' hard hearts were moved. There were a great many creditors hovering about the left wing of the Palm Palace and for a time it was thought that "la Bagration" was permanently ruined. Happily a rich stepfather in Russia came to her rescue, enabling her to remain in her splendid apartment mourning her lost prince.

It must have pleased Catherine to hear that her rival, Wilhelmina Sagan, was also in financial straits, having made fearful inroads on her fortune during the preceding reckless years. It was Metternich who saved her. Passion spent, he no longer sat up all night writing despairing letters to the duchess, but he could never meet her in society without finding her the most attractive woman in the room. When she asked him to help her sell her jewels during April, he was delighted to be of service to her, but even the large sum Wilhelmina received from the sale of the Courland sapphires was inadequate to meet her needs. To the delight of Catherine Bagration, Wilhelmina was later obliged to move out of the Palm Palace into a smaller apartment in the Windischgraetz Palace.

Having changed residences, Wilhelmina dismissed Prince Alfred Windischgraetz, of whom she was growing tired, and threw herself into the arms of that vain, arrogant, badly behaved figure, Sir Charles Stewart. Princess Bagration was beside herself. One of her accomplishments had been to keep several love affairs going at the same time without friction or difficulty, but the all-absorbing romance with the crown prince had blinded her to the danger of losing Stewart. The Sagan-Stewart affair was partly the fault of the Duke of Wellington, who was fond of the soldier-diplomat who had served under him in Portugal with outstanding gallantry. Before leaving Vienna he had instructed him to keep an eye on Wilhelmina: "Help her, Charles, if she needs any help. For my sake don't lose sight of her." [22]

Charles Stewart obeyed his commander's orders promptly and literally. Hager's reports are crammed with descriptions of the rendezvous that spring between the lovers. Probably Wilhelmina was happier with Charles than she had been with the complex Clemens Metternich. He was violent, he could display boorish manners, he was spoiled, but he was a simple, straightforward man, extremely handsome and very brave—just the sort of uncomplicated companion her earthy nature demanded. Their flamboyant affair was to be the talk of Paris that summer when they were there together after Waterloo.

Stewart and his new mistress were among the few carefree persons in Vienna during the last days of the congress. The 100,000 visitors were tidying up, preparing for departure—worrying about the tips they should leave, the presents they should give, and the debts they had accumulated. Gentz and his minions toiled over the draft of the Final Act that would be signed on June 9. This was a backbreaking task, for the results of the work of the many committees filled volumes which Gentz was obliged to condense into a single document. He succeeded admirably.

The representatives of the convening powers met in the Hofburg to sign the tremendous treaty on the day appointed. This was the only time in the entire nine months that the delegates to the congress had ever gathered together officially. There was little fanfare or celebration, for men's minds were occupied with the great battle that was about to take place near Brussels. Francis I was represented at the signing by Metternich; the emperor had left Vienna for Allied Headquarters at Heilbronn in Germany on May 27. He was followed the next day by the tsar and the king of Prussia, who had also deputized their ministers to sign the agreement. Talleyrand reluctantly departed for the Low Countries on June 10 to join his sovereign, who had been demanding his presence insistently, writing: "It does not matter who signs the treaty." [23]

On June 11 Charles Stewart climbed into his carriage for a fast run to Brussels. There the diarist Creevey encountered him sauntering about the town in the august company of the Duke of Wellington. Wilhelmina joined other worried women friends in the summer resort of Baden outside Vienna. Laure Metternich and her children were also there waiting in suspense for news from the theater of war. Clemens was at headquarters, writing cheerfully enough, but it was almost the end of June before the tidings arrived for which everyone had been praying. Wilhelmina was the first to receive them. Frantic with anxiety, devoured with impatience, she could no longer remain in Baden with the women and children. She therefore drove into Vienna to find a letter that had just arrived by special courier from Charles Stewart. Opening it with trembling hands, she read that the war was over following a great Allied victory. The battle had been a bloody one and the duke had said to Creevey: "It has been a damned nice thing—the nearest run thing you ever saw in your life." [24] Charles himself was unharmed, but the

British and Prussian forces had probably lost thirty thousand men.

The streets of Vienna seemed very peaceful as Wilhelmina started back to Baden in the June twilight. The Viennese were strolling about in family groups exchanging the gossip of the day without a foreign voice among them. Their city had been regained and "a world restored."

On her return to Baden Wilhelmina found the women she had left there gathered together in joyous reunion, reading and rereading Metternich's letter to his wife containing the great news. It had just arrived, and carried more details of the battle of Waterloo than Stewart had been able to supply in his hurried bulletin. Laure Metternich was radiant. Now Clemens would be returning, perhaps in time for the baby she expected in late summer, the product of the reconciliation that had taken place following his devastating love affair with the Duchess of Sagan. Knowing her husband, Laure could not hope that he would remain faithful to her indefinitely, but she instinctively felt that nothing could ever be as terrible again as his passion for Wilhelmina Sagan. She settled down to a serene time of waiting, attended by her loving daughters and cheered by tender letters from Clemens in Paris.

She was the only one among the women central to this story to know tranquillity in the ensuing period. It is interesting that the men who had formed the Allied Coalition that brought down Napoleon and had gone on to bear the strain of the peacemaking appear to have continued their lives without a backward glance at the congress. Their future careers belong to European history and will not be recounted here. Less well known and well worth describing are the destinies of those remarkable women: Princess Bagration, the Duchess of Sagan, and the Duchess of Dino, as Dorothea de Talleyrand-Périgord was to be known from 1816 on. When the curtain came down on the stage at Vienna all of them wandered as if uncertain of their roles. For them the nine months of the congress had been a time of hectic, exhilarating frenzy, when anything could happen at any moment. The men who dined at their tables might seize a pencil to draw frontiers on the damask cloth which would alter the lives of millions of people. The arrival of a messenger carrying a letter might signify the dismissal of an ambassador or even a new threat of war. Nothing was as it had been before and, in the heady climate in which they lived, a light flirtation could turn overnight into an erotic intrigue in which politics were intermixed with physical passion. It had become a habit for these women at the center of the stage to live among characters who were larger than life-size, among events of high drama and charged emotions. No wonder they found it hard to return to normal existences. Of the three it was Wilhelmina Sagan who managed least well in the post-congress years.

She had always been considered the most beautiful and the most talented of the four Courland sisters. In their youth, little Dorothea had been intimidated by her, almost afraid of the glamorous Wilhelmina. Now, at the age of thirty-four, she was as lovely as she had ever been and was still extremely rich despite the temporary financial embarrassments she had brought upon herself by her reckless extravagance. The vast castle and estate of Sagan in Silesia was hers, as was the huge castle of Nachod in Bohemia and the nearby manor house of Ratiborzitz with its hundreds of acres. When she went to Paris during the month after Waterloo it was to join Charles Stewart and to partake with him of the merrymaking that accompanied the second restoration of Louis XVIII. The Duke of Wellington was there, delighted to see her again and eager to introduce her to the fashionable English society which had flocked across the Channel to celebrate the victory. There were dressmakers to visit by day and dinners and balls every night; on the surface the Duchess of Sagan's life was one of dazzling pleasure.

However, behind the gleaming appearance she presented to

the world, Wilhelmina was not happy. Alfred Windischgraetz
had pursued her to Paris, tormenting her with anguished re-
proaches. She broke with him at last in the middle of August,
writing him a final letter in which she reminded him that she
had severed her relationship with Metternich for his sake—
"the inclination of my heart and the truest attachment I have
perhaps ever encountered."[25] The scenes with Alfred were
wearing enough, but worse still were Charles Stewart's out-
bursts of jealous temper. In September she left for Italy to join
her sisters Pauline and Dorothea. Stewart went to meet her
there, but the affair was coming to an end. It is probable that
she would have liked to marry him and settle down, but there
could be no question of marriage with a twice-divorced woman
for the ambitious Charles. He was soon to abandon the army to
undertake a diplomatic career, with his first post British ambassador at Vienna. The wife he chose was a very young heiress,
Lady Frances Vane-Tempest, much as Alfred Windischgraetz
was to marry about the same time a young Schwarzenberg princess, a niece of the field marshal's.

These conventional marriages were predictable enough, but
the duchess led a lonely life during the years 1816–19. Avoid-
ing Vienna, she drifted aimlessly about Europe without ever
settling anywhere for long. She was never to see Gustava, the
daughter by Armfelt for whom she had longed and for a sight of
whom she had begged the tsar during the congress. There were
rumors that she had taken another lover, Prince Paul Esterházy,
the Austrian ambassador to England, but in the summer of 1819
came a new piece of gossip concerning her. It was said that she
had ended the affair with Esterházy and was going to remarry.
The story was true. Her third husband was Count Karl Schulenberg, an Austrian officer seven years younger than she. Metternich was appalled when he heard the news: "Of all the men I
know Schulenberg is least suited to remain even for a year the
husband of the duchess. He is weak, a good fellow, patient and
yielding, while to be husband to this woman he needs to have

above all other qualities an iron hand, energy, yes, even a kind of impudence."[26] Metternich was not the only one to be horrified by the marriage. Wilhelmina's sisters wept throughout the wedding service. The pessimists were justified. The marriage was as unsatisfactory as the duchess's first two had been, and after years of futile drifting about with Schulenberg she lived separately from him. In her later years she sank into depression and illness and died in Vienna at the age of fifty-eight. Princess Metternich* wrote that her husband had been so distressed by the news of the duchess's death that his anguish had quite alarmed her.

Jeanne d'Acerenza, writing to Dorothea in Paris of their sister's beauty and charm and of the happiness that she had brought to those around her, questioned sadly whether she herself had ever been happy.[27] We do not know what Dorothea replied, but she might have said that, while Wilhelmina had in the main wasted the gifts that had been bestowed on her, she had known moments of intense happiness during the turbulent years 1813–15.

Dorothea was the steadiest and most serious of the sisters, yet even she had been completely thrown off her stride by her discovery during the congress of what life could offer. It would be more than a year before she was to find her way out of the emotional confusion into which she had been plunged on her return to Paris after Waterloo. What did she want? She knew only what she did not want: reunion with Edmond. Consequently she removed herself and her two boys to Talleyrand's house in the rue St. Florentin, leaving Edmond in the house they had formerly shared. Her uncle was only too delighted to welcome her, but the summer of the second restoration was a bad time for him. Napoleon was safely on his way to far-distant

---

*Melanie Metternich, the prince's third wife. Laure had died some years earlier of tuberculosis, and he remarried only to lose his young second wife in childbirth.

St. Helena, but Louis XVIII's ramshackle government was as weak as his first one had been and Talleyrand found his role as foreign minister a hard one. The Allies' peace terms were harsher than they had been in 1814 and the French particularly resented the restitution to their original homes of the objects of art that Napoleon had looted from all over Europe. It was said that the Duke of Wellington himself spent his nights unhooking pictures from the walls of the Louvre. Dorothea, who had never felt herself a Parisian, took little pleasure in the entertainments she attended, finding the voices of the fashionable Englishwomen strident and the ambiance of the city a disagreeable contrast to the elegant hedonism which had reigned in Vienna. For once she was too self-centered to absorb herself in Talleyrand's worries and work, and by autumn she could stand it no longer. Her lover, the handsome Count Clam, had for months been imploring her to join him and was waiting for her in Italy. On the pretext of her sisters' need for her she crossed the Alps once more, running away from husband, children, and uncle. Wilhelmina and Pauline were indeed in Italy, but it was Clam with whom she lived, at first in a state of ecstatic delight. They moved back to their beloved Vienna, and it seemed probable that the relationship would be a permanent one.

Talleyrand was desolate. His friends and his enemies noted that he seemed suddenly to have withered and aged. Never comfortable with the king, he offered his resignation in the course of the autumn and when, to his astonishment, it was instantly accepted he did not struggle to fight back. It appeared that loss of power was secondary to his graver loss of the one person who was indispensable to him. Naturally he bombarded Dorothea with appeals to return, yet she lingered in Vienna, unable to bring herself to break with her lover. Clam was different from most of the attractive young officers who had danced away the nights of the congress with Dorothea and her friends. He was cultivated and intelligent—just the sort of man she had been looking for since girlhood. It will be remembered that her mother had tricked her out of her early infatuation with Czartoryski in order that she should make "a better match." Here was a second Adam Czartoryski—Clam was not only brave and noble but a great future was predicted for him. Already he was the star of Field Marshal Schwarzenberg's staff, and it was said that he himself would reach the rank of field marshal before he was forty. Furthermore, he adored Dorothea. How could she leave him?

Eventually she did so, partly out of her strong sense of duty and loyalty to the uncle to whom she owed so much, partly because Talleyrand truly fascinated her. By the fall of 1816 she was back in Paris, and would never leave Talleyrand again. Was she his mistress? In 1821 she had a child, Pauline, and, while Edmond had moved back to the rue St. Florentin to regularize the birth, the world assumed that Talleyrand was the father. People were shocked, for he was by now sixty-seven and considered physically repulsive, while she was a ravishing beauty of twenty-eight. We will never know, but Talleyrand showed especial tenderness to Pauline and she became her mother's favorite child, far closer to her than the two Périgord boys.

For the next fourteen years the incongruous pair divided their time between Paris and Talleyrand's great Renaissance château of Valençay in the province of Berry. The boys grew up and fine titles and fortunes were conferred on them by Talleyrand. They married appropriately, and Dorothea early became a grandmother. It was a luxurious life, with both houses filled with guests of every nationality who welcomed the opportunity to sit at the feet of the great statesman. Yet, old as he was, Talleyrand was restless out of power. In 1830 the Bourbons were overthrown and their Orléans cousin, Louis-Philippe, became king. When he offered Talleyrand the post of French ambassador to England the former foreign minister accepted the mission with alacrity. Dorothea and he remained in London for four years, during which she played her role as diplomatic hostess as deftly as she had done in Vienna. She would have liked to stay there longer, but in 1834 she felt it her duty to persuade Talleyrand to resign. He was now eighty years old and tiring fast. He died in 1838, and Dorothea felt that it was the triumph of her life to have reconciled him with the church at the end. After his death, she was to feel that life had lost its savor, and to write: "My long intercourse with Monsieur de Talleyrand has made it difficult for ordinary people to get on with me. I meet minds which seem slow, diffuse and ill-developed. . . . "[28]

She was now forty-five—a bad age to be left to lead what had become a meaningless life after the marriage of her beloved Pauline to the charming Henri de Castellane. Too young to devote herself entirely to being a grandmother, too old to start a new career, she wandered between France and the Germany she had known so well as a girl. She never had been quite at home in Paris; now she felt herself a bit of a has-been, owing her position to her uncle-by-marriage. In Berlin she was welcomed as a princess of Courland and therefore a great lady in her own right. She renewed her acquaintance with the Prussian royal family and was soon on intimate and affectionate terms with them and treated almost as a relation. Gradually her visits to France became merely brief interruptions to her happy German life, journeys made only out of her sense of duty to her children and grandchildren. In 1834 she bought Sagan, Wilhelmina's great castle southeast of Berlin, from their sister, Pauline, to whom it had been left. With it came the title, and she was known for the rest of her life as the Duchess of Sagan.

In Paris her admirers missed her: "Still beautiful at sixty-five," wrote the statesman Guizot after meeting her again in 1859, "the same eyes, the same figure; still Circe. And the same spirit: always free, firm, flexible and understanding. How sad it is that once more she has become a German grande dame. . . ."[29] He was to describe her even more poignantly after her death at Sagan in 1862: "I find it almost impossible to convince myself that I shall never again see those eyes, by turn so brilliant and so profound; that I shall never again enjoy that conversation, rich and yet simple, which concealed strength in its very grace and which always left more to be understood than was actually said. When a brilliant light goes out, for some time afterwards one seems to see it shining; one does not pass at once into the darkness. . . ." [30]

We have no record of any such tribute being paid to Princess Bagration when she died at what was then considered the great age of seventy-four, but her life in the post-Vienna years was so startlingly dramatic that, in contrast, the careers of the two Courland sisters seem almost conventional.

The end of the congress found the poor princess mourning her lost love and hounded by creditors, but saved at the last moment by her rich Russian stepfather. Yet her financial situation was truly precarious; unlike the Duchess of Sagan with her vast holdings in land and possessions, Catherine Bagration had no resources to fall back on should Count Litta cease to concern himself with the stepdaughter he had not seen for many years. She had long since run through her Russian inheritance, and her mother, disapproving of her daughter's dissolute life, had cut off relations with her. The tsar, whose pension to his cousin, mistress, and agent had been an important source of revenue during the preceding years, appears to have cooled toward the princess before he left Vienna and the steady flow of imperial rubles ceased. Then there was her responsibility for Clementine, who bore the name Bagration but was in fact the child of Metternich. Clementine never comes into the story of the Palm Palace during the congress, but when we pick up her mother's trail again in Paris in 1818 she was very much on the scene as a sixteen-year-old whose education was being completed by a faithful tutor, the Abbé Brot. Where were Princess Bagration and her daughter in the intervening three years? We have no idea, and there are many gaps in the story that is about to begin.*

* My source of information on Catherine Bagration is a monograph written by Louis Hastier called *Les Bagration,* which was kindly sent me by the princess's descendant, Teymuraz K. Bagration. This led me onto other memoirs, but Hastier was indispensable.

The reputation of the princess in Vienna during the congress had evidently preceded her to Paris, for she was considered a possibly subversive character by the police and put under strict surveillance. According to their reports she had received another advance of 135,000 rubles from Count Litta which enabled her to take a small furnished house in the fashionable rue Chaussée d'Antin, just off the Grands Boulevards. There she entertained some of the greatest names in France, the Duc de Mouchy, the Duc de Guiche, the Duc d'Escars, the Vicomte de Chateaubriand, mixing these *grands seigneurs* with liberal writers and politicians like Benjamin Constant and Mathieu Dumas. Aristocratic friends from Poland and Russia made her house their headquarters when they were in Paris, and to it also came the diplomats she had known in Vienna: Comte Alexis de Noailles, the Duc de Dalberg, the Marquis de la Tour du Pin, Count Nesselrode, Lord Clancarty and Lord Stewart (Charles Stewart had succeeded to this title). While a great many ladies adorned the salon they were either slightly shabby relics of the Napoleonic past or belonged to the brassy new world of businessmen and bankers who were clawing their way up the Parisian social ladder. The Duchesse de Mouchy and the Marquise de la Tour du Pin most definitely did not accompany their husbands to the little house in the rue Chaussée d'Antin. The Russian ambassador occasionally went there but the princess was almost never invited to his embassy. This must have hurt, especially as the ambassador was Pozzo di Borgo, that jolly old friend we have seen welcoming Lady Burghersh to headquarters at Frankfurt and cheering up Adèle de Boigne and her family after the entrance of the Allied armies into Paris in 1814. As Russian ambassador, Pozzo could not afford to take chances in the early 1820s, for Catherine was still out of favor with the tsar and her house had a reputation for shadiness.

To the police spies who watched it the scene was a brilliant one, and they wrote admiringly in their reports of the princess's sparkling conversation. She was fond of reminiscing about the Congress of Vienna, and those who had not been there hung on her words as she recounted the story of the marvelous days and nights during which, according to herself, she had engineered the success of the coalition through her influence over Prince Metternich. Catherine was a good actress and a brave woman. During these years she was sailing very close to the wind and there must have been many a night when she lay awake wondering what would happen to Clementine and herself if Count Litta withdrew his support. Above all, how would Clementine find a husband? In the harsh world of nineteenth-century Paris there was little chance that their new friends would come to their help if they fell into poverty, and their old friends, the Polish and Russian aristocrats, had enough needy relations of their own.

After the first two years the police surveillance was discontinued and all we know of the princess is that she moved a great deal, from apartment to house and again to an apartment, and while her salon continued to be filled with the most interesting men in Paris there is no record of a permanent lover. Then a miracle occurred. In 1825 a new assistant military attaché, aged twenty-six, arrived at the British embassy. His name was John Hobard Caradoc, the son of an exceptionally rich man, Lord Howden. "Le beau Caradoc," as he was known in Paris, is a shadowy figure. We do not know how or when he met Princess Bagration, who was sixteen years his senior, but the historian Louis Hastier has published a copy of what he calls "l'incroyable déclaration" of March 15, 1830. It is indeed an incredible document, written in the form of a will by Catherine Bagration. In it she declares that she has secretly and religiously married John Hobard Caradoc, and wishes to acknowledge the fact that she owes his father, Lord Howden, the sum of 3,008,726 francs which he has lent her in several installments. She asks that on her death he should be repaid from her estate in Russia. Why did Howden lend her this gigantic sum? Perhaps he had hoped to buy off his son's mistress. We can only guess, but what we do know is that in the year 1828 Princess Bagration, now one of the richest women in France, gave her daughter Clementine a dowry of 800,000 francs on the occasion of her marriage to Count Othon Blome, chamberlain to the king of Denmark.

The wedding was a splendid affair, attended by all the grandest men and women in Paris society. The marriage act was signed by the Russian and Austrian ambassadors as well as three Cabinet ministers and a covey of dukes. The ceremony was followed by a ball and supper, with Carême serving as caterer. For the occasion he created two new dishes, "potage Bagration" and "salade Bagration." During the course of the evening the guests wandered about the house admiring the furnishings, and some of the staider ladies were shocked to come on a room displaying the bridal bed, bedecked with the finest of linen sheets embroidered with royal crowns. Showing off the bed was considered vulgar, but Princess Bagration was now in a position in which she could well permit herself a touch of flamboyance. At the age of forty-five she had at last achieved security, and she made the most of it.

Her new home was the Hôtel de Brunoy, at 45 rue du Faubourg St. Honoré. There was no more impressive address in all Paris. Today the house no longer exists, but one can judge what it must have been like by looking at its close neighbors, the majestic British and American embassy residences, or the Palais de l'Elysée a couple of hundred yards down the street. Behind these magnificent houses are vast gardens extending toward the Champs-Elysées. Princess Bagration paid 366,000 francs for the property; a large sum but not a severe drain on her ever-increasing fortune. During the late 1820s her stepfather had sent her enormous gifts amounting to a million rubles in response to her pleas for money to satisfy her creditors and marry Clementine appropriately. Count Litta surely didn't know that she was being supported by Caradoc's father, but evidently he found out later, as Catherine received no further funds from him.

Among the visitors to the salon in the Faubourg St. Honoré

was the great writer Honoré de Balzac, who was fascinated by the princess. No one could mistake the protrait he drew of her as Foedora, "la belle Foedora, la femme à la mode," the heroine of his novel *La Peau de Chagrin,* written in 1830–1831.

> She presented a sort of feminine problem, a Parisian who was half-Russian, a Russian half-Parisian. The most beautiful woman in Paris, the most graceful! . . . When I went to call on her I found a woman of about twenty-two [Balzac cut her age in half], of medium height, dressed in white, surrounded by a circle of men while she relaxed on a soft ottoman, holding a feather fan in her hand. . . . I met everyone there, scientists, men of letters, diplomats, Cabinet Ministers, aristocrats.

In another passage he mentions the contradictions in the character of the adventuress who so intrigued him: "Miserly yet luxurious, vain yet without affectation, defiant yet warm of heart. . . ."

Caradoc did not live in the noble house that had been bought with father's money, preferring to retain his bachelor apartment across the street. As time went on his life and that of Catherine drew apart and she did not accompany him on his various missions abroad. As the years progressed he rose in rank, serving as a colonel in Brazil in the 1840s, as British ambassador to Spain in the early 1850s, later as a major general with several commands. Except that he was popular in Madrid while ambassador there, we know nothing more of that mysterious figure, "le beau Caradoc."

Princess Bagration was anything but lonely without her husband. Her middle years were the happiest of her whole life. She remained the fashionable hostess whom Balzac described, retaining her interest in politics and the conversation of clever men, and she traveled about Europe with a luxurious retinue of servants. Yet it might have been better for her if, instead of living on into her seventies, she had died in her fifties like her rival the Duchess of Sagan, for the descriptions of her in old age are heartrending. In 1848 she was in London, and there she went to see Metternich who had been thrown out of power by the Austrian revolution earlier that year. His granddaughter Melanie described the old lady who tottered in:

> We saw arriving the Princess Bagration, whose beauty was celebrated at the time of the Congress. Who has not seen her has seen nothing remarkable. . . . She has forgotten to grow old and thinks that she still lives in that magical time when Isabey painted her crowned with roses, enveloped in veils and surrounded with clouds. Only the veils and roses remain. The clouds have gone as has her beauty. The mass of curly blond ringlets has been reduced to four or five thin yellow hairs. Her skin is the color of a lemon; her body, yes—her body, one could see it—is a crackling skeleton. The poor princess covers herself with a sort of transparent chemise, tied with a knot of pale rose or blue ribbons. One couldn't speak, and prayed that the two light ribbons would not come undone. The aged head was covered with a hat that an eighteen year old shepherdess would have hesitated to wear. It was dressed like this, if one can call it dressed, that she arrived to visit Grandpapa. What a spectacle to see my grandfather, so perfectly dignified and distinguished, with this embalmed mummy on his arm as we went to the table! During the meal she leaned towards him and regarded him with such a dreamy look in her faded blue eyes that it was all the rest of us, young and old could do, not to burst out laughing." [31]

This is such a merciless portrayal that we can only guess that Melanie Metternich must have known of the liaison in Dresden nearly half a century before and resented it. Yet a man who had no reason to be malicious, the tenor Roger, was passing through Berlin in 1852 and wrote after seeing Princess Bagration at her hotel:

> It is really a dead person who talks and walks. She lives on sherbets and biscuits. . . . Yet she is very excited about going to Potsdam and asked me the details about how one is pre-

sented to the King. So close to the tomb, how can she care about such worldly things?

Her last journey was to Venice in June 1857. There she died and is buried. Metternich was by now re-established in his Rennweg villa in Vienna. When his household learned of the death of the princess they did not have the courage to tell him for three days, remembering the terrible shock that the death of the Duchess of Sagan had given him. Finally, fearing that he would read the story in the newspapers, they broke the news as gently as they could. All he said was: "Really? I am amazed that she lived so long." Then he went on to talk of other things.

Prince Metternich himself was to die three years later at the age of eighty-four, and with him went the last echoes of the waltzes that were played so that the congress could dance.

Notes

1. *Lady Burghersh's Adventure*

Page 2. 1. Alastair Horne, *Napoleon, Master of Europe* (New York: Morrow, 1979), 14.

5. 2. Harold Nicolson, *The Congress of Vienna* (London: Constable, 1946), 19.

7. 3. Horne, *Napoleon*, 99ff.

9. 4. Nicolson, *Congress of Vienna*, 45.

12. 5. Ibid., 35.

12. 6. C. K. Webster, *The Congress of Vienna, 1814–1815* (London: Oxford University Press, 1919), 6.

12. 7. Nicolson, *Congress of Vienna*, 34.

13. 8. Henry A. Kissinger, *A World Restored* (Gloucester, Mass.: Peter Smith, 1973), 13.

14. 9. Ibid., 24.

14. 10. Ibid., 45.

15. 11. Ibid., 73.

16. 12. Ibid., 75.

2. *Into France*

Page 20. 1. Nicolson, *Congress of Vienna*, 58.

21. 2. Webster, *Congress of Vienna*, 9, 10.

24. 3. François-René de Chateaubriand, *Mémoires d'outre-tombe* (Paris: Pléiade, 1962), 1:853.

25. 4. Kissinger, *World Restored*, 109.

26. 5. Nicolson, *Congress of Vienna*, 87.

28. 6. Kissinger, *World Restored*, 114–115.

28. 7. Webster, *Congress of Vienna*, 22.

29.   8. Dorothy Gies McGuigan, *Metternich and the Duchess* (New York: Doubleday, 1975), 197.
29.   9. Ibid., 199.
30. 10. Ibid., 185.
31. 11. Henri Troyat, *Alexandre 1er: le sphinx du nord* (Paris: Flammarion, 1980), 58.
31. 12. Ibid., 81.
32. 13. Nicolson, *Congress of Vienna*, 9.
32. 14. Troyat, *Alexandre 1er*, 363.
32. 15. Nicolson, *Congress of Vienna*, 279.
33. 16. Troyat, *Alexandre 1er*, 233–254.
34. 17. Ibid., 245.
34. 18. H. Montgomery Hyde, *Princess Lieven* (London: Harrap, 1938), 79.
36. 19. Nicolson, *Congress of Vienna*, 82.
36. 20. Boigne, *Mémoires de la Comtesse de Boigne* (Paris: Plon, 1908), 283.
38. 21. Wendy Hinde, *Castlereagh* (London: Collins, 1981), 210.
38. 22. Nicolson, *Congress of Vienna*, 87.
38. 23. Hinde, *Castlereagh*, 152.
38. 24. Ibid., 153.
39. 25. Ibid., 117.
39. 26. Ibid., 165.
40. 27. Nicolson, *Congress of Vienna*, 79.
40. 28. Ibid.
40. 29. Friedrich von Gentz, *Dépêches inédites aux Hospodars de Valachie* (Paris: Plon, 1876), 1:74.
41. 30. Jean Orieux, *Talleyrand, ou le sphinx incompris* (Paris: Flammarion, 1970), 563.
43. 31. Duff Cooper, *Talleyrand* (London: Cape, 1932), 23.
45. 32. Ibid., 176.
45. 33. Ibid.
46. 34. Troyat, *Alexandre 1er*, 248.
46. 35. Ibid., 250.

3. Paris in the Spring

Page 49.   1. Charles Maurice de Talleyrand, *Talleyrand Intime: Unedited Letters to the Duchess of Courland* (Paris: Kolb, 1891), 200.
54.   2. Orieux, *Talleyrand*, 568.
54.   3. Ibid., 569.
55.   4. Troyat, *Alexandre 1er*, 256.
55.   5. Ibid., 257.
58.   6. Charles Maurice de Talleyrand, *Mémoires du Prince de Talleyrand*, ed. the Duc de Broglie (Paris: Lévy, 1891), 2:165.

60.	7.	Cooper, *Talleyrand,* 226.
60.	8.	Chateaubriand, *Mémoires,* 1:863.
62.	9.	Boigne, *Mémoires,* 1:281.
62.	10.	Ibid., 287.
63.	11.	Ibid., 294.
64.	12.	Ibid., 297.
66.	13.	Nicolson, *Congress of Vienna,* 93.
68.	14.	Boigne, *Mémoires,* 1:300.
69.	15.	Ibid., 308.
69.	16.	Chateaubriand, *Mémoires,* 1:895ff.
70.	17.	Elizabeth Longford, *Wellington: The Years of the Sword* (New York: Harper & Row, 1969), 340.
71.	18.	Boigne, *Mémoires,* 1:359.
71.	19.	Hinde, *Castlereagh,* 215.
71.	20.	Ibid., 216ff.

4. *Visit to England*

Page 74.	1.	Arthur Bryant, *The Age of Elegance: 1812–1822* (London: Collins, 1950), 103.
75.	2.	Nicolson, *Congress of Vienna,* 106.
77.	3.	Troyat, *Alexandre 1er,* 65.
77.	4.	Ibid., 66.
78.	5.	Ibid., 102.
79.	6.	Ibid., 100.
80.	7.	Nicolson, *Congress of Vienna,* 111.
81.	8.	Bryant, *Age of Elegance,* 104.
82.	9.	Nicolson, *Congress of Vienna,* 112.
83.	10.	Ibid., 113.
83.	11.	Bryant, *Age of Elegance,* 109.
84.	12.	Ibid., 113.
85.	13.	Ibid., 114.
86.	14.	Nicolson, Congress of Vienna, 115.
86.	15.	Ibid.
86.	16.	Ibid.
87.	17.	Bryant, *Age of Elegance,* 122.

5. *Vienna*

Page 96.	1.	Hilda Spiel, *The Congress of Vienna: An Eyewitness Account,* trans. Richard H. Weber (Philadelphia: Chilton, 1968), 75–76.
100.	2.	Talleyrand, *Mémoires,* 2:207.
101.	3.	J. F. Bernard, *Talleyrand: A Biography* (New York: Putnam's, 1973), 363.
102.	4.	Philip Ziegler, *The Duchess of Dino* (London: Collins, 1962), 127.

103.   5. Ibid., 11.
103.   6. Ibid., 14.
103.   7. Ibid., 19.
106.   8. Orieux, *Talleyrand,* 505.
106.   9. Ibid., 506.
107. 10. Boigne, *Mémoires,* 1:247.
109. 11. Troyat, *Alexandre 1er,* 290.
109. 12. Ibid.
110. 13. McGuigan, *Metternich and the Duchess,* 26.
112. 14. Ibid., 17.
114. 15. Ibid., 135.

6. *The Congress Opens*

Page 117.   1. Nicolson, *Congress of Vienna,* 137.
118.   2. Cooper, *Talleyrand,* 240.
119.   3. Ibid., 249.
119.   4. Ibid., 250.
120.   5. Ibid., 252.
120.   6. Ibid., 253.
122.   7. McGuigan, *Metternich and the Duchess,* 340.
123.   8. Clemens Metternich, *Clemens Metternich–Wilhelmine von Sagan,* ed. Maria Ullrichová (Graz: Hermann Bohlaus Nachf., 1966), 267.
124.   9. Commandant M. H. Weil, *Les dessous du Congrès de Vienne* (Paris: Payot, 1917), 1:221ff.
124. 10. Ibid., 139.
124. 11. Ibid., 127.
126. 12. Comte Auguste de la Garde-Chambonas, *Souvenirs du Congrès de Vienne* (Paris: Vivien, 1901), 116.
127. 13. Ibid., 141.
127. 14. Spiel, *Congress of Vienna,* 82.
130. 15. Webster, *Congress of Vienna,* 99.
130. 16. Ibid.
131. 17. Nicolson, *Congress of Vienna,* 120.
132. 18. Cooper, *Talleyrand,* 240.
132. 19. Ibid., 242.
132. 20. Ibid.
133. 21. Talleyrand, *Mémoires,* 2:335.

7. *The Approaching Crisis*

Page 137.   1. Weil, *Les dessous du Congrès de Vienne,* 1:321.
139.   2. Ibid., 1:234.
140.   3. Troyat, *Alexandre 1er,* 295.
140.   4. Ibid.

141. 5. Ibid., 294.
142. 6. Weil, *Les dessous*, 1:267.
142. 7. Troyat, *Alexandre 1er*, 292.
143. 8. Kissinger, *World Restored*, 154.
143. 9. Ibid.
144. 10. Webster, *Congress of Vienna*, 102.
145. 11. Hinde, *Castlereagh*, 223–224.
146. 12. Nicolson, *Congress of Vienna*, 183.
146. 13. Ibid.
147. 14. Ibid., 184.
147. 15. Ibid., 176.
147. 16. Ibid.
147. 17. Webster, *Congress of Vienna*, 107.
149. 18. McGuigan, *Metternich and the Duchess*, 358.
150. 19. Metternich, *Metternich–von Sagan*, 267.
151. 20. McGuigan, *Metternich and the Duchess*, 369.
152. 21. Metternich, *Metternich–von Sagan*, 267.
153. 22. McGuigan, *Metternich and the Duchess*, 362.
153. 23. Ibid., 389.
153. 24. Nicolson, *Congress of Vienna*, 13.
154. 25. McGuigan, *Metternich and the Duchess*, 386.
154. 26. Ibid.
155. 27. Ibid., 366–367.
156. 28. Ibid., 367.
157. 29. Ibid.

8. Crisis Surmounted

Page 160. 1. Ziegler, *Duchess of Dino*, 20.
161. 2. Orieux, *Talleyrand*, 614.
161. 3. Ibid., 615.
162. 4. Jean-François Revel, *Culture and Cuisine*, trans. Helen R. Lane (New York: Doubleday, 1982), 251.
162. 5. M. A. Carême, *Le Maître d'Hôtel Français* (Paris: Firmin-Didot, 1823), 215–218.
163. 6. Orieux, *Talleyrand*, 614.
163. 7. Ibid., 609.
164. 8. Ibid., 602.
166. 9. McGuigan, *Metternich and the Duchess*, 409–410.
167. 10. Hinde, *Castlereagh*, 225.
167. 11. Bryant, *Age of Elegance*, 203.
169. 12. Nicolson, *Congress of Vienna*, 178.
169. 13. Cooper, *Talleyrand*, 255.
169. 14. Ibid., 256.
169. 15. Bryant, *Age of Elegance*, 213.
171. 16. Nicolson, *Congress of Vienna*, 181.
171. 17. Ibid., 183.

172. 18. Bryant, *Age of Elegance,* 211.
172. 19. Ibid., 213.
172. 20. Ibid., 210.
173. 21. Nicolson, *Congress of Vienna,* 187.
173. 22. Ibid.
173. 23. Bryant, *Age of Elegance,* 210.
174. 24. Kissinger, *World Restored,* 143.

9. Final Acts

Page 179. 1. Spiel, *Congress of Vienna,* 118.
179. 2. Ibid.
180. 3. Longford, *Wellington,* 378.
180. 4. Ibid.
180. 5. Ibid.
180. 6. Ibid.
180. 7. Bryant, *Age of Elegance,* 186.
181. 8. Longford, *Wellington,* 381.
181. 9. Ibid.
183. 10. Nicolson, *Congress of Vienna,* 119.
186. 11. Norman Mackenzie, *The Escape from Elba* (London: Oxford University Press, 1982), 166–167.
187. 12. Nicolson, *Congress of Vienna,* 225.
187. 13. Mackenzie, *Escape from Elba,* 154.
187. 14. Ibid., 211.
189. 15. Nicolson, *Congress of Vienna,* 227–228.
189. 16. Ibid., 229.
189. 17. Ibid., 230.
190. 18. Ibid.
190. 19. Ibid.
190. 20. McGuigan, *Metternich and the Duchess,* 448.
193. 21. Longford, *Wellington,* 389.
195. 22. Clemens Brühl, *Die Sagan: Princessin von Kurland* (Berlin: Steuben-Verlag, 1941), 251.
196. 23. McGuigan, *Metternich and the Duchess,* 472.
196. 24. Longford, *Wellington,* 489.
199. 25. McGuigan, *Metternich and the Duchess,* 485.
200. 26. Ibid., 506.
200. 27. Ibid.
203. 28. Ziegler, *The Duchess of Dino,* 284.
203. 29. Ibid., 346.
204. 30. Ibid., 348.
209. 31. Mélanie Metternich, *Souvenirs d'enfance et de jeunesse* (Paris: Dunod, 1924), 22–23.

Bibliography

Aldington, Richard. *The Duke.* New York: Viking, 1943.

Arblay, Madame d'. *Diary and Letters.* London: Macmillan, 1905.

Austellung veranstaltet vom Bundesministerium für Unterricht bemeisam mit dem Verein der Museumsfreunde. *Der Wiener Kongress.* Wiener, 1965.

Bartlett, C. J. *Castlereagh.* New York: Scribner's, 1966.

Basily-Callimaki, Madame de. *J. B. Isabey: sa vie, son temps.* Paris: Frazier-Soye, 1909.

Bernard, J. F. *Talleyrand: A Biography.* New York: Putnam's, 1973.

Boigne, *Mémoires de la Comtesse de Boigne.* 2 vols. Paris: Plon, 1908.

Bourgoing, Freiherr von. *Vom Wiener Kongress: Zeit-Und Sittenbilder.* Brünn: Verlag Georg D. W. Callwey, Verlag Rudolph M. Rohrer, 1943.

Brühl, Clemens. *Die Sagan: Princessin von Kurland.* Berlin: Steuben-Verlag, 1941.

Bryant, Arthur. *The Age of Elegance: 1812–1822.* London: Collins, 1950.

Burghersh, Lady. *The Letters of Lady Burghersh.* Edited by Lady Rose Weigall. London: Murray, 1895.

Carême, M. A. *Le Maître d'Hôtel Français.* Paris: Firmin-Didot, 1823.

Castlereagh, Viscount. *Correspondence, Dispatches and Other Papers.* Edited by the Marquess of Londonderry. 4 vols. London: Murray, 1848–1852.

Chateaubriand, François-René de. *Mémoires d'outre-tombe.* 2 vols. Paris: Pléiade, 1962.

Cole, Hubert. *Fouché, the Unprincipled Patriot.* London: Eyre and Spottiswoode, 1971.

Cooper, Duff. *Talleyrand.* London: Cape, 1932.

Creevey, Thomas. *The Creevey Papers.* Edited by John Gore. London: Murray, 1948.

Fischer, H. A. L. *A History of Europe.* London: Arnold, 1936.

Fyppe, C. A. *A History of Modern Europe.* New York: Holt, 1890.

La Garde-Chambonas, Comte Auguste de. *Souvenirs du Congrès de Vienne.* Paris: Vivien, 1901.

Gentz, Friedrich von. *Depêches inédites aux Hospodars de Valachie.* Paris: Plon, 1876.

Herold, J. Christopher. *Mistress to an Age: A Life of Madame de Staël.* London: Hamilton, 1959.

Hinde, Wendy. *Castlereagh.* London: Collins, 1981.

Horne, Alastair. *Napoleon, Master of Europe.* New York: Morrow, 1979.

Hyde, H. Montgomery. *Princess Lieven.* London: Harrap, 1938.

Kissinger, Henry A. *A World Restored.* Gloucester, Mass.: Peter Smith, 1973.

Leigh, Ione. *Castlereagh.* London: Collins, 1951.

Lieven. *The Private Letters of Princess Lieven to Prince Metternich.* Edited by Peter Quennell. London: Murray, 1937.

Ligne, Prince de. *Fragments de l'histoire de ma vie.* Paris: Plon, 1928.

Longford, Elizabeth. *Wellington: The Years of the Sword.* New York: Harper & Row, 1969.

Mackenzie, Norman. *The Escape from Elba.* London: Oxford University Press, 1982.

McGuigan, Dorothy Gies. *Metternich and the Duchess.* New York: Doubleday, 1975.

Maurois, André. *Chateaubriand.* New York: Harper, 1938.

Metternich, Clemens. *Memoirs of Prince Metternich.* Edited by Richard Metternich. New York: Scribner's, 1881.

———. *Clemens Metternich–Wilhelmine von Sagan.* Edited by Maria Ullrichová. Graz: Hermann Bohlaus Nachf., 1966.

Metternich, Mélanie. *Souvenirs d'enfance et de jeunesse.* Paris: Dunod, 1924.

Nicolson, Harold. *The Congress of Vienna.* London: Constable, 1946.

Orieux, Jean. *Talleyrand, ou le sphinx incompris.* Paris: Flammarion, 1970.

Revel, Jean-François. *Culture and Cuisine.* Translated by Helen R. Lane. New York: Doubleday, 1982.

Rosebery, Archibald Philip Primrose, Lord. *Napoleon, the Last Phase.* New York: Harper, 1900.

Rudé, George. *Revolutionary Europe, 1783–1815.* New York: Harper & Row, 1964.

Spiel, Hilda. *The Congress of Vienna: An Eyewitness Account.* Translated by Richard H. Weber. Philadelphia: Chilton, 1968.

Strakhovsky, Leonid I. *Alexander of Russia, the Man Who Defeated Napoleon.* New York: Norton, 1947.

Talleyrand, Charles Maurice de. *Talleyrand Intime: Unedited Letters to the Duchess of Courland.* Paris: Kolb, 1891.

──── . *Memoires du Prince de Talleyrand.* Edited by the Duc de Broglie. 2 vols. Paris: Lévy, 1891.

La Tour du Pin, Marquise de. *Journal d'une femme de cinquante ans.* Paris: Chapelot, 1916.

Troyat, Henri. *Alexandre 1er: le sphinx du nord.* Paris: Flammarion, 1980.

Webster, C. K. *The Congress of Vienna, 1814–1815.* London: Oxford University Press, 1919.

──── . *The Foreign Policy of Castlereagh, 1815–1822.* London: Bell, 1925.

Weil, Commandant M. H. *Les dessous du Congrès de Vienne.* 2 vols. Paris: Payot, 1917.

Ziegler, Philip. *The Duchess of Dino.* London: Collins, 1962.

Index